EARLY ENGLISH ORGAN MUSIC
FROM THE MIDDLE AGES TO 1837

EARLY ENGLISH ORGAN MUSIC FROM THE MIDDLE AGES TO 1837

by

FRANCIS ROUTH

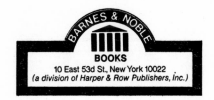

BARNES & NOBLE
BOOKS
10 East 53d St., New York 10022
(a division of Harper & Row Publishers, Inc.)

Contents

Preface

The Festival of Britain in 1951, following the end of the second world war, gave rise to two far-reaching musical developments, which were to prove of permanent and widespread importance. The first was the building of the Royal Festival Hall* on the South Bank of the Thames; the second was the publication of 'an authoritative national collection of the classics of British music', under the title *Musica Britannica*.

Both these developments concern the student of early English organ music very directly. The organ built in the Royal Festival Hall in 1954 represented a fresh departure in organ design (as far as this country was concerned) in several essential respects; it also helped to advance the general public interest in organ music. The *Musica Britannica* volumes provide the definitive text, both scholarly and practical, of early music. As far as Organ Music is concerned, this comprises the Mulliner Book, and the complete keyboard works of those four monumental composers of the Renaissance, Byrd, Bull, Gibbons and Tomkins. The similar excellence of certain other editions, of Mediaeval and Renaissance music, also stemmed from the same source; the volumes of Early English Church Music, for instance, published by the British Academy. It is these, and some other, publications which have provided much of the basic material for the present study.

Unfortunately there still remains a large amount of music, equally part of the early English tradition, and therefore referred to in the text, which remains unpublished, and unavailable so far in any modern edition. The most blatant example of a major

* Later extended to include the Queen Elizabeth Hall and Purcell Room.

composer, whose works are thus generally unobtainable today, is Samuel Wesley.

The rediscovery of the glittering world of early English music has been one of the most marked achievements of the twentieth century. It was a process which began in the early years of the century, and its pioneers included such visionary musicians as E. H. Fellowes, Margaret Glyn, Van den Borren, Peter Warlock, and many others. It is largely thanks to their essential work that the scholars of the next generation, notably Professor Thurston Dart, were able to make the authoritative texts of the *Musica Britannica* series.

Two immediate results ensue. The first is that, out of the truly immense quantity of keyboard material now available, it becomes possible to discern the thread of an unfolding, immensely variable, yet continuous, tradition, which gave rise over the years to a greatly contrasted outpouring of music, and to a gradual assimilation of an instrument that is both highly complex in character, yet at the same time impersonal. Moreover the term is seen to extend from *c.* 1400 until the death of Samuel Wesley in 1837. The early tradition thus sprang from the stark but exuberant grandeur of the mediaeval church, and the monarch's itinerant Household Chapel; it terminated with the gradually encroaching stranglehold of that urban, industrial society, which marked the accession of Victoria.

The second result is that, in pursuance of the work of scholarship since 1951, it becomes possible to experience the music directly and aurally. The work of the composers here discussed may now be lifted down, as it were, from the shelf of musicological research, and translated into sound. For the music of past periods—indeed of any period—can be much more than a matter of merely scholastic concern, essential though this is. An *Offertorium* of Preston, or a *Voluntary* of Greene, are now seen to be art-works originating from one vital, cultural tradition; therefore they make legitimate demands on the listener's attention today.

The work of Samuel Wesley marked both the culmination and the conclusion of this early organ tradition. Indeed the symptoms of decay were already apparent well before his death. He had no successor, and after him that degeneracy set in which was to extend

far into the twentieth century. It was a degeneracy that was reflected not only in the organs that were built during and after the
Victorian period, but in the wider musical life of the country. It
was a deep-rooted process of decline which could not easily be
reversed. The developments of the 'Organ Reform Movement'
(*Orgelbewegung*) which took place in the 1920s, particularly in
Germany and North America, passed unnoticed and without effect
in this country. It was not really until 1954 that a spectacular and
unique attempt was made to catch up with the past, when the
organ already mentioned was built in the Royal Festival Hall.★

Unfortunately this organ had two serious shortcomings. First,
the dry, somewhat clinical acoustics of the auditorium proved unsuited and unsympathetic to the complex sonority of full organ
tone; second, the instrument belonged to no vital tradition. On
the contrary, its designer proudly, if inconsistently, claimed alleg-
iance to many various traditions—with their many conflicting and
contradictory demands.

Less spectacular, but more far-reaching, certainly as far as organs
of the early period in England are concerned, has been the highly
skilful work of Mr Noel Mander. Many are the instruments of the
seventeenth and eighteenth centuries that he has restored to playing
condition; organs by such builders as Father Smith, Renatus Harris,
John Byfield. Thus for the first time authentic performances are
possible of the music of this period.

And it is with the music rather than with the instruments that
this study is primarily concerned. Each section of the book ends
with a short chapter on 'The Organ of the period', but the organs
are throughout seen as the means, not the end. They are referred
to only in so far as they are relevant to an assessment of a composer's
work. Many are the books which treat the organ from the mechanical point of view; any further such study would be repetitive and
superfluous. Yet no instrument has ever been made to exist *in
vacuo*, without reference to its corresponding literature. It was
precisely such a *rapport* which was the great strength of the early
period; it was precisely such a lack of *rapport* which lay partly at
the roots of the vulgarity of the Victorian organ.

★ Designed by Ralph Downes, built by Harrison.

In order to evaluate fully a composer's keyboard works, I have included lists of repertoire under each section; these lists occasionally cover works for other instruments than the organ, such as the virginal or harpsichord, or, in the case of Wesley, the piano. Similarly, for the sake of completeness, I have not omitted Clarke's famous 'Prince of Denmark's March', though any whose acquaintance with early English organ music begins and ends with 'Purcell's Trumpet Voluntary' may in this way be disconcerted to see that this singularly ill-fated piece is not by Purcell, nor is it for the Trumpet stop, nor is it a Voluntary; nor indeed is it for the organ at all. *Sic transit gloria.*

In the text, works in manuscript are referred to by an identifying letter; works in printed editions by an identifying number. These letters and numbers are listed in the keys on p. 281 and 284. When a composition exists in more than one printed edition, they are all usually referred to under the appropriate column in the list of repertoire. Editions are only omitted if they are seriously unreliable, and distort the composer's original, or if they have been superseded. In those few cases where an unreliable printed edition is the only source of a piece, it is necessarily referred to. The chief source of unreliability was the addition by nineteenth-century editors of a third stave for the pedals, and the addition of an extra part. Mainly for this reason John E. West's series *Old English Organ Music*, and W. T. Best's *Cecilia* editions, both very characteristic of their time, have been omitted from this study. Fortunately all the pieces covered by these two editors are found elsewhere.

London, October 1971   FRANCIS ROUTH

Acknowledgements

I am grateful for the assistance and co-operation of the staff of many libraries and colleges; particularly of the British Museum, the Royal College of Music, the Bodleian Library and Christ Church Library, Oxford. I acknowledge with gratitude the helpful advice of Mr Oliver Neighbour, Mr John Marsh, Mr David Scott, Mr Jeremy Caulton, and Mr Austin Hall. Specific kindnesses were rendered by Mrs Elisabeth Skinner, Dr Antony Milner, Mr Noel Mander, and Mr Barry Ferguson.

The Liturgical Use of the Organ in the Mediaeval Period up to 1400

English organ music originated from the complex and highly sophisticated ritual of the mediaeval church. The existence of organs in the British Isles is well attested from at least the eighth century onwards, though their precise function is open to question. It was not until the fifteenth century that organ music began to assume an individual identity, independent of the singers, a thing in its own right; and from then up to the death of Samuel Wesley in 1837, its history is that of a continuous and accumulating tradition covering a period of some four hundred years, and surprisingly little affected by schism or upheaval. An art-form which was strong enough to survive the religious civil wars of the sixteenth century, to say nothing of the political civil wars of the seventeenth, was to decline only during the comparative stability and prosperity of Victoria's reign. 1837 is indeed a fateful year, for more than one reason.

In the early mediaeval period, and up to the fourteenth century, more is known about the design of organs, their positioning and their structure, than about their use. We know how much they cost, from contemporary accountsheets; we know what they looked like, from contemporary illustrations. We do not know the most important thing of all, what their sound was; nor can we do more than surmise what their precise purpose and function was in the mediaeval liturgy. We know what qualifications, both moral and musical, were required of an organist; we do not know for certain what he was called on to play. Mediaeval developments in style and form of composition, were almost entirely vocal, mainly for solo voices; examples of organ music *per se* are extremely scarce. The *Robertsbridge Codex* (*c.* 1330), MS k², is the earliest and so far the only known surviving manuscript of the period in England, and is thus unique.

Yet, in spite of this, it can hardly be disputed that the organ was accepted as making an essential contribution to the performance of the mediaeval liturgy; it was central to the ritual of churches and cathedrals, from their very foundation in the tenth and eleventh centuries. Moreover its position in the building was decided by the liturgical requirements of its use; thus organ music sprang from the very centre of the mediaeval ritual.

Among mediaeval foundations, it seems to have been those under Benedictine rule which first, and chiefly, encouraged the use of organs, as they did also of polyphony. Reading, Worcester and Bury St Edmunds are known to have made early use of music in the liturgy.* There is evidence too of a lead being taken by monasteries in Ireland, whose influence spread to England, particularly to Western districts. The abbeys of Malmesbury, Abingdon, and Glastonbury received organs from St Dunstan, that remarkable mediaeval artist and theologian (*c.* 924–988), who eventually became Archbishop of Canterbury, and was equally skilled in music, painting and the mechanical arts, and in addition to organs also made chime-bells, and other instruments. He was shown the art of organ-building by 'Irish masters in Glastonbury', and his instruments were the earliest known examples in this country of the *hydraulis*, the water-operated organ that was invented by Ktesibios of Alexandria in the third century B.C., and was very popular in the days of imperial Rome.†

Thus through St Dunstan, and probably through Irish influence, there is a direct link between the music of the mediaeval English Church and that of the ancient world. Though the *hydraulis* continued to be made up to the ninth or tenth centuries, it was gradually superseded by the pneumatic organ, particularly in the Eastern provinces of the Roman world. This first appeared in the

---

* See Harrison *Music in mediaeval Britain* p. 135.
† Partly because of its loudness.
  See Reese *Music in the Middle Ages*, p. 15 (Latin spelling—*hydraulus*); also Bragard and de Hen, *Musical instruments in art & history*, p. 36.

third century, and its first known example in England is the famous and much-quoted instrument at Winchester. This was the gift of Bishop Alphege, who was later canonised after his martyrdom at Canterbury in 951. It was built in the Saxon church, which stood on almost the same site as the later Norman Cathedral, and has been described by the monk Wulstan (d. 963) in his *Life of St. Aethelwold*, who was a monk at Glastonbury, and worked as a pupil, or apprentice, to St Dunstan. He 'made with his own hands' an organ at Abingdon Abbey, where he became Abbot in 955. He became Bishop of Winchester in 963 and died in 984.

Twelve bellows are ranged in a row above and fourteen below. These, by alternate blasts, supply an immense quantity of wind, and are worked by seventy strong men, labouring with their arms, covered with perspiration, each urging his companion to drive up the wind with all his strength, that the full-bosomed box may speak with its four hundred pipes, which the hand of the organist controls. Some when closed he opens, others when open he closes, as the individual nature of the varied sound requires. Two brethren (religious) of concordant spirit sit at the instrument, and each manages his own alphabet. [There are also hidden holes in the forty tongues (sliders), and each has ten (pipes) in their due order. Some are conducted hither, some thither, each preserving the proper point (or situation) for its own note. They strike the seven differences of joyous sounds, adding the music of the lyric semitone.*]

Like thunder the iron tones batter the ear, so that it may receive no sound but that alone. To such an amount does it reverberate, echoing in every direction, that everyone stops with his hand to his gaping ear, being unable to approach and tolerate the sound, which so many combined tones produce. The music is heard throughout the town, and the widespread fame of it is gone out over the whole country.

The passage between brackets is, in the original Latin:

Suntque quaterdenis occulta foramina linguis
Inque suo retinet ordine quaeque decem;

* i.e. B flat.

Huc aliae currunt, illuc aliaeque recurrunt
Servantes modulis singula puncta suis;
Et feriunt jubilum septem discrimina vocum
Permixto lyrici carmine semitoni.

Linguae: sliders

The instrument was clearly something of a curiosity. The absence of a wind-chest made the large number of bellows necessary, to supply air direct to the 400 pipes. The absence of a keyboard meant that each of the three operators (the organist and his two assistant monks) made the pipes speak by working the levers and slides, which were each named by a letter of the alphabet. Each of the forty levers opened and closed ten pipes; thus each note was a ten-rank mixture, whose deafening volume Wulstan, not unreasonably, describes as sounding 'like thunder'.

Other Benedictine foundations where the use of the organ is specifically referred to in contemporary records, include the monasteries of St Mary's, York, and St Peter's Westminster, and the Cathedrals at Durham and Canterbury. The thirteenth-century *Customary of St Augustine's, Canterbury*,[*] refers to the use of the organ at certain times on chief festivals and Saints' days: St Thomas's day, the Epiphany, the Feast of St Adrian, the Purification, the Annunciation, the Translation of St Augustine and the Feast of St Michael.

The use of the organ at this period was probably confined to playing the plainchant in single notes. All ranks of pipes would sound with each key, and the effect must have been an instrumental equivalent of the contemporary style of vocal *organum*, with parallel fourths and fifths. Organ music reflected vocal music in style, texture and sonority; and just as the early vocal organum had its instrumental counterpart, so did the later polyphony, after 1400. Just as the vocal parts separated from the monodic plainchant, and each voice was given equal importance in a homogeneous polyphonic texture, so the ranks of the early mediaeval mixture were later separated into independent pipes by means of

---

[*] Referred to by Harrison *op. cit.* p. 205.

stops, and so allowed organ music to develop into a texture of homogeneous instrumental polyphony, based on the unison. The introduction of the keyboard may probably be dated from about the twelfth century, though clearly this varied from place to place. The organ in Magdeburg Cathedral, for instance, had a keyboard at the end of the eleventh century. Each key, we are told, was an ell long and three inches broad.

Large cathedrals and collegiate churches had more than one organ, each of varying size, and for use on different occasions. The fullest and most detailed account of the disposition of organs in a mediaeval cathedral under Benedictine rule is found in *Rites of Durham.** This, though written in the later sixteenth century, clearly refers to the practices of the pre-Reformation period.

Durham Cathedral possessed no fewer than five organs. On the north side of the nave, between two pillars, there was:

> A looft for the master and quiresters to sing Jesus Mass every fridaie conteyninge a paire of orgaines to play on, and a fair desk to lie there books on in tyme of dyvin service.

In the Galilee, the chapel at the west end of the nave:

> being all of most excellent blewe marble stood our Lady's altar, a verie sumptuous Monument fynly adorned with curious wainscott woorke . . ., the wainscott being devised and furnished with most heavenly pictures so lyvely in cullers and gilting as that they did gretly adorne the said altar where our Lady's Mass was song daily by the master of the song schole, with certain decons and quiristers, the master playing upon a paire of faire orgaines the tyme of our Lady's Masse.

Besides these two organs, which were outside the choir, Durham also had:

> 3 paire of organs belonginge to the said quire for maintenance of gods service . . . one of the fairest paire of the 3 did stand over the quire dore only opened and playd uppon at principall feastes, the

* Quoted by Harrison, *op. cit.* p. 188.

pipes being all of most fine wood . . . there was but 2 paire more of them in all England of the same makinge, one paire in Yorke and another in Paules . . . also there was a letterne of wood like unto a pulpit standinge and adjoyninge to the wood organs over the quire dore, where they had wont to singe the 9 lessons in the old time on principall dayes standinge with their faces towards the high altar.

The second paire stood on the north side of the quire being never playd uppon but when the 4 doctors of the church was read, viz. Augustine, Ambrose, Gregorye and Jerome, being a faire paire of large organs called the cryers.

The third paire was dayly used at ordinary service.

This organ, we learn from another source, was placed on the south side of the choir, opposite 'the cryers', and was called 'the white organs'.

Finally, we are told in *Rites of Durham* that the master of the choristers:

> Was bound to plaie on the orgains every principall daie when the mouncks did sing ther high Messe and likewise at evinsong, but the mouncks when thei weare at there mattens and service at mydnighte thene one of the said mounckes did plaie on the orgains themeselves and no other.

Furthermore, Durham accounts show that an organ in 1377 cost 10s; while in the early 1400s the cathedral paid £26.13.4. for 'making several organs', (clearly much larger).

Mediaeval services were sung in choir, in the nave, or in chapel, according to the occasion. The choir was an enclosed space, bounded on its west side by a stone choir-screen, or *pulpitum*, with a central door, *ostium chori*. The layout varied in different buildings. The pulpitum was surmounted by a large crucifix, the rood, and its upper level enclosed by a parapet to form a rood-loft, or *solarium* (*soler*). Another screen separated the choir from the nave, which was intended for the laity, who in a monastery were not members of the monastic community. Except in the case of the largest instruments, such as that at Winchester, organs were placed in the pulpitum, or in a gallery; thus the organ in accepted use was the *Positive* in a fixed position, in preference to the *Ninfali* or *Portative* organ, which was very small, played with one hand, and intended, as its name implies, for use out of doors, or in processions. The Positive organ was placed in the centre of the pulpitum and the singers grouped round the player, facing the altar.

The organist was in no sense a specialist. On the contrary, he was simply one of the worshipping community. Clerks, chaplains, vicars, monks were expected to be proficient in organ-playing; that is to say instrumental polyphony, of no great technical complication. In the mediaeval hierarchy, they were of lower status than abbots or deans, in just the same way as an artisan was looked on as lower than a man of letters. The best-known example of the prevalence of this attitude was the case of John Taverner, who when he was accused of heresy at Oxford in 1528 was merely imprisoned.

'The Cardinal', we are told, 'for his musick excused him, saying that he was but a musitian, and so he escaped.'

As well as the Benedictine monasteries and cathedrals, many secular cathedrals and churches had organs by the thirteenth century. Indeed the pulpitum with its organ was essential for carrying out the Sarum rite in larger collegiate churches. The function of the organ, which clearly varied from place to place, was probably to play in those ceremonial parts of the Mass which were sung in the pulpitum. Important festivals required polyphony for various parts of the Mass, while for the performance of the motet, which took place during the canon of the Mass, the organ played the plainchant, or *tenor*, in single notes. This feature of organ music is, once again, a reflection of the vocal polyphony of the early middle ages, which was a polyphony of solo voices, based on a *cantus firmus*. Choral polyphony, and the evolution of balanced choirs, was a later development, and one which was particularly associated with the secular cathedrals.

The main purpose of the organ before 1400 was thus probably two-fold; firstly to alternate and combine with the voices in polyphony, and thereby enrich the ritual; secondly to remove occasionally the strain of continuous chanting from the singers. Both of these uses of the organ are specifically mentioned in the *Exeter*

Ordinal, which Bishop John Grandisson drew up in 1337, and in which, with extreme precision, he laid down the exact form in which the liturgical ritual was to be conducted on different occasions and feast days; what proportion was to be chanted, and by whom; he also stipulated such matters as the relative importance of feast days, and the positioning of the various participants.* It is the most detailed surviving account of the form of liturgical ritual established by a secular cathedral in the early mediaeval period, and complements that of Salisbury, whose influence was the most widespread of any secular cathedral. The *Use of Sarum* describes the ceremonial procedures adopted by numerous other cathedrals, both monastic and secular, and by collegiate churches.

Bishop Grandisson provided for the organ to be played during those sections of the Office and the Mass which were sung in polyphony. These sections are listed by Dr Harrison;† as far as the Mass is concerned, on greater double feasts, such as Christmas and Easter, they included the Introit (when sung for the third time), Kyrie, Gloria, Sequence or Prose, Credo, Offertory, Sanctus, Agnus Dei, Deo Gratias; on lesser feasts, only the Kyrie, Sequence, Sanctus and Agnus Dei; on *ferias*,‡ nothing.

In practice, the proportion that was chanted, or sung in polyphony, or played on the organ, varied from Sunday to Sunday, and from place to place, over the mediaeval period. There was no fixed and uniform procedure. Various licences were even allowed by Bishop Grandisson; for instance instead of the *Benedicamus* at Vespers and Matins, and after the Sanctus at Mass, 'polyphony might be performed either by voices or organ, provided those in authority approved' (*si placet senioribus . . . poterunt organisare cum vocibus vel organis*).

The ruling is quite specific. If polyphony, with the organ, is to be performed, instead of the *Benedicamus*, it must be in the *pulpitum*, 'and the response§ (*Deo gratias, Alleluia*) will then be chanted by those in the choir'; but if a single plainchant is used, and not poly-

---

* Other ordinals may be compared, e.g. Norwich.
† *Op. cit.* p. 110.
‡ p. 11.
§ Not to be confused with a *respond*; see p. 11.

phony, it will be sung 'by three voices as usual'. (*Vel in pulpito cantetur aliquod canticum, si placet, organicum, loco Benedicamus. Et respondeatur a choro Deo gratias, Alleluia. Benedicamus a tribus more solito vel organicum loco Benedicamus.*)

The commonest case of a performance *alternatim*, between voices and organ, was that of the *Te Deum*, which was the hymn sung 'solempniter' at the end of Matins, on Sundays and most festivals. It was also used to mark any time of special rejoicing or festivity, such as the occasion at Winchester in 1334 when Adam of Dalton was restored as Bishop after a dispute with Edward III. The Prior ordered the community to ring the bells and sing 'a solemn *Te Deum* to the accompaniment of the organ'. On another occasion, at St Albans in 1396, 'the *Te Deum* was sung solemnly and devoutly by the community, alternating with the organ' (*alternantibus organis*).

Examples of such a composition, dating from the early sixteenth century, are included in *Early Tudor Organ Music (I)*.* If surviving examples of organ music of the pre-1400 period are practically non-existent, that is insufficient reason in itself for our assuming that it did not, in fact, exist. A very large number of manuscripts was destroyed with the suppression of the monasteries under Henry VIII (1536-40). Moreover it is a patently reasonable assumption, for no other reason than that the instrument itself existed, that the mediaeval organist would indulge his innate musical curiosity, and proceed to improvise upon it—whether his superiors required him to or not. We can safely assume this to have been the case; indeed it would be highly surprising if it were not; yet how could we expect records to have been conveniently left behind for us to discover? All music at this time had to be copied by hand, and it is entirely probable that if an organist were to attempt to write down his improvisation, it would become either lost or defaced. It is interesting to note that when Professor Dart tracked down a short piece of what appears to be an early fifteenth-century organ piece, an anonymous setting of the offertory *Felix namque* of 29 bars in length, the manuscript was so faded

* Ed. 25, see p. 286

that it could only be read under ultra-violet light.* Had some monk or clerk attempted to preserve his improvisation? It seems likely.

But if this is speculation, there are two aspects of the early mediaeval tradition, matters of fact, which were the soil from which grew the keyboard styles of later periods; carried over into the fifteenth century and beyond, they formed the twin pillars on which rested the immensely rich heritage of organ music from the Tudor period onwards.

The first of these cultural achievements was the gradual development and codification of ritual based on plainsong; that framework of liturgy within which the mediaeval organist and composer worked. Highly disciplined and ornate, and varied according to different Sundays and festivals, it formed the background and occasion for all organ composition, and indeed for most other compositions of any kind, up to the time of the Reformation, when the mediaeval period came to an end with the abandonment of the Latin rite, and the introduction of the English Prayer Book in 1549.

The second main cultural achievement consisted of those developments of musical style and form, mainly of vocal music, that characterise the period up to 1400. Though these were largely dictated by liturgical requirements, nevertheless those roots can be seen to have been struck which were later to grow into independent life.

EARLY MEDIAEVAL LITURGY

For ritual purposes, the year was divided into six seasons:

1. Advent—Four Sundays to Christmas Eve.
2. Christmas to Epiphany
3. Sunday *Domine ne in ira*† to Septuagesima
4. Septuagesima to Easter Eve (or Lent)
5. Easter to Whitsunday
6. Sunday *Deus omnium* to Advent.

* Dart, R. T.: *A new source of Early English Organ Music* (*Music & Letters*, July 1954).
† The words of the first respond at Matins.

Festivals and Saints' days were graded into double or single (*duplex, simplex*), the former having a procession, and more elaborate ceremonial than the latter. A week-day with no festival was called ferial (*feria*). Days were divided between the canonical Hours and the Mass.

Organ Music for the Office

Beginning with Vespers followed by Compline, there followed the night-hours of Matins and Lauds, and the day-hours of Prime, Terce, Sext, None, Vespers and Compline. Vespers, Matins and Lauds (*horae majores*) called for the presence of the choir; the others were known as little hours, and generally were musically less important.*

The liturgical scheme of the monastic office was as follows:

Vespers	Invitatory
&	Psalms with Antiphon
Lauds	Lesson with Responds
	Hymn (with versicle)
	Magnificat with Antiphon (Vespers)
	Benedictus with Antiphon (Lauds)
	Benedicamus—Deo gratias
Compline	3 Psalms with Antiphon
	Lesson
	Hymn
	Nunc dimittis with Antiphon
Matins	Sentences
	Respond and *Venite*
	Hymn (with versicle)
	1 or 3 Nocturns

* Though hymns were allotted:
Prime: Jam lucis orto sidere
Terce: Nunc sancte nobis Spiritus
Sext: Rector potens verax Deus
None: Rerum Deus tenax vigor
Two organ versions of the *Prime* hymn appear in the *Mulliner Book*, Nos 75 & 86 (see repertoire list p. 36).

3 Psalms with Antiphons ⎫
3 Lessons with Responds ⎬ each nocturn
Te Deum ⎭

Within this liturgical framework, various musical forms and patterns evolved during the early mediaeval period. Those parts of the Office in which polyphonic treatment resulted in the establishment of recognisable musical forms were the Hymn, the *Te Deum* and *Magnificat*, and the Antiphon. Hymns form the item most favoured by organists, and the two chief later collections of Tudor organ music, *The Mulliner Book* and *Early Tudor Organ Music*,* contain a large proportion of hymns, many of them set more than once, even by the same composer. They were sung *alternatim*, starting with the organ, with alternating plainchant for the even verses. Many of the polyphonic organ settings of hymns were based on *faburdens*, and others on the plainchant itself. Harrison suggests,† on the basis of surviving examples of organ hymns in comparison with vocal settings, that one purpose of the organ may have been to play polyphonic settings on those less important occasions when the choir was not present. There are no organ settings for the hymns of the festivals of Epiphany, Ascension, Whitsunday, Trinity, Corpus Christi, or any feasts of the *Proprium Sanctorum*. He applies the same principle to organ Antiphons. The *alternatim* style is exemplified by Ludford; the solo organ alternates with the choral polyphony of the voices.

The *Te Deum* is somewhat different from other parts of the mediaeval rites, partly because of its lengthy and unusual construction, partly because in addition to its place in the liturgy, it was also used for special ceremonial occasions. The beginner, the senior person present, sang the opening *Te Deum laudamus*; in the case of an organ *Te Deum*, the organist then played the remainder of the first verse *Te Dominum confitemur*. Thereafter voices and organ alternated. Surviving examples of polyphonic settings of the *Te Deum*, in the *Mulliner Book* and *Early Tudor Organ Music* (*I*) date from the sixteenth century. There is also one example of an organ

* Ed. 24, 25.
† *Op. cit.* p. 217.

setting of the *Magnificat*, the Gospel canticle sung at Vespers with its Antiphon.

The Antiphon was originally a choral chant sung before and after a psalm or canticle, or between the verses. As with the hymns, Antiphons varied according to the day, season or festival. The Antiphon later became an independent polyphonic composition, for voices or organ. Examples of Antiphons, of which several survive in the later organ collections already mentioned, are the Antiphon sung with the *Nunc dimittis* at Compline, *Lucem tuam, Domine, nobis concede* and the much set Compline Antiphon, sung with the Psalms, *Miserere mihi, Domine.*★ The Antiphon *Glorificamus te Dei Genetrix* was sung at feasts of the Virgin, and at commemorations. Other examples are the canticle-Antiphon *Clarifica me, Pater,* sung at Lauds on the vigil of the Ascension, and on Palm Sunday; and the *Beatus Laurentius,* sung at the first Vespers of St Laurence's day. *Gloria Tibi Trinitas* was the Psalm-Antiphon sung at Vespers on Trinity Sunday, and also at Prime when there was no choir. This plainsong is used both for organ settings, and later, even as late as the seventeenth century, for numerous other instrumental settings (over 150) under the generic name of *In Nomine.*

At the end of Vespers and Lauds, on feast days, which meant roughly one day in three, was sung the *Benedicamus Domino.* The particular melody for this, of which there were several, would be taken from a *neuma* of one of the responds after the Lesson. The repetition of a melodic phrase was a practice which occurred elsewhere in the liturgy; for instance the *Christe Eleison* trope at the beginning of the Mass was used again for the *Ite missa est* at the end; and the *neumae* of the responds in the Mass (such as the Gradual and Alleluia) were used as the basis of clausulae.

Substitutes for the *Benedicamus* were allowed, whether vocal, such as a *conductus,* or organ polyphony, and it is more than likely that an organist would make use of such an opportunity of licence to play a short improvisation, whether using the plainchant of the *Benedicamus,* or its *faburden;* or indeed neither. Such may have been the earliest origin of the later Voluntary.

★ See also the *Fitzwilliam Virginal Book* (Bull, Byrd).

Organ Music for the Mass

Mass was celebrated several times daily. Mass of the day was celebrated after Terce, about 10 o'clock; other votive Masses would be for the community, or in memory of the dead; Masses celebrated daily outside the choir were the Lady-Mass, in the Lady Chapel, the Chapter-Mass, for past members of a community, at a side altar, or a Jesus-Mass, which was an occasion for popular devotion.

The scheme of the Mass was as follows:

(the Ordinary, or invariable parts, are in italics; the Proper, or variable parts, are not.)
Introit
Kyrie
Gloria (not in Advent or Lent)
Epistle
Gradual
Alleluia and verse (during Lent & other occasions the Tract)
Sequence (on certain festivals)
Gospel (Evangelium)
Credo (except on ferial days)
Offertory
Sanctus
Agnus Dei
Communion
Ite missa est, (or *Benedicamus Domino* when *Gloria* is omitted)

Although the first surviving manuscript of an organ Mass, that of Philip ap Rhys, dates from the early sixteenth century, there is no doubt that the organ was essential to the liturgy of the Mass in the early mediaeval period, particularly in its roles of sustainer of the plainchant, and as a relief for the singers. That part of the Mass which provided the greatest scope for the organist was the Offertory, and of all organ settings of the offertory that which was most common was the tune *Felix namque es, sacra Virgo Maria,* which belonged to the Lady-Mass *Salve sancta parens.* This Mass to the Virgin, performed in the Lady Chapel daily between the feast of the Purification and Advent, was more often sung than any other, which no doubt explains the prevalence of this particular offertory.

The earliest surviving example of the offertory *Felix namque* is an early fifteenth-century manuscript,* in discant style, and based on the Brigittine version of the tune, which differs slightly from that of Sarum. Later composers were to develop the *Felix namque* into much longer and more elaborate solos. Tallis's two versions, for instance, written about a century later, are of fantasia-like proportions.

The early mediaeval Motet, performed during the Mass in the pulpitum, required the organ, or perhaps other wind instrument, to sustain the plainsong in the Tenor part. This use of the organ, as something complementary to the voices, ceased when the mediaeval Motet based on a *cantus firmus* gave way to the later votive Antiphon and polyphonic Mass. It was resuscitated however, much later, in the seventeenth century when the organ was used in *continuo* style in the later Anthem.

In summary, it will be apparent that the early mediaeval period was one of preparation, as far as the repertory of English organ music, as such, is concerned. Not only was the role allotted to the organ entirely concomitant with the voices, and anything but independent; but the very few surviving manuscripts, of which, strictly speaking only one falls into the pre-1400 period, do not indicate that organ music was thought of by the mediaeval composer as anything in its own right, which could be performed except in conjunction with the vocal part. Nevertheless it was from this background that organ music later grew and burgeoned on its own.

MUSICAL STYLES AND FORMS

Parallel with the codification of an established liturgical ritual by both monastic and secular cathedrals in this period, ran the gradual evolution and development of styles of composition. All were naturally based on plainchant, and almost all were concerned

---

* In Trinity College, Dublin MS L.1.13. See footnote p. 10.

with vocal styles of composition, and were therefore not necessarily relevant to the requirements of organ music; nevertheless the mediaeval organist would be expected to be conversant with all the musical aspects of the ritual.

As far as composition techniques were concerned, the twelfth and thirteenth centuries saw great developments; mainly, but not entirely, in France. The chief styles of the period were Organum, Discant, Gymel, and Rondellus; the chief forms of composition were Clausula, Conductus and Motet. Each of these developments concerned the organist, either directly or indirectly.

The earliest established mediaeval style was that of simple Organum;* the parallel movement of two parts, at a slow tempo, in fourths or fifths. The part allotted the plainsong was the *vox principalis*; the other the *vox organalis*. Either part might be doubled at the octave, to make composite Organum. The Unison, as a point of departure and arrival, was inherent in the use of Organum; Free Organum, the very earliest form of polyphony, in which oblique as well as parallel movement was envisaged, was also used from the beginning.

Organum was the first systematised response to an innate harmonic sense. It has long been debated whether it arose from the nature of plainchant itself, or whether it was brought in from some outside source, such as folk-song,† and, as it were, imposed on it. Though this may be as unanswerable as the familiar riddle 'which came first, the chicken or the egg?', nevertheless the explicit realisation of the harmonic factor within a modal, monodic, flexible and free melodic line (which is what polyphony implies), could only lead to radical developments, a transformation of Gregorian chant, to say nothing of problems of performance,‡ and the gradual evolution of new styles, as well as rhythmic modes.

The earliest polyphony was in two parts. An example of this is seen in the first extant manuscript of polyphonic music in this

* Described in *Musica Enchiriadis* (see *New Oxford History*, Vol. II, 277–9)
† See Reese *Music in the Middle Ages*, p. 256 foll.
‡ See Apel *Gregorian Chant*, p. 196 foll.

country, the eleventh century (pre-Norman) Winchester Troper.*
Normally Organum would be sung by soloists, plainsong by the
choir.

Broadly speaking, there were only two basic ways in which the
melody of a plainchant could be treated polyphonically. There
could be, against every note in the plainsong, either one note, or
more than one note, in the added part. Again, the vox organalis
could be above, or below, the vox principalis; movement could
be contrary, oblique or parallel.

The enormous range of Gregorian chant contained a wide
variety of melodies; some of great simplicity, akin to folk music,
of which there was a long-standing tradition in mediaeval Britain;
and others much more flexible rhythmically, and richer in their
harmonic implications. So different forms of extra-liturgical composition arose.

Among these separate musical forms developed by composers
as ancillary to the liturgy, the Conductus, French in origin, had a
metrical text, and was not necessarily based on the plainchant. It
was a free composition, originally used for Tropes, or processions,
or where the ritual required some extra music. Though most
Conducti were religious, this was not necessarily so.† They were
originally monodic, but the Notre Dame School of Leonin and
Perotin (1170–1250) wrote polyphonic Conducti in as many as
four parts, in which the music moves largely in block chords.

The Conductus in discant style was for voices, all of which sang
the same metrical text. More relevant perhaps, to the organist, was
the other main French innovation, the Clausula, and its successor
the Motet, if for no other reason than that he was required to play
the plainsong melody which made up the *Tenor*. This received its
name because each of its notes was held‡ against a group of notes,
sometimes quite elaborate, in the second part, *Duplum*. In the
Clausula of the Notre Dame School, the Tenor and Duplum each
have rhythmic patterns, based on the modes. This chiefly distinguishes the Clausula from the Conductus, which did not use the
held-note technique.

* Cambridge, Corpus Christi College, MS 473.
† See Reese *op. cit.* p. 202.   ‡ Lat. *tenere* = to hold.

If the Clausula was more suited to instrumental performance, and was rhythmically derived from a folk-dance such as the *Estampie*, the Motet was the logical vocal continuation of it. There might be a third part, *Triplum*, and different words in each part. When the Tenor was played on an instrument, the next part above it, Duplum, to which words were sung, was called Motetus;* thus this particular musical form acquired its name. As with the Conductus, in France it was not confined to sacred use only, though in England there are no examples of secular Motets.

If the Clausula and Motet were primarily French innovations, certain characteristics of style, and certain uses of these newly-discovered techniques, appear at this time as specifically English. The most pronounced is a preference on the part of English composers for the 'imperfect' intervals of the 3rd and 6th, as distinct from the 'perfect' intervals of the 5th and 4th. This was to remain a constant feature of English style in later periods such as the Tudor, and it can be noticed as early as the thirteenth century.

A striking example of this trait is in the 2-part discant style known as Gymel,† in which the two voices are close together, use the same clef, and therefore have an equal range. The music moves largely in thirds, closing on the unison; or in sixths, closing on the ocsave. Though this style was not given the name of gymel until the fifteenth century, it can be traced back much earlier than that. The characteristically English style of adding a discant to a plainsong was to allow a group of parallel thirds, (or sixths with a third added), ending with the Unison, (or octave with a fifth added)‡. Later, in the fifteenth century, contrary movement was also used, with mixed perfect and imperfect intervals, between the plainsong and the lower part. The highest part was added last, with 'merry' effect. As one fifteenth century writer says, with refreshing candour: 'The mo imperfit tones that a men synges in the trebyll the merrier it is.'§

Another of the commonest techniques among English composers of the thirteenth century was the Rondellus, or the repetition by one part of the words and melody of another. It is indeed

* From *mot* = a word.   † From *gemellus*, a twin.
‡ Harrison *op. cit.* p. 150.   § Reese *op. cit.* p. 401.

probable that this style had some influence over French and other thirteenth-century composers, who make use of canon—particularly in view of the close interchange that existed between Britain and the continent at this time.

Finally, the establishment, and the general acceptance, of organs in places of worship, is well attested by that most representative poet of the early mediaeval period, Geoffrey Chaucer—who, it may be noted, in addition to his other functions at Court, was also appointed in 1390, at the age of fifty, as Clerk of the Works at St George's Chapel, Windsor; he was thus directly concerned with the maintenance of the organ in that royal foundation.* He had also been appointed Clerk of the King's Works at Westminster the previous year.

In *The Nonne Preestes Tale*, written about this time, Chaucer says of the cock Chauntecleer:

> His vois was merier than the mery orgon
> On messe-dayes that in the chirche gon;

If Chaucer's earlier work reflects the influence of, and interchange with French writers, this is something, as has already been said, that was shared by composers also; particularly in the case of the only known extant example of fourteenth-century organ music in this country, the *Robertsbridge Codex*.

---

* The first actual mention of an organist as such, as distinct from an *Informator*, or Master of the boys, refers to the year 1406, when the organist was Walter Whitby, who received 13s. 4d. for playing during Christmastide. This does not necessarily mean, of course, that there was no organ before that date. (See Fellowes, E. H. *Organists of St George's Chapel*.)

2

1400—1558
Tudor Organ Music (I)

If surviving examples of fifteenth-century organ music are extremely scant, this dearth is amply compensated for in the following Tudor period, which is one of the richest in British musical history. The sixteenth century, the golden age of the Renaissance, was one of particularly marked advances in keyboard composition, in which England was the foremost country in Europe.

The output of the Tudor composers is approximately divided into two groups by the accession of Elizabeth in 1558.

The composers of the earlier group, who form the subject of this chapter, still worked mainly within the liturgical framework of the mediaeval church. Their material was the repertoire of plainchant; their function the extra adornment of the ritual. Yet on this basis they laid the foundation of a form and a style specifically suited to the organ, and extended the range of keyboard technique in a way which was to bear rich fruit in the later Elizabethan period. In the years up to Elizabeth's accession, because the strongest influence on composers was liturgical, the keyboard instrument they chiefly wrote for was the organ. After 1558 secular and domestic influences vied with those of the church, and composers wrote also for the virginal, the secular equivalent of the organ. This later group will be discussed in the next chapter. But no such division can be clear-cut. Organ and virginal music are largely interchangeable. Many pieces of secular origin appear before 1558; many liturgical pieces after.

Moreover several composers straddled both groups, and adapted the techniques of each; Blitheman and Tallis, for example. Nevertheless the basic dividing-line of the Tudor period, which decided the two main groups into which composers were divided, was the abandonment of the Latin rite at the Reformation, followed by the Act of Uniformity under Elizabeth in 1559, and the subsequent growth of music in directions other than those of the preceding centuries.

In the period up to the death of Dunstable (1453), the organ was used in those parts of the Mass that were sung in the pulpitum; and more especially in the performance of the Motet—the mediaeval liturgical form *par excellence*.

Various ways of integrating a plainchant into a polyphonic composition were created by Power and Dunstable. For instance a part might be added above the plainchant, in discant style, in notes of lesser value and varied rhythm; and a part might be added below the plainchant, the *Faburden*, which provided a harmonic succession of $\frac{6}{3}$ chords. The plainchant might appear in any part in a polyphonic composition, and not necessarily in the *Tenor*. Sometimes it was so decorated that it became almost unrecognisable.

After 1450, and for the next hundred years until the Reformation, composers developed polyphony in various other directions, such as the festal Mass, the votive Antiphon, the Magnificat and the Carol. This expansion of vocal polyphony, in the hands of such composers as Fayrfax, Ludford, Taverner, and those of the Eton Choirbook, made the growth of a balanced choir inevitable. This was particularly the case in secular Cathedrals, where choral polyphony was sung on Festivals. It also made the use of the organ gradually more redundant, as far as the performance of vocal music was concerned, since the instrument did not accompany or support polyphonic music, but rather alternated with the singers, or was used as a substitute for them on lesser festivals.

This progressive independence of vocal polyphony necessarily obliged the organist also to pursue a separate path. From this point therefore can be traced a specifically organ style; a keyboard interpretation of those principles of polyphony which had been established by vocal composers. For the most part organists based their work on a plainchant, though they might set the *Faburden*, or paraphrase of the melody, instead of the melody itself; this was always the case, for instance, in those organ settings of the *Te*

Deum that have survived. And just as the vocal repertoire contains pieces not based on a plainchant—Conductus for example—so is this also the case with early organ music.

Of the twenty-four composers listed in this first group, those whose work came to fruition earliest, that is to say by *c.* 1530, included chiefly Burton, Preston, Redford, Rhys and Taverner; the largest extant output, and the most representative of this period, is that of Redford.

But pride of place must go to the single surviving organ piece by John Taverner, his *In nomine* (Ed. 24, No. 35) which proved to be the prototype of a long line of works written under this title, which extended right down to the end of the seventeenth century, and included other instruments apart from the organ, such as the lute, and the newly-invented consort of viols.

Taverner's *In nomine* is a keyboard transcription of the vocal parts, taken from his festal Mass *Gloria tibi Trinitas,*★ which is the first Antiphon at Vespers on Trinity Sunday. The straightforward plainchant, which is given throughout in even notes in the *Mean* part, not the *Tenor*, presents a certain structural unity and implied harmonic richness of the melodic contour, with an apex in the second half. Thus was Taverner able to avoid that structural fragmentation, which, together with a lack of tonal variety, is the besetting problem of the organ composer—of this, or indeed of any period.

From the surviving repertoire of this period two large works stand out, which consist of a composer's making several different settings of the same plainchant. Blitheman's six settings of *Gloria tibi Trinitas* form a remarkable work. Whether the composer thought of them consecutively is open to question, though his pupil Bull later wrote a set of twelve; and Tomkins and John Lugge each wrote six. Blitheman's settings show remarkable resource; more ornate than Taverner's, partly because they are later chronologically, partly because they are specifically keyboard pieces. They particularly exploit rhythmic and metrical patterns, or 'proportions', and blend *Tempus perfectum* and *imperfectum*—a peculiarly English speciality.

★ See Reese *The Origin of the English 'In Nomine'* (JAMS ii, 1949).

The position of the plainchant varies; in the first setting (Ed. 24, No. 91) it forms the bass, with two quicker moving parts above; in the second (No. 92) it forms the upper part, with varied rhythmic patterns in the lower voices. In the third, fourth and fifth (Nos. 93, 94, 95) it is the middle of three parts, which develop increasingly complex counterpoint, while the sixth (No. 96) provides the release-moment of the set, in imitative counterpoint of great simplicity, which could only have been written by an English composer of this tradition.

Considered as a whole, like a suite in six movements, the plain-chant itself becomes progressively more concealed. In the central pieces (Nos. 3–5) the rhythmic and figurative interest of the more prominent outer parts somewhat blanket the inner part; and this textural complexity finds its match in the more homogeneous polyphony, and simpler counterpoint, with a reiterated point, of the sixth setting, which is the only one of the set to use four parts; all the rest use three.

Blitheman's organ, almost certainly of one manual, made possible only the simplest variations of dynamics. But the organist himself, now as then, would be expected to improvise to create interest; to realise, from the shorthand of the score, the accidentals, the tempo, the dynamics. In addition to the conventional demands of *musica ficta*, he might make use of octave transposition of either or both hands in the second piece, and vary the tempo of each piece in accordance with the nature and character of the part-writing.

Another work of substance, and comparable brilliance, consists of the eight settings of the Offertory *Felix namque** by Thomas Preston, (Ed. 26, Nos. 12–19). These are considerably earlier than the Blitheman pieces, and more substantial, because the plainchant is longer. It also lacks a point of structural or melodic climax, and, in contrast to the festal tune of *Gloria tibi Trinitas*, is more subdued in character.

Without the rhythmical interest and colour of vocal entries of a choral work, to say nothing of the force of the words, the organ composer can only rely on the vigour and variety of his counter-

* For the Lady-Mass *Salve sancta parens*.

point, his sense of sustained architectural growth, harmony, unity and rhythmic movement, over a long span. Preston varies harmony, metre and movement. The first three pieces are in A, the fourth in D, the fifth in G, the sixth in A, the last two in D. The metre varies widely, starting with triple metre* in the first piece, with quick passages, and a more sustained duple metre in the second and fourth pieces. Imitation between the parts abounds, and the position of the plainchant constantly varies, starting in the bass part in equal notes. The first piece also presents an additional interesting difficulty which is shared by certain other organ compositions of this period;† it is practically impossible to perform by one player on a single manual. There are several possible solutions; the most likely is that an assistant organist would play the held notes of the *cantus firmus*, either on the same manual, but possibly, where it was available, on a second manual, called, appropriately, the *Tenor*. Several composers of the later Tudor period, such as Carleton, Byrd, Farnaby and Tomkins, specifically called for two players.

As many churches and cathedrals had more than one organ, there is the further possibility that the assistant might play not on another manual of the same instrument, but on another instrument. Such an antiphonal performance would be a perfectly logical extension of the *alternatim* style between voices and organ.

A third less likely possibility, though one not entirely to be dismissed, is that where the *cantus firmus* occurs in the lower notes, these could also be operated by pedal keys. The existence of such pedal-keys in the early sixteenth century is most doubtful, though not to be definitely ruled out.‡

Preston's *alternatim* setting of the Proper of the *Missa in Die Paschae*, in which the organ is used like a soloist, alternating with the singers, is unusual in many respects. Normally composers of organ Masses, in Europe as well as in England, set the Ordinary.

---

* *Tempus perfectum* of mensural notation.

† For instance the anonymous *Felix namque* (Ed. 26, No 11).

‡ It goes without saying that an organist today would play the *cantus firmus* on the pedals, but not necessarily with independent pedal stops drawn. See Maslen *The earliest English Organ Pedals* (MT Sept 1960).

Bishop Grandisson in the early fourteenth century* had laid down the points at which the organ might be played, on principal double feasts. But there can be little doubt that the order of the liturgy varied from place to place throughout the mediaeval period; and now, two centuries after Grandisson's stipulations for Exeter Cathedral, Preston in his organ Mass for Easter Day, introduces the organ also at the first appearance of the Introit, as well as for the Gradual and Alleluia—the only surviving setting of responsorial chants for the organ. The Sequence, *Fulgens praeclara*, uses twelve out of the sixteen verses; and the manuscript, which is incomplete, contains no *Offertorium*.

The liturgical organ works of minor composers such as Rhys or Burton are interesting more for historical and musicological, than for artistic reasons. Burton's *Te Deum* and Rhys's Mass for the Feast of the Holy Trinity, viewed as musical entities in themselves, are too fragmentary, too innately bound up with the rituals which gave them birth, to possess much distinctive identity. Rhys, the later of the two, was a Marian composer; the *Offertorium* of his Mass, *Benedictus sit Deus Pater,* in spite of a certain monotony, possesses something of the harmonic movement, based on the interval of the third, which is so characteristic of the Redford school. But Preston's setting of the same plainchant (Ed. 26, No. 6) has much greater rhythmic variety and structural strength. An example of this is his use of rising fourths, which mount in sequence to a climax over crossing metres; the polyphony matches the melodic contour of the plainchant.

John Redford c. 1486–1547

John Redford was far the best-known and most representative, of the organ composers of the early sixteenth century. The most important institution at this time was unquestionably the Chapel Royal, where composers and organists enjoyed official patronage, and the status that went with it. But it is a reasonable conjecture that St Paul's Cathedral, under Redford's guidance, also represented a significant musical focal point; several composers were

* See p. 8.

assistants there, perhaps his pupils, and there was a close link with the various musicians who sang or played at nearby St Mary-at-Hill, Billingsgate—Thorne, Wynslate, Tallis and Rhys among them. Sheppard, and possibly Byrd,* were choristers. It is perhaps fortuitous that we are comparatively well acquainted with Redford's work, since on his death in 1547 his successor as Almoner was Thomas Mulliner, whose collection of pieces, *The Mulliner Book*, is a uniquely valuable source for the music of this period. Indeed it is probable that in committing to paper his collection of works for the organ, Mulliner was attempting to preserve something of the achievement, whose importance he appreciated, of that active group of composers centred round his much-admired predecessor, possibly also his teacher, John Redford. Later at Oxford he was associated with Blitheman, a former St Paul's chorister.

St Paul's was the hub round which the life of the City of London, in all its several aspects, revolved. And it seems that here John Redford, by the force of his personality as much as by his reputation as a composer, gathered round him a group of his contemporaries, composers and musicians, who between them carried forward the polyphonic and liturgical heritage of the late mediaeval period into the newly-forming keyboard and instrumental style of the Renaissance.

It is probable that many of the documents and records, to say nothing of the musical manuscripts, of old St Paul's were later lost in the fire of 1666; and this must have been the case with the libraries of other churches as well. The Great Fire, which lasted for five days in September 1666, ravaged the entire residential and commercial heart of the City of London, between the Tower and the Temple. Eighty nine churches, in addition to St Paul's Cathedral, were entirely destroyed.†

In the early years of the sixteenth century, when the spirit of the Reformation was gathering strength in Europe, the English Church produced several stern critics; Erasmus for example; but no Martin Luther. Indeed that greatest of all church reformers possessed a

---

* Fellowes doubts this. See *William Byrd*, p. 1. Nevertheless Byrd's musical debt to Redford is undoubted.

† See G. M. Trevelyan *English Social History*, pp. 289–92.

vision and a courage which outshone that of any of his contemporaries, whether in England or elsewhere. The spirit of Lutheranism, and the 'new learning', had many adherents—Miles Coverdale's first English Bible appeared in 1535. But whereas the Lutheran chorale acted as a fresh creative focus in Northern European church music, the English church was subject to a gradual increase of Puritanism.

As far as the liturgy was concerned, the organ music that Redford and his contemporaries were required to write at this time continued to be the Latin hymns and Antiphons handed down from the earlier mediaeval period. Hymns in the vernacular, such as Luther's *Geistliche Lieder* ('Spiritual Songs') of 1527, which had such a direct and fervent popular appeal in Germany, did not exist in England. Songs with English words which were such a pronounced feature of the later Tudor period, were to be almost entirely secular.

For this reason, whereas the Lutheran tradition, popularly based, was to lead directly, two centuries later, to the consummation of J. S. Bach, the school of Redford and his contemporaries, though in many respects the foremost among the countries of musical Europe, could only be transitional; their role was to lay the foundation of an organ style, which later composers, particularly Byrd, might adapt and direct into fresh channels. In the event, the work of this school was the starting-point for the later sixteenth-century instrumental composers in England.

Redford's style, which may also be detected in the work of many of his contemporaries, has certain pronounced and recurring characteristics; his fondness for harmony based on the interval of the third—a peculiarly English feature—and a more clearly defined tonality than is usually found hitherto; his preference for conjunct movement and scale-passages; his use of a motif, or 'point', sometimes derived from the plainchant, which may be treated by imitation in different parts, or in sequence, or repeated like an *ostinato*, though not with the polyrhythm of Blitheman; his introduction of ornaments, so inherent a part of keyboard music. Many of his pieces are, of necessity, short, yet within a brief span the composer can establish a wide range of interest, as well as a unified structure.

The simplest example of repetition of a point is seen in his setting of the Ascension hymn *Aeterne Rex Altissime* (Ed. 24, No. 26); another similar one, which also introduces an ornament, is *Jam lucis orto sidere* (Ed. 24, No. 75); in this case the figure is repeated ten times, each time at a different pitch, and with different harmony at the cadence. A point is always given a characteristic feature, which becomes the focus of interest throughout a piece. This feature may be ornamental, as in *Chorus novae Jerusalem* (Ed. 25, No. 33); or rhythmic, as in *Salvator mundi Domine** (Ed. 25, No. 54).

Consistency is achieved from much more than merely the repetition of a figure or sequence. Redford seems to have been the first organ composer to effect a sustaining of mood as well as a sustaining of tone; both are so much characteristics of the instrument. An example of his achieving this occurs in *Justus ut palma* (Ed. 26, No. 23), where the comparatively high pitch is maintained throughout as part of the composer's overall musical thought.

An example of canonic imitation is seen in the Compline Antiphon *Lucem tuam* (Ed. 25, No. 8), in which Redford's fondness for scale passages, combined with a sureness of tonal direction, lead to an extreme expressiveness within the limited duration of a short piece. In mood and texture this particular work bears an uncanny resemblance to Bach's Chorale Prelude *Christe du Lamm Gottes* in the *Orgelbuchlein*—which was written almost exactly two hundred years later. It is pure speculation whether Bach could directly have heard, or even heard of, Redford's work; but the creative impulse, and technique employed, are very similar.

Redford's direct successor was without question William Byrd, particularly in so far as the continuity and consistency of mood in a piece are concerned, as well as the contrapuntal imitation, the harmonic resource, and the use of ornaments. And Byrd was to exert a direct and strong influence on seventeenth-century German composers.

Redford's other settings of *Lucem tuam* are more intricate, and admit more chromaticism. At one point (in Ed. 24, No. 37, bar 9) he even alters the plainchant, with the result that a cadence is more clearly defined. The melodic climax of the plainchant is subtly realised.

* Ascribed as 'Anon' in Ed. 25.

Redford's hymns and Antiphons were fundamentally very distinct from the German chorale. They were not harmonisations of a tune for singing in parts, such as we associate with the Lutheran tradition. They were, on the contrary, organ pieces in their own right, more akin to Chorale Preludes, played in alternation with the singers. As they had Latin words, they represented more a late flowering of the old mediaeval tradition rather than the first step towards something new. It was certain that this was not a form which could long survive the Reformation in England; but within its confines Redford achieved a distinctive organ style, which was to affect later composers. He avoids monotony by means of a considerable rhythmic resource; usually the last of the organ verses of a hymn is at a steadier pace, and uses longer note-values than the preceding verses; thus he suggests finality. This technique does not seem to have been followed by other composers, whose settings of the final organ verse is often the most elaborate; for example the anonymous *Primo dierum omnium* (Ed. 25, No. 50).

Apart from direct settings of the melody of a plainchant, Redford frequently used the *faburden*; for instance for O *lux beata Trinitas* (Ed. 24, No. 28), and the Compline hymn *Salvator mundi Domine* (Ed. 24, No. 26, 72). The reason why composers preferred the *faburden* had to do with tonality, and the sense of harmonic direction that was gradually evolving at this time. A plainchant was primarily melodic, and in many cases was thus incompatible with a distinct tonal progression; one example has already been mentioned. The *faburden*, primarily harmonic, could often supply a much more secure foundation on which the tonality could rest. The organ composers thus frequently omitted the plainchant itself; it could be taken for granted; if the added parts fitted with the *faburden,* they would automatically also fit the plainchant itself, which was assumed.

As well as composing either on a plainchant or a *faburden*, composers also wrote works of their own free invention, whose material was entirely independent. Such a piece might be called a 'Meane', a 'Point', or a 'Voluntary'. All occur in the *Mulliner Book*; Blitheman's *Excellent Meane* (Ed. 24, No. 32) is the plainchant Offertorium *Felix namque,* but Redford's short *Meane*, (Ed. 24, No. 67) like his several short improvisations which he calls *a Point,* has no such plainchant basis. A longer non-liturgical piece of this category in the *Mulliner Book* is Allwood's *Voluntary* (Ed. 24, No. 17) which like Taverner's *In nomine,* is a precurser of many later compositions under this title. The Voluntary, as a form, was to continue right through to the nineteenth century. Unlike the *In Nomine,* but like the Lutheran Chorale Prelude, it remained confined to the organ, and from its first appearance in the *Mulliner Book* runs like a continuous stream, with many tributaries, through the whole course of the early English organ tradition. The title *Voluntary* is derived from this fact of its origin, namely, that it was written on material of the composer's own invention, and not based upon either a plainchant or *faburden.* In the event, for this very reason, it was to prove the most capable of subsequent growth of any of the forms created by organ composers of this period.

Allwood's other piece in the *Mulliner Book, In nomine* (No. 23), is a vocal transcription, though it does not use the generally-accepted *Gloria tibi Trinitas* tune. Farrant's short piece, however, under the title *Voluntary,* is really indistinguishable from one of Redford's *Points.*

More interesting, and considerably more puzzling to a number of commentators, is the short, free piece in two parts, (Ed. 26, No. 3) under the mysterious title *Orma vulte.* It was quite possibly the work of Redford,★ and it can be explained as a study or technical exercise. Taking a *Kyrie* melody, (which also appears in the *Kyrie* and *Christe* immediately preceeding it in Ed. 26, No. 2), the composer has written a part above it in such a way that the piece may be played either in its ordinary form or in retrograde. Played *al rovescio* it is as follows:

Example 1

Orma Vulte *[al rovescio]*   [Redford?]

★ Though it is attributed anonymously in Ed. 26.

Retrograde movement, like inversion, canon and so on, was commonly practised by composers in the fourteenth and fifteenth centuries. They frequently called their riddle canons by somewhat surprising names; *Nusmido* for instance, which is an anagram of *Dominus*, or Machaut's *Ma fin est mon commencement*. It is not in the slightest surprising therefore that Redford should describe his short study in retrograde by an unusual Italian name. By adapting *Orma vulte* into *Orma volta* it would mean 'retrace your footsteps',★ which exactly describes the piece.

Contrapuntal ingenuity, involving inversion, canon, or retrograde, was nothing uncommon in the 16th century, and among later composers it was carried to greater lengths by Byrd, particularly in his Latin Motets.

Many organ works of this period are transcriptions; those of Tye for instance are chiefly transcribed from vocal compositions.

The *Mulliner Book* also contains many keyboard transcriptions; from vocal works, such as Taverner's and Allwood's *In nomine*; or from compositions for viols, such as the *In nomine* of Johnson and White. The secular, instrumental form that was chiefly to take root, next to the *In nomine*, was the *Fancy*, or *Fantasia*, represented in the *Mulliner Book* by a transcription of such a work by Newman; his *Pavan* is another piece in similar vein, of dance origin. The collection also includes many arrangements of secular or lute songs, such as the song, or 'complaint', attributed to Anne Boleyn, 'Defiled is my name'. Thus were sown the seeds of another important musical form that was to be pursued by later sixteenth-century composers—variations for keyboard on a lute, or secular, song.

Thomas Tallis *c.* 1505–1585

Little of Tallis's life is known. The date of his birth is uncertain, as well as the facts surrounding his early years. A reasonable

★ Orma = a footstep.   Voltare = to turn round.

conjecture would be that he was born *c.* 1505–1510, and that he received his early musical training at the St Paul's Cathedral school. If so, he would have been one of the musicians in the group centred round Redford.

Already in 1525 he was a member of the Household Chapel under Henry VIII; and before the King's death in 1547 he was a gentleman of the Chapel Royal. He retained this position under succeeding monarchs. In 1556 Mary also granted him, and Richard Bowyer,* a joint lease for twenty-one years, in the Manor of Minster, Isle of Thanet.

Tallis continued to serve the Chapel Royal, where he was also one of the organists, until his death on 23rd November, 1585. He lived the latter part of his life at Greenwich, where he was buried, near the Royal Palace.

The most remarkable aspect of his work was his close, continuing association and partnership with William Byrd. The latter, who was some thirty-five years his junior, was first his pupil; later, in 1572, his colleague as organist at the Chapel Royal; finally his partner in the music-printing licence granted to them by Queen Elizabeth in 1575. But much more enduring than their business dealings—which do not appear to have been marked by any notable commercial acumen—was nothing less than the evolution of the musical art in this country, that took place as a result of their acquaintance. Indeed the musical history of England can show few if any parallel examples. The collaboration of Gustav Holst and Vaughan Williams in the early years of the twentieth century perhaps alone invites any sort of comparison, though this happened in a radically different situation.

Tallis and Byrd between them bestride a century of English music. When the former was a young musician in Henry VIII's Household Chapel, the prevailing style of music for the Latin rite was liturgical, modal, largely vocal—in a word, mediaeval; when the latter died a hundred years later, in 1623, the prevailing style had broadened out to include secular, domestic music-making, as well as compositions for the reformed English church; it had moreover a more secure and better developed tonality, and it gave

* Master of the children of the Chapel Royal, (d. 1563).

greater scope to instruments, as well as voices; it heralded the Baroque.

It is therefore not entirely surprising that Tallis, who was about forty when Henry VIII died, and whose formative years were spent before the Reformation, should not compose music for domestic use, but should write exclusively for the church. His vocal compositions are to either Latin or English texts; his keyboard compositions are comparatively few, and, like those of his contemporary Blitheman, are a continuation of the Redford style of liturgical organ composition.

Apart from two transcriptions in the *Mulliner Book*, his organ pieces total seventeen. Fourteen are, at least in origin, liturgical pieces based on Latin words, while of the remaining three pieces, the *Lesson* is a technical three-part exercise in canon, which the composer maintains right through between the two upper parts, against a free part for the left hand. In spite of the unifying device of canon, the structure is loose. This diffuseness is less noticeable in the shorter, free compositions, the *Fantasy*, and the *Point*, the last of which is in the nature of a small interlude, very much after the Redford manner.

Structural diffuseness is also the most immediate feature of the two enormous Latin Offertories, *Felix namque*, in which canonic and imitative entries, and rhythmic ingenuity, are the chief means whereby the composer seeks to impose order upon the long, intractable plainchant. The second of these settings was a much quoted source-work for later organists and composers.

But it is in the Antiphons and Hymns that Tallis combined the greatest unity of structure with an individual organ style. They are not so much statements of a plainchant as meditations, or commentaries ,on it. The three settings of *Clarifica me Pater* well illustrate this. The 'point' is through-composed in each of the four parts, and treated in the manner of a counter-subject, rather than simply repeated, like an *ostinato*, in the style of Redford. Each short but highly concentrated Antiphon gives rise to a different point, and the plainchant is freely integrated with the four-part polyphony, not maintained in equal notes, somewhat as a thing apart, as in the *Felix namque* settings.

Another aspect of Tallis's style which marks him out from others of the Redford school, is his pronounced tonal sense. Each of the Antiphons and Hymns is approximately divided into two halves by a full close, or 'perfect' cadence. This forms a structural link, a hinge, and often changes the music into a related tonality. Of the three settings of *Clarifica me Pater*, which have a D final, the first and third modulate to G, the second to F, at this central point. Tallis's harmonic thinking marks the changeover from modality to tonality, and leads to some asperities of *musica ficta*.

The other two Antiphons are slighter, in two parts; one of them, *Gloria tibi Trinitas*, a somewhat laboured canon.

The seven Hymns, however, like *Clarifica me Pater*, consist of concentrated, polished counterpoint; all but one, *Iste confessor*, in four parts. This one amply illustrates the composer's style, which was best suited to the shorter keyboard piece.

The 'point' is a bold one:

Example 2

It runs like a thread throughout the piece, in each of the three parts, and is used in inversion, and 'stretto', or overlapping entries:

Example 3

Tallis does not call for any virtuoso keyboard technique in these organ pieces. He is not so much seeking for effect in the use of the

instrument, as for the effective working-out of the musical material, and the construction of a harmonic unity.

He was, we are told, a mild and quiet man; certainly no revolutionary, though his work took place in a revolutionary situation. As far as his all-too-few organ pieces are concerned, particularly the Hymns and Antiphons, subdued and grave they may certainly be, yet, within their short compass, they are perfect.

COMPOSERS AND EXTANT REPERTOIRE
UP TO 1558

Composer	Work	MS Source★	Printed Editions★
ALLWOOD,	Claro paschali gaudio I & II	zz	24, 29
Richard	In nomine	zz	24
	Untitled piece	zz	24
	Voluntary	zz	24, 29
	In nomine I & II	d	30
AMBROSE,	Untitled piece	yy, r^1	
John			
ANONYMOUS	*Music for the Mass*		
	Kyrie and Christe	a^1	26
	Communion: Beata viscera	a^1	26
	Offertory:		
	Felix namque (incomplete)	a^1	26
	Felix namque (incomplete)	b^1	26
	Felix namque I & II	a^1	26, 29
	Music for the Office		
	Antiphon:		
	Miserere	a^1	25
	Hymns:		
	A solis ortus cardine	t	25
	Aeterne rerum conditor	t	25
	Audi benigne conditor	t	25
	Bina coelestis I & II	t	25
	Christe qui lux es et dies I, II	t, u	25
	Christe Redemptor omnium	t	25
	Conditor alme siderum	t	25
	Deus creator omnium	t	25
	Ex more docti mystico	t	25
	Hostis Herodes impie I, II	t	25
	Primo dierum omnium	t	25
	Salvator mundi Domine	h, t	25
	Sancte Dei pretiose	t	25
	Summi Largitor praemii	t	25
	Veni Redemptor gentium	t	25
	Verbum supernum prodiens	t	25
	Vexilla Regis prodeunt	u	25
	Vox clara ecce intonat	t	25

Felix namque	Non expecto	a^1	
Beata viscera	3 unnamed pieces		
Kyrie, Christe, Miserere			
2 unnamed pieces	Apre(s) de vowse		
Dum vincella	2 unnamed pieces		
Grace & virtue	A solis ortu cardine		
Fortune unkynde	Myne cuckes co		
Jesu, Redemptor omnium	A litell God Fayth		
La bell fyne	Hornpipe 'Hughe Aston' r^1		33
My Lady Carye's Dompe			
My Lady Wynkfyld's rounde			

★ For key to manuscripts and printed editions see p. 281.

Composer	Work		MS Source	Printed Editions
	The empororse pavyn	A Galyarde	r[1]	33
	King Harry the VIII pavyn			
	The crocke	The Kyng's marke		
	A Galyarde			
BLITHEMAN, William	*Music for the Mass* Offertory:			
	Felix namque (an excellent meane)		zz	24
	Music for the Office			
	Antiphons:			
	Gloria tibi Trinitas I–VI		d, a, zz	24, 29
	Hymns:			
	Aeterne rerum Conditor I–VI		zz	24
	Christe qui lux es et dies		zz	24
	Christe redemptor omnium		zz	24
	Untitled piece		zz	24
BURTON, Avery	Te Deum		t	25
CARLETON, Nicholas	Audi benigne Conditor		zz	24
	Gloria tibi Trinitas		zz	24
COXSUN, Robert	Laetamini in Domino		t	26, 29
	Veritas mea		t	26,
FARRANT, Richard	Felix namque		zz	24
	Voluntary		zz	24
HEATH, Thomas	Christe qui lux es et dies		zz	24
JOHNSON, Robert (?)	Benedicam Domino		e[1], zz	24
	In nomine		f[1], g[1], zz	24
	Defiled is my name		n[1], zz (*et al.*)	24
KYRTON, ?	Miserere		t	25
MUNDY, William	Tres partes in una		zz	24
NEWMAN, ?	a Fansye		zz	24
	a pavan		zz	24
PRESTON, Thomas	*Music for the Mass* Mass Proper:			
	'In Die Paschae'		t	26
	Offertory:			
	Benedictus sit Deus Pater		t	26
	Confessio et pulchritudo		t	26
	Diffusa est gratia		t	26
	Felix namque I–VIII		t	26, 59
	Reges Tharsis		t	26
	Music for the Office Antiphon:			
	Beatus Larentius		t	25
REDFORD, John	*Music for the Mass* Agnus Dei		u	26, 28

Composer	Work	MS Source	Printed Editions
REDFORD, John—*contd.*			
	Offertory:		
	Felix namque I, II	t	26, 28
	Justus ut palma	t	26, 28
	Precatus est Moyses	t	26, 28
	Tui sunt Coeli	xx, yy	26, 28
	Music for the Office		
	Te Deum I	xx, zz	24,★ 25, 28
	Te Deum II	t, xx	25, 28
	Antiphons:		
	Glorificamus te Dei genetrix	xx, zz	24, 28, 78
	Lucem tuam I	t	25, 28
	Lucem tuam II, III	zz	24, 28, 29
	Miserere I, II	t, u	25, 28
	Miserere III	t, zz	24, 28, 29
	Hymns:		
	A solis ortus cardine	t	25, 28
	Ad cenam Agni providi	xx	25, 28
	Aeterne rerum Conditor I	t, xx	25, 28
	Aeterne rerum Conditor II	zz	24, 28
	Aeterne rex altissime	zz	24, 28
	Angulare fundamentum	u	25, 28
	Aurora lucis	zz	24, 28
	Christe qui lux es et dies I	t, zz	24, 25, 28
	Christe qui lux es et dies II	zz	24, 28
	Christe redemptor omnium	t	25, 28
	Conditor alme siderum	t, xx	25, 28
	Deus creator omnium	t	25, 28
	Exultet coelum laudibus	zz	24, 28
	Iam lucis orto sidere	zz	24, 28
	Iste confessor I, II	zz	24, 28
	O lux beata Trinitas I, II	zz	24, 28, 29
	O quam glorifica	v	25, 28
	Primo dierum Omnium I, II	t, xx	25, 28
	Salvator mundi Domine I, II	zz	24, 28
	Te lucis ante terminum	zz	24, 28
	Veni Redemptor gentium I	t, zz	24, 25, 28, 75
	Veni Redemptor gentium II	u	25, 28
	Verbum supernum prodiens	t, zz	24, 25, 28
	Miscellaneous pieces		
	A meane	zz	24, 28
	A point, I–IV	zz	24, 28
	Pieces whose authenticity is open to question		
	Antiphons:		
	Glorificamus, I, II	t	28, 'anon' in 25
	Miserere I, II	t, u, zz	28, (Redford) in 24
	Miserere III–IX	t	28, 'anon' in 25
	Hymns:		
	Chorus novae Jerusalem	t	28, 'anon' in 25

★ Parts included in 24 are: *Salvum fac, Te per orbem terrarum, Tibi omnes, Tu ad liberandum.*

Composer	Work	MS Source	Printed Editions
REDFORD, John—*contd.*			
	Ex more docti mistico	zz	24, not in 28
	Exultet coelum laudibus	zz	24, not in 28
	Iste confessor	t	28, 'anon' in 25
	Lucis creator optime	t	28, 'anon' in 25
	Salvator mundi Domine I, II	t	28, 'anon' in 25
	Sermone blando anbelus	zz	24, not in 28
	Te lucis ante terminum	t	28, 'anon' in 25
	Magnificat	t	'anon' in 25, 28[*]
	Miscellaneous pieces:		
	Orma vulte (?)	u	28, 'anon' in 26
	Unnamed piece	zz	24, not in 28
RHYS, Philip ap	*Music for the Mass*		
	Missa in die Sanctae Trinitatis[†]	t	26, 29
	('Deus Creator Omnium')		
	Offertory:		
	Felix namque	t	26
	Music for the Office		
	Antiphon:		
	Miserere	t	25
SHELBYE, ?	Felix namque	zz	24
	Miserere	zz	24
SHEPPARD,	I give you a new commandment	m^1, n^1, zz	24
John	Point	zz	24
	Quia fecit mihi magna	m^1, zz	24
	Versus I–III	zz	24
STROWGER,	Miserere	t	25
E.			
TALLIS,	*Music for the Mass*		
Thomas	Offertory:		
	Felix namque I, II	a, d, p	1, 27
	Music for the Office		
	Antiphons:		
	Clarifica me Pater I–III	zz	24, 27
	Gloria tibi Trinitas	u	27, 78
	Natus est nobis	zz	24, 27
	Hymns:		
	Ecce tempus idoneum I, II	zz	24, 27
	Ex more docti mistico	zz	24, 27
	Iam Lucis orto sidere	zz	24, 27
	Iste confessor	zz	24, 27, 78
	Per haec nos	c^1, zz (*et al.*)	24
	Veni Redemptor I, II	b, zz	24, 27
	Miscellaneous pieces		
	Fantasy	u, yy	27
	Lesson	a, d	27
	Point	zz	24, 27
	Remember not O Lord	d^1, zz	24
TAVERNER,	In nomine	u, f^1, c^1, g^1,	24, 29
John		n^1, zz (*et al.*)	

[*] Called in 28 'The VIII tune in C faut'.
[†] 'Gloria' is attributed to Redford by 28.

Composer	Work		MS Source	Printed Editions
THORNE,	Offertory:			
John	Exsultabant sancti		t	26, 29
TYE,	I lift my heart		g^1, h^1, i^1, j^1,	24
Christopher			k^1, zz (*et al.*)	
	Madona		u	
	Point	} prob. Tye	u	
	Amor me poynt		u	
WHITE, Robert	In nomine		l^1, zz	24
	Ut re m: fa		u	
WOODSON, ?	Miserere		u	25
WYNSLATE,	Lucem tuam		t	25

BIOGRAPHICAL NOTES ON THE COMPOSERS

ALLWOOD, Richard (or Alwood).
 Priest. Fl. mid-sixteenth century; Chorister at St Paul's Cathedral under Mulliner. Nothing otherwise known.

AMBROSE, John.
 Nothing known.

BLITHEMAN, William (or Blytheman).
 153?–1591. Chorister at St Paul's Cathedral. 1564 Master of choristers at Christ Church, Oxford. 1585 Organist of Chapel Royal, after death of Tallis. Teacher of John Bull (q.v.), who succeeded him at Chapel Royal.

BURTON, Avery.
 147?–154? 1509 Prob. gentleman of Chapel Royal under Henry VII. 1513 travelled with him to France. A *Te Deum* of his was performed after Mass at Tournai, on 17th September. 1525 Member of the Royal Household Chapel.

CARLETON, Nicholas (or Carlton).
 Fl. mid-sixteenth century. Nothing otherwise known. See under *Carleton*, Chap. III.

COXSUN, Robert.
 Fl. mid-sixteenth century. Nothing otherwise known.

FARRANT, Richard.
 c. 1530–1580. 1564–80 Master of choristers St George's Windsor. ?–1564 and 1569–80 Gentleman of Chapel Royal.

HEATH, Thomas.
 ?–1584. 1558–1584 Organist and Master of the choristers at Exeter Cathedral.

JOHNSON, Robert?
 (i) Scottish priest, fl. early sixteenth century, banished to England before the Reformation. Possibly chaplain to Anne Boleyn. (ii) Lutenist composer 1569–1633. See Chap. III.

KYRTON, ?
 Fl. early sixteenth century. Nothing otherwise known.

LUDFORD, Nicholas.
 c. 1485–1557. 1547 Possibly at St Stephen's, Westminster at its dissolution. 1520–30 His seven Lady Masses are an example of *alternatim* performance with choir and organ.

MULLINER, Thomas.
 152?–158? Associate (pupil?) of Redford at St Paul's Cathedral. 1563

(3rd March) Organist Corpus Christi College, Oxford. *Mulliner Book* compiled in two parts, first at St Paul's, second (after No. 77) at Oxford, where he knew Blitheman.

MUNDY, William.

See under Chap. III.

NEWMAN, ?

Fl. mid-sixteenth century. Chorister at St Paul's Cathedral under Mulliner. Nothing otherwise known.

PRESTON, Thomas.

Fl. fifteenth/sixteenth century. 1493 The Precentor William Charite's Inventory of Music in the Augustinian Abbey of St Mary of the Meadows, Leicester, contains a polyphonic Antiphon by Preston. A Preston (Thomas?) was also: ? 1543 Organist and informator at Magdalen College, Oxford. ? 1558–59 Joint organist with John Marbeck at St George's, Windsor. 1559–1563 Organist St George's, Windsor.

REDFORD, John.

c. 1486–1547. 1532 Organist and Almoner, Elemosinarius, of St Paul's Cathedral*, in succession to Thomas Hickman. 1534 Vicar Choral. Thomas Mulliner was perhaps his pupil, certainly his associate. 1537 (13th Oct.) Te Deum sung at St Paul's for the birth of Prince Edward. 1538/9 'Play of Wyt and science'. 1543 (20th June) signed the Act of Supremacy.

RHYS, Philip ap.

?–c. 1559. Contemporary (and associate?) of Redford. Welsh composer and organist, 'off Saynt Poulls in London'. Organist at St Mary-at-Hill, Billingsgate, which he left in 1547 to go to St Paul's (following the death of Redford?).

SHELBYE, ?

Fl. mid-sixteenth century. Chorister at St Paul's Cathedral under Mulliner. 1543 Master of the boys at Canterbury Cathedral.

SHEPPARD, John (or Shepherd).

151?–? Chorister at St Paul's Cathedral. 1542–56 at various times *Informator* at Magdalen College, Oxford (see Preston).

STROWGER, E(dward?).

Fl. early sixteenth century. Nothing otherwise known. See under Chap. III.

---

* His duties perhaps included play-producing for the boys. His 'Play of Wyt and science' survives in a British Museum manuscript (Add. 15233), which also contains poems by him, John Thorne and others.

TALLIS, Thomas.

15?–1585 Chorister at St Paul's Cathderal. 1525 Member of Royal Household Chapel under Henry VIII, subsequently under Edward VI, Mary and Elizabeth. 1537–8 sang at St Mary-at-Hill, Billingsgate. 1540 Master of singers at Waltham Abbey at its dissolution. Teacher of William Byrd (q.v.) and joint organist with him of Chapel Royal; granted exclusive patent with him to print music.

TAVERNER, John.

c. 1495–1545. 1525 Clerk-fellow of Collegiate Church of Tattershall, Lincs. 1526–30 First *Informator* and organist at Wolsey's Cardinal College, Oxford. This huge foundation, calling for a 'peritissimus informator', was re-named after Wolsey's fall. Taverner's festal Masses date from this period. But he was involved in religious controversy, and was imprisoned for heresy (see p. 7). He became an agent of Thomas Cromwell in the destruction of monasteries, and eventually abandoned music.

THORNE, John.

?–1573 (Associate of Redford?). 1540 Organist at St Mary-at-Hill, Billingsgate. 1543–1573 Organist at York Minster.

TYE, Christopher.

151?–1572. Born at Westminster. 1537–9 Lay clerk at King's College, Cambridge. 1541–62 Organist at Ely Cathedral. 1545 Gentleman of Chapel Royal. After 1562 became priest. 1564 Rector (simultaneously) of Little Wilbraham, Newton and Doddington-cum-March, all in the diocese of Ely. Compositions almost exclusively vocal.

WHITE, Robert (or Whyte).

153?–1574. (organist and ?) Master of Choristers at Westminster Abbey. 1562–67, Organist at Ely Cathedral in succession to Tye. Chief composition: *Lamentations*, sung at *Tenebrae* in Holy Week.

WOODSON, ?

Fl. early sixteenth century. Nothing otherwise known.

WYNSLATE, Richard (or Wynslade).

?–1572. 1537–8 Singer at St Mary-at-Hill. 1540–72 Organist and Master of choristers at Winchester Cathedral after it became a Cathedral of the 'new foundation' at the Reformation. A statute of Henry VIII, dated 20th June 1544, provides for the appointment of ten boys and an organist. Wynslate was therefore the organist at the Royal wedding of Mary with Philip II of Spain, in July, 1554.

THE ORGAN OF THE PERIOD (1400–1558)

The Positive organ of the fourteenth and fifteenth centuries appears in numerous illustrations with a single keyboard, and a double row of pipes, one larger than the other. From this probably came its common description, 'a pair of organs'.* The fact that many divergent sources present such a uniform impression suggests that the Positive organ had reached a generally accepted common standard in Northern Europe by this time, after a preceding period of development.

Other notable advances, which seem to have been particularly marked in France, Switzerland, Holland and Scandinavia, were mainly concerned with the extension of the keyboard, the introduction of pedal keys, and the separation of the ranks of pipes by means of stops, There is no evidence to suggest that British organ builders did not take full advantage of these developments; indeed, what evidence there is suggests that they did. The steady interchange between England and the continent, particularly France and the Low Countries, has already been mentioned as one of the prevailing features of the whole mediaeval period.

But although it is quite possible that a few organs in English Cathedrals, by the early sixteenth century, had a second short-compass manual, called the *Tenor*, they probably had no pedal keys. These did not appear in England until the early eighteenth century, perhaps as much as 400 years after their development on the Continent. Pedal keys were introduced as early as 1306 by Lodewijk van Valbeke of Louvain.†

The compass of the keyboard, which in the twelfth century generally covered two octaves, was extended downwards to CC, so that by the thirteenth–fourteenth century three octaves were the general compass, and by the sixteenth century four, that is to say CC–c², though no doubt this varied with different instruments. In England the lowest note was GG. To start with, in the earliest organs the only chromatic was B♭. Gradually this was increased,

* Which means 'a pair of pipes' (*organum* in the Vulgate = pipe).
† Bragard & de Hen *Musical Instruments in Art & History*, p. 74.

until the keyboard was fully chromatic by the fifteenth century. The lowest octave made use of the so-called 'short octave', probably to save space, pipes and money, by leaving out unnecessary pipes. The appearance of the lowest keys of an English Positive might be: G-C-A, with A appearing in the position of C♯ chromatic. Another arrangement might be ..

```
   |'F#|G#|
   |D|E|B♭|
C|F|G|A|B|
```

The key placed in the position of the chromatic F♯ sounded D; the key in the position of the G♯ sounded E. When, later, the missing chromatic notes (F♯, G♯) became necessary, 'split keys' were made which supplied them. The front part of the key played one note, the back part another. This practice was taken over by makers of stringed keyboard instruments, such as the virginal, spinet, and harpsichord, and remained in some cases even as late as the eighteenth century.

The invention of stops enabled the player to separate the different ranks of pipes, hitherto indivisible. From the simultaneous sounding of more than one pipe for each note arose the principle of the Mixture, which has been described by Praetorius in his *Syntagma Musicum* (1615–19). The rank of pipes on the front of the windchest were known as *Vordersatz*; those behind, *Hintersatz*; the pipework as a whole as *Blockwerk*. Underlying this trend in tonal design was the continental *Werkprincip*, which was later to develop into the conception of organs made up of separate but complete divisions, such as are particularly associated with the North German School of Arp Schnitger in the late seventeenth century. But this lay in the future, and little hint of it was reflected after the sixteenth century in England, where the Reformation acted as a barrier to the interchange of ideas so far as organ design is concerned. It is reasonable to suppose, moreover, as Sumner suggests, that after the Reformation the organ became somewhat discredited in England through its association with the mediaeval Latin liturgy, and that partly for this reason attention focussed more on the other domestic keyboard instruments. Certainly, in the event, British organ builders after the Reformation lacked a stimulus, just at the very moment when their continental colleagues were beginning to reap rich rewards from their innovations.

But the names of several British organ-builders at the beginning of the sixteenth century are known; William Wotton was an organ-builder in Oxford, where he built instruments in Magdalen College (1486) and Merton College (1489). The Howe family, of whom John Howe was the most prominent, covered three generations between 1485 and *c.* 1560; their work whether as builders or repairers took them into numerous London churches, such as St Mary-at-Hill, St Michael's Cornhill, St Martin-in-the-fields, and further afield, for instance to York Minster. The instrument built at Holy Trinity, Coventry in 1526 is mentioned on p. 48.

The Chappington family extends over a somewhat later period, from *c.* 1536 to *c.* 1620. They came from Devonshire, and most of their work was therefore in the West country. Richard Chappington built an organ in St Olave's Exeter in 1536, and at Woodbridge in Devon in 1538, and (his son ?) Hugh was well known in the area, to judge from his numerous contracts for maintenance and repair, particularly in Salisbury.

Henry VIII's Household Establishment included an organ-maker, William Beton, whose duties included maintaining and tuning the collection of regals that the King and the Princess Mary seem to have enjoyed.

But of all these builders' work nothing more is known than the barest facts. The only pre-Reformation instrument whose specification has survived was one built by Anthony Duddyngton in 1519–20 for the church of All Hallows, Barking, Unfortunately the details of this much quoted organ are not without ambiguity, owing to the somewhat sphinx-like wording of the agreement, which has caused much contradictory speculation by several commentators.*

---

* First quoted in full in Rimbault *The early English Organ builders*, (1864) App. III p. 75.

See Glyn, preface to *Early English Organ Music* (1939). Also Williams, *Diapason* (MT, June 1965), Caldwell, *Duddyngton's Organ* (MT March 1967), *et al.* (Clutton and Niland *The British Organ*, pp. 48, 60, is not very reliable).

This endenture made the yere of oure lorde god M¹ V⁰ XIX and in the moneth of July XXIX day. Witnesseth that Antony Duddyngton, Citezen of London, Organ-maker, hath made a full bargayn, condycionally, with Maister Willm. Petenson, Doctour in Divinite, Vicar of Alhalowe Barkyng, Robt. Whytehed and John Churche, Wardeyns of the same Churche, and Maisters of the P'isshe of Alhalowe Barkyng, next ye Tower of London, to make an instrument, that ys to say a payer of organs for the foresed churche, of dwble Ce-fa-ut that ys to say, XXVII playne keyes, and the pryncipale to conteyn the lenth of V foote, so folowing w^t Bassys called Diapason to the same, conteyning length of X foot or more: And to be dowble pryncipalls thoroweout the seid instrument, so that the pyppes w^t inforth shall be as fyne metall and stuff as the utter parts, that is to say of pure Tyn, w^t as fewe stoppes as may be convenient.

And the seid Antony to have ernest VI^li XIII^s IIIJ^d. Also the foresaid Antony askyth V quarters of respytt, that ys to say, from the fest of Seynt Mighell the Archaungell, next following to the fest of Seynt Mighell the day twelvemonth following. And also undernethe this condicion, that the foresaid Antony shall convey the belowes in the loft abowf in the seid Quere of Alhalowes, w^t a pype to the sond boarde. Also this p'mysed by the said Antony, that yf the foresaid Maister, Doctour, Vicaire, Churche Wardeyns, Maisters of the p'isshe, be not content nor lyke not the seid instrument, that then they shall allowe him for convaying of the belows xl^s. for his cost of them, and to restore the rest of the Truest agayn to the said Maisters. And yf the seid Antony decesse and depart his naturall lyf w^tin the forseid V quarters, that then hys wyff or hys executours or his assignes shall fully content the foresaid some of iij^li. Xiij^s. iiij^d. to the seid Vicare, and Churche Wardeyns, and Maisters of the p'isshe w^tout any delay. And yf they be content w^t the seid instrument, to pay to the seid Antony fyfty poundes sterlinge. In Wittnesse whereof the seid p'ties to these endentures chaungeably have set their sealls. Geven the day and yere abovesaid.

Anthony Duddyngton was clearly a shrewd man of business. He could not afford to be slipshod, as the instrument was an important one, for a wealthy London church, not far from St Paul's, where there were already two organs, one in the Lady

Chapel. So he allowed for its construction to take fifteen months, and to cost the comparatively large sum of £50. Various contingencies were taken into account by the contract, including his own possible death, in which case part of the initial deposit of £6.13.4. would be repayable. This rather suggests that Duddyngton was an elderly man in 1519, as well as an experienced craftsman. At all events the instrument seems to have been satisfactorily installed, and on 22nd March 1520, he received a further £30 on account.

The compass of the single keyboard was 3 octaves and a sixth, GG–a^{ll}; it would have included 17 chromatic as well as the 27 'playne' keys. This was standard; six years later John Howe built an instrument of the same compass, with seven stops, at Holy Trinity Church, Coventry.

Probably Duddyngton's *Blockwerk* consisted of three ranks of pipes, which extended over the whole range of the instrument. The upper ranks were called *Principal*; the lower rank was called *Diapason*. All the pipes were tin; there were no wooden ones, such as at Durham and St Paul's.* The tone-quality was therefore clear and well-defined, suited to a building of moderate size. The pipe-lengths, five and ten feet respectively, were standard for a keyboard whose lowest note was GG. The pipes of the two Principal ranks would have been of different scales, and could be used either together or independently; the stops were levers or knobs—'as few as may be convenient'. There must have been at least three such stops, to operate each of the ranks.

There is no mention in this otherwise very thorough and business-like contract of any chromatic keys; only 'playne' ones; but it is inconceivable, as the music of this time shows, that the keyboard should have consisted of only white notes.† What is most likely is that certain fundamental standards of design were accepted and assumed.

Though it is clearly a mistake to draw general conclusions from one specific instance, particularly when the evidence is not entirely clear, it seems probable that Duddyngton's unique specification

* See p. 6.
† As Margaret Glyn suggests *op. cit.*

and compass were standard for a church organ of moderate size. The upward compass of the keyboard might extend, in some cases to c^{11}, but rarely if ever beyond; and there might well be more ranks making up the *Blockwerk*. But the repertoire of this period could be played on such a keyboard as Duddyngton's, with the simplest registration; the only contrast in dynamics was that provided by the unison and the octave, which could be either used separately or in combination. In certain compositions, for instance Redford's *Tui sunt coeli* (EECM 10, No. 27), where the upward compass extends above c^{11}, the organist would play the piece an octave lower, with only the upper stop (*Principal*) drawn. In no such case does the lowest note go below C. It goes without saying that alterations of stops in the course of a piece, particularly a piece based on a plainchant, would have been most uncommon.

As far as it is possible to judge, the pipes of the early organ produced a loud tone, and the Diapason had a strong, flute-like quality. The lower rank of Duddyngton's organ would provide the foundation for either of the two Principals; the resulting choruses could be contrasted in volume and quality.

As far as pitch is concerned, in this country GG remained the lowest note right through to 1837; generally the diapason of ten foot was the standard for this compass, which gave the organ a pitch approximately comparable to the standard pitch to-day (A = 440). But there was no fixed and uniform procedure; the pitch of organs varied, along with other details of specification, from place to place and builder to builder. It was not standardised, as it is now. Occasionally the same builder used different pitch for different instruments?

3

1558–1656
Tudor Organ Music (II)

THE BACKGROUND

The hundred years between the accession of Queen Elizabeth I and the death of Thomas Tomkins, saw a great release of creative energy, and formed a period most rich in musical development. Pronounced advances were made in styles and techniques of composition; the invention and enlargement of instrumental ensembles gathered pace; the acceptance and establishment of music, to say nothing of its printing and publication, became more widespread. And while many of these developments did not necessarily directly concern the organist, they all nevertheless contributed to the background against which organ music of a new kind was written and played.

In addition to the fresh requirements of the English liturgy, many styles and techniques of secular composition grew and flourished at this time. Among the new *genres* which, though they were major musical achievements, did not directly concern the organist, were, first, those various categories of vocal music, such as the lute song, the madrigal, and its derivatives such as the ballet and part-song; second, those multifarious and widespread types of dramatic and theatre music, culminating in the court masque. The first of these categories came to fruition under Elizabeth; the second under the Stuarts.

If some of these important musical innovations were initially of Italian or French derivation—though later coloured with peculiarly English characteristics, in the course of their naturalisation—the same cannot be said for the two other chief areas of musical growth in this country, which involved the organist more directly. The first of these was the exploitation of keyboard composition; the second was the growth of concerted chamber music.

The gradual evolution of the art of keyboard composition in the hands of British composers at this time has been already well attested, and although composers of other countries in Europe were writing for the keyboard—notably the Spaniard Cabezon, the Italians Gabrieli and Frescobaldi, and above all the Dutchman Sweelinck—nevertheless it was the political, social and religious circumstances arising from the Reformation in this country that combined to cause the British composers to originate, develop and propagate a unique style of keyboard work.

The circumstances prevailing in this country from Elizabeth's accession, caused particular emphasis to be laid on domestic music-making, which gave the keyboard composer a vastly wider scope. The organist became also a virginalist, and the repertoire of keyboard music was as a result enormously enriched.

The forms that were exploited will be discussed shortly.

One of the immediate results of these developments was the acceptance of the chamber organ. It came to be used both as a solo and as a concerted instrument in Court entertainment, and the 'Private Musick'. Henceforward therefore organ music falls under two headings, the secular and the sacred.

The secular keyboard music of this period was intended either for the virginal or for the chamber organ. The two are largely interchangeable. The virginal tradition can be traced quite precisely. Beginning with such a piece as Hugh Aston's *Hornpipe*, or *My Lady Wynkfyld's rounde*,* it flourished towards the end of the sixteenth century with such collections as Byrd's *My Ladye Nevells Booke* (1591), *Cosyn's Virginal Book* (c. 1600), *Parthenia* (1612), *The Fitzwilliam Virginal Book* (1609–19); its decline towards the middle of the seventeenth century can be almost exactly dated; 1656. This year saw not only the death of Thomas Tomkins, but also the last of the chief collections of virginal music, *Elizabeth Rogers' Virginal Book*. By this time dances such as the *Saraband* and *Courante* had practically replaced the earlier Elizabethan *Pavan* and

* MS r¹.

Galliard, and with the addition of a *Prelude*, already foreshadowed in *Parthenia*, the form of the later harpsichord *Suite* or *Lesson* was gradually evolving.

But if the virginal tradition came to an end, the use of the chamber organ did not. For domestic music-making, mainly at the Court of James I and others of the nobility, had meanwhile developed in fresh directions still. The growth in popularity of the viol consort, and the violin, led composers to invent new forms for such music. They found them in the existing *In nomine*, *Fantasia*, and dances of the keyboard composers. But the composers at James's court, among whom may chiefly be mentioned Ferrabosco, Cooper,★ and Henry and William Lawes, added several fresh dimensions to this newly-growing chamber music, by using the chamber organ both as a continuo and as a concerted instrument.

The use of the organ in conjunction with viols was perhaps, in retrospect, inevitable. Other instruments than the organ were also used as continuo—the harp and theorbo for instance. But the fact that the viol was not given to maintaining a *sostenuto* tone over any length of phrase, and that its characteristic speech consisted of short figures, made the sustained quality of organ-tone the perfect foil for it. Moreover the chamber organ was capable of considerable agility, as the technique of the virginalists had shown; so the composer of the new chamber music could expect the violinist, violist and organist to discourse on equal terms. The new concerted music was a partnership between the players.

Thus grew the chamber sonatas and fantasias for violins, viols and organ, whose chief exponents, among many others, were Alfonso Ferrabosco, John Cooper, William Lawes, John Jenkins, and Christopher Simpson. It was a new form of music, which proved to be both durable and capable of later development. It continued in the later seventeenth century in the form of the Trio Sonata; it developed in the eighteenth century into the Organ Concerto.

Both these developments must be kept for a later chapter, but two consequences of their growth are of immediate importance. The first is that the pronounced trend towards secular, domestic

★ *Alias* Coperario.

music-making at this time, combined with the anti-clericalism that gathered such pace under Elizabeth, and found its outlet in the philosophy of Puritanism, naturally reduced the importance laid on the sacred, liturgical use of the organ in churches and cathedrals. Moreover the adoption by chamber music composers of the forms that hitherto were the preserve of the organist, such as the *In Nomine* and the *Fantasia*, to say nothing of the song-variation, meant that the composer of organ music for sacred use henceforward was required in his turn to seek new forms, if he was not merely to revert to basing his music on a well-worn plain-chant such as *Miserere* or *Felix namque*—which by the seventeenth century were wearing somewhat thin, if they were wearing at all.

Organists found a two-sided solution to this problem; first the *Verse*, second the *Voluntary*. Originally the terms were interchangeable, describing as they did a piece of free composition, not based on a plainchant, or pre-arranged theme, such as a hexachord or ground. Gradually, however, the term *Voluntary* came to be used exclusively to refer to any free (non-liturgical) composition for the organ, which was intended to be played in church or cathedral.

Henceforward therefore the twin prongs that make up organ music develop independently; the secular in the direction of the Sonata and Concerto, the sacred in the direction of the Voluntary.

The second immediate consequence was that organ music was securely enough based, in court and chamber, to withstand the onslaught of the Commonwealth. The Parliamentarians might remove organs from cathedrals, and places of public worship; they were not able to eradicate a tradition of private music-making. In the event, the effects of the revolution, on either of these two aspects of organ music, were slight.

The extent of the change brought about in the musical art in general, and organ music in particular, during this most splendid hundred-year period, may be measured in two other ways; first by the composers' idiom and style, particularly so far as the discovery and exploitation of tonality is concerned; second by the increase of instrumental music at Court, and in other houses of the nobility.

As far as idiom and style are concerned, the outward forms of liturgical organ composition that marked the work of the Redford school, only survived the Reformation in a few cases, such as Tallis, and one or two others. However the discovery of a true organ style by Redford was not lost by his successors, who built on the foundations laid by him, particularly so far as polyphonic keyboard textures were concerned. The assimilation of virginal technique helped rather than hindered this process, because it created a greater textural interest in the music. The organ both preceded and outlived the virginal, and greatly benefited from its domestic equivalent.

There was no hard and fast difference between an organ and a virginal piece; rather the distinction lay in the style of performance, and in the suitability of a piece for a particular occasion. In the list of repertoire,* those pieces shown as 'organ works' would be chiefly suitable for sacred use; those shown as 'other keyboard works' would be intended for secular performance, and more appropriate for the chamber organ or virginal. The embellished and ornamental style called for by the virginal, with its single wire to each note, was unnecessary and inappropriate when applied to the fuller sound of the organ, in which the sustained tone implied a simpler style. The light sonority and the refined texture which characterise so much virginal music, and are derived from the lutenist song-writers, can well sound ridiculous if transposed directly to the organ. So the same piece would be played differently on each instrument; the skill and taste of the player were the criterion.

The change from modality to tonality was effected during this period. At one end of the period, Tallis, working still in a modal tradition, developed a stronger tonal sense than his fellow church composers, particularly in his shorter organ pieces; at the other end, composers had discovered in tonality a unifying element for an entire structure. This sense of tonality is most marked in the extrovert and brilliant masques of the early seventeenth century; indeed it is difficult for us to conceive of a Baroque spectacle whose music was not based on a sense of key. The clearest example of this

* See p. 112.

assimilation of the tonal sense is shown in a work such as William Lawes' most lavish and extravagant masque *Triumph of Peace* (1634), in which Edward Dent* noticed 'the composer's strong sense of balanced tonality'.

But this progressive key-sense was chiefly applicable to the secular composers, when writing chamber music and Court spectaculars. As far as the organ composer was concerned, particularly if his music was intended for church use, the link with modality was naturally stronger, the assimilation of tonality more gradual.

At the end of one of his manuscripts† Bull wrote a table of tones then in general use:

TONE	TONALITY	KEY SIGNATURE
1	D minor	—
2	G minor	one flat
3	A minor	—
4	E minor	—
5	C major	—
6	F major	one flat
7	D major	—
8	G major	—

The tone of a piece is decided not by the key-signature, but by the starting note, and final note. A major scale was formed from a minor scale by starting it one tone lower. Thus, starting from G, with the key-signature of B flat, would make a minor tonality; starting one tone lower, from F, still with the key-signature of B flat, would make a major tonality. The table shows four minor tonalities, four major ones, and this scheme may be taken to apply to all the organ pieces of this period.‡

The greater general acceptance of music in the sixteenth to seventeenth centuries ran parallel to these more technical develop-

* E. J. Dent *Foundation of English Opera*, p. 39. See also M. Lefkowitz *William Lawes*, p. 224.

† MS o.

‡ It has also been used to decide their distribution order in the *Musica Britannica* volumes (see Dart, Introduction to Vol. XIX).

ments. Under Henry VIII, music was in effect an embellishment of church or court. With the overthrow of the monasteries, and more particularly after the Reformation, the performance of music spread far wider; it became popular in private houses, theatres and taverns. Composers wrote for, or dedicated their pieces to, specific individuals. Musicians who had hitherto been employed by the monastic foundations now found it necessary to ply their trade outside; while within the church itself a new repertoire of services and anthems was needed to replace the former masses and motets.

Foreign influence and contacts continued under Elizabeth, though invariably these were now tempered and refashioned by the assertiveness of British composers, whose work covered all the existing *genres*, and several others besides. There had always been foreign influences in English music, whether that of the Flemish motet, the French chanson, or the Italian madrigal; there have always been those in England for whom the music of foreigners possesses a spell-like *mystique*; not for nothing did John Cooper return from Italy as Giovanni Coperario. By the time of the Stuarts music was much more securely established as a part of court and social life than it had been in the sixteenth century. Many houses of the nobility employed musicians, and in addition to the long-established Chapel Royal, musicians were also employed in the 'Private Musick' at the Court of James I. This group of instrumentalists were available for Court entertainments, masques and other private performances; and at the end of his reign, in December 1641, Charles I could challenge any prince of the Baroque in the lavish extent of his musical establishment:*

Trumpettors	20
Drummes and Phife	9
For the Wind Instruments	18
For the violins	13
For Lutes, violls & voices	23 (incl. Henry & William Lawes, Giles & Robert Tomkins)
Master of the Musique	Nicholas Lanier

* Lafontaine *The Private Musick*, pp. 109/11.

For the Harp	Mr Le Flelle
Organ keeper and tuner	Edward Norgate
For the Virginall	Mr Warwick
Musical Instrument maker	George Gill
Musician extraordinary and stringer of the lutes	William Allaby

It is natural to expect that important state occasions would be celebrated by the finest collection of musicians available; and a comparison of the singers and instrumentalists at the funerals of Henry VIII (1547) and James I (1625) is doubly instructive,* as it not only illustrates the increased size of the later ceremony, but enables a comparison to be made between the 'Private Musick' of James and that of his son Charles I, which has been already referred to;

Funeral of Henry VIII

Gentilmen of the Chapell†	20
Trumpettors	18
Singing men and children under Philips	9
Mynstrells	7
Musytyans	5
Shackebuttes	4
Vyols	6
Fluttes	5
Vialls	2
Fyfer	1
Drume player	1
Harper	1
Bage piper	1

Funeral of James I
'The chamber of our late sovereign Lord King James'

Trumpettors	21
Drums and Phife	4
Musitians for Violins	13
Musicians for windy instruments	21
The Consorte	11

The Chappell

William Heather, Doctor	
Nathaniel Giles, Doctor & Master of the children	
John Stephens, gentleman, recorder of songes	
Thomas Tomkins, Organist	
Gentlemen of the Chappell	19
Children of the Chappell	12
Orlando Gibbons, privy organ	
Sampson Rowdon, bellringer	
Singing men of Westminster	18

* Lafontaine *op. cit.* pp. 7–8, pp. 57–8.
† c.f. also Le Huray *Music and the Reformation in England* pp. 68, 73–4.

Two Shagbutts, Two
    Cornitors   4
Choristers of Westminster   10
Bellringers   4

THE MUSIC

Against such a background we may consider the music itself.
Four major figures dominate the period—Byrd, Bull, Gibbons
and Tomkins. These composers are therefore treated separately.
But as the list of repertoire shows, many other composers contributed important works to it, and developed the organ, whether
as a sacred or secular instrument. Their music falls into the following broad categories:

1. The *Fantasia*, or (slighter) *Fancy*.
   This single-movement piece might be free, and (increasingly)
   chromatic, or based on the six notes of the hexachord.

2. The *Verse* or *Voluntary*; originally shorter than the *Fantasia*, and
   more akin to the *Ricercar* of the continental schools.

3. Pieces based on dances, which gradually evolved into the movements of the later Harpsichord *Suite* or *Lesson*.

4. Pieces, usually in variation form, based on songs.
   a) Secular, such as folk songs, lute songs or viol songs.
   b) Sacred, such as traditional plainchant. The technique was
   derived from that used by mediaeval composers for the Hymn
   and Antiphon.

Virginal music originally sprang from organ music, from which
it derived its basic forms, until it assumed an individual style.
Generally speaking pieces for both instruments occur in all these
four categories particularly when, as the seventeenth century progressed, the organ came to be used more as a secular instrument,
interchangeable with the virginal.

Prominent among those composers who developed the *Fantasia*, whether for keyboard or viols or both, were those composers whose work centred round the Court of James I or Charles I; John Cooper, Charles Coleman, Alfonso Ferrabosco, Thomas Lupo. Sometimes their instrumental compositions were transcribed for organ.

In the hands of John Cooper the *Fantasia* is usually a substantial movement, whose style is harmonic rather than contrapuntal, and in which there is little sustaining of the 'point'. The music is usually in four parts. Indeed the examples contained in MS p¹, though they are described as 'Three fantasias of six parts' and 'Two fantasias a 5', are all however reduced to four parts for performance on the organ. The fifteen 'Fancies of 5 parts' in MS s¹ are probably based on Italian madrigals, to judge from their titles; certainly their style is one of vocal polyphony; only very occasionally are more than four parts used. The twenty-four untitled pieces, which might well be called fantasias, all show an embryonic fugal technique, though the 'point' is not, generally speaking, maintained beyond the first entry of the voices, and the phrases are somewhat short-winded. Cooper's style is lightweight.

A much greater spaciousness, and feeling of the *sostenuto* quality of organ music, is shown in the *Fantasias* of Cooper's contemporaries Ferrabosco and Lupo. The eleven 4-part *Fantasias* of Ferrabosco contained in MS p¹ are brilliant. The 'point' almost amounts to a fugue subject, while the composer shows a developed sense of tonality. His two *Fancies* in MS d are equally effective; the one substantial, steadily moving, the other shorter, and opening with quick scale passages. Of the six untitled pieces in MS s¹, three are *In nomine* settings, with the plainchant in the mean part, and the other parts freely based on it; the remaining three are short, free pieces in fantasia style; each of them falls into three sections, like a Pavan or Galliard, of which the middle section uses a related tonality.

The seven substantial pieces by Lupo in the same manuscript also achieve the sustained consistency of characteristic organ music. Three of them are freely based on the *In nomine* theme. This also provides the basis for White's single work, which uses more

chromaticism than those of the other composers, and is marked
by the somewhat obvious devices of syncopated entries, and wide-
ranging scale passages. Such a work bears no similarity to the very
short and uninteresting hexachord piece in MS u—if indeed it is
by the same composer.

Experiments with chromaticism occur frequently at this time.
Ferrabosco's *Hexachord Fantasia*, in MS t, is a substantial piece in
two parts, in which the 6-note phrase starts on a different degree
of the scale with each successive entry, rising a semitone each time.
In the first part of the work, it is used ascending, in the second part
descending; considerable chromaticism is the unavoidable result.

Chromaticism also contributes to the expressiveness of Nicholas
Carleton's music, particularly in his chromatic study *A verse upon
the 'sharpe'*. His other free compositions include a short but highly
expressive *Prelude* in D minor, and *A verse of four parts*, which is
chiefly characterised by the independent movement of the inner
parts; one part, however, usually has a longer-held note, derived
from the *cantus firmus* technique. Carleton's only use of traditional
plainchant occurs in his duet, which is an *In nomine*, set as 'A verse
for two to play on one virginall or organs'. It is altogether a
weightier work than the Tomkins duet.* Each player has three
parts; the composition is thus in six parts, with the *In nomine*
theme in the middle of the upper three.

Two considerable pieces, which also effectively explore chromaticism, are the work of Emanuel Soncino. He is an otherwise
unknown composer, though it requires no great powers of divina-
tion to deduce that he was an Italian who worked close to, or was
in some way connected with, the Court at this time—along with
numerous others of his fellow-countrymen. His *Prelude*, in MS a,
achieves consistency by the repetition of the same figure, and
brilliance by such means as a powerful sequence of rising fourths,
and chromaticism. The same characteristics appear more explicitly
in his *Cromatica*, in MS c, which exploits the chromatic fourth,
both harmonically, and as a source of melodic material.

The single four part *Fantasia* by another unknown composer
William Simmes, in MS o¹, maintains a full texture throughout;

* See p. 108.

only occasionally do imitative entries appear, and the left hand is used in *continuo* style, against the two right hand parts.

But of the composers about whom nothing is known, far the most tantalising is the family of Strowger. It seems unlikely that the E. Strowger whose *Miserere* appears in MS t, is the same as the Nicholas Strowger whose works appear in later collections, such as the *Fitzwilliam Virginal Book*. Perhaps Nicholas was the son, E(dward?) the father. At all events, the music is of an excellence that quite belies their obscurity.

The Miserere in MS t is a strict canon in two parts over a *cantus firmus*; a remarkable short piece which, within the limits of fourteen bars, achieves a homogeneous texture without recourse to a 'point'. But the four complete works of Nicholas Strowger are much more substantial, and brilliantly extend the limits of organ composition of this time. His hexachord piece is a free 2-part interpretation of the scale-pattern. Starting with a downward scale in the left hand, in long notes, it changes in the second half to quicker notes in ascending patterns, and sequences between the parts.

This rhythmical technique of progressive lessening of the metrical unit is also used in the *Fantasia* in the *Fitzwilliam Virginal Book* (MS p). Here the process of diminution of note values is a more gradual one, and the effect of brilliance correspondingly more marked. But Strowger also introduces the more far-reaching principle of varying the material, and using contrasted *motifs*. His countersubject at bar 30 is an extension of the *faburden* principle of an earlier age, and an exciting discovery which clearly anticipates the later development of the fugal countersubject:

Example 4

Fantasia (*Fitzwilliam Virginal Book*, LXXXIX)   Nicholas Strowger
(Opening)   (bars 30-31)

etc.   etc.

(a and a¹ show the rhythmic connection)

The MS u contains two complete *In nomine* by Nicholas Strowger, and one incomplete, anonymous *In nomine*, which because of its style may confidently be ascribed to him also. The first *In nomine*, with two imitative parts, also ends like the *Fantasias* with quicker movement, while the second *In nomine*, in four parts, builds to a full climax. The unfinished *In nomine* starts like the first with two imitative parts against the *cantus firmus*; but its texture and counterpoint have more sustained brilliance, which make this a most tantalising fragment, and one which positively invites completion.

John Mundy's two *Fantasias* in the *Fitzwilliam Virginal Book* are widely contrasted. The first is essentially an organ piece, spacious in its phrasing and full of variety; though constructed sectionally, the same material is used throughout the work. The second, also in sections, is primarily a virginal piece, and is an early example of programme music: '*Fair wether*', '*Lightning*', '*Thunder*' are the titles of the sections.

Two organists associated with the West Country also enriched the repertoire in different ways. Elway (or Edward?) Bevin at Bristol Cathedral was a small-scale composer, and preoccupied with technical matters. His *Brief and Short Instruction* (1631) earned very wide circulation; while his explanation of ornaments is of particular interest to us today.

The following explanation of ornaments occurs in MS a, f. 5, (c.1630) where they are written immediately after Prelude (No. 2) by Gibbons:

'Graces in play'   Elway Bevin

'The Graces before is here exprest in notes'

The contemporary (1971) view of the interpretation of ornaments of this period is expressed by Professor Dart, and appears in
all his editions, as well as those of other editors:*

Ornaments: the interpretation of these still remains a matter of
some dispute. $\natural$ seems to mean ♫, and $\ddagger$ may mean ♫ or
♫ or ♩ or ♪ , according to the context. Ornament-signs often
seem to be used for no other purpose than to draw attention to an
accented note—to point an unusual harmony or to bring out some
of the many cross-rhythms that add such a sparkle to the music—
and in performance they are sometimes best omitted altogether.
(The notation used in the present volume has been chosen to throw
some of the more important cross-rhythms into relief. In general
the music calls for a light, singing style.)

Bevin's compositions are for the most part short and simple;
for instance the first of the two *Preludes*, in MS a, uses a straightforward toccata-style passage, with short notes, in one part against
longer held notes in the other; the *Fancy*, in MS c, is a piece in
triple metre, like a *Galliard* or *La Volta*, with a melody in the right
hand and accompaniment in the left. This straightforward formula
also occurs in the only known examples of Hugh Facy's work,
which appears in the same manuscript. Bevin's other short pieces
are largely technical studies of one sort or another. His canon on
the *Miserere* has more rhythmic interest than the earlier Strowger
example; his other studies in canon are effective as well as ingenious. The 'Dubble Canon' (4 in 2) is strictly maintained, unlike the
other single canon; both alternate red and black ink in the manuscript.

The other West Country organist was John Lugge, of Exeter
Cathedral, whose compositions are much more substantial and
important than those of Bevin. His work covered three of the four
categories of keyboard composition already mentioned. His solitary
Fantasia is a large piece, which uses the hexachord like a *cantus
firmus* in the inner of the three parts, 'canto in diapente'.

* Of *Musica Britannica*, and other Stainer & Bell publications.

Lugge's three *Voluntaries*, in one substantial movement, like the fantasia, alternate 'double' and 'single'—that is to say the Great and the Chayre, which make up the 'Double organ'. The first two voluntaries are in three parts, while the third uses four, and is both broader in conception and more brilliant in its integrated counterpoint.

The remainder of Lugge's organ works fall into the fourth category, of pieces based on traditional plainchant. He strongly favours three-part writing. Of the six settings of *Gloria tibi Trinitas*, only one—the second—uses four parts. He also seeks to introduce variety, particularly of rhythm; the third piece maintains a rhythmic 'point', while the second (in four parts) uses a 2-against-3 pattern. And while Lugge's range of note-proportions is not so wide as Bull's,* he frequently varies the ratio between the held-note and the shorter ones. He evidently felt that the use of a traditional plainchant tended to fetter his free invention, and in *Christe qui lux es* he introduced an embellishment of the *cantus firmus* in bar 11–12.

Lugge was organist at Exeter for more than forty years, until the Commonwealth, and his compositions are entirely conceived in terms of the instrument. There were at least two organs in the cathedral, and frequently other instruments (Cornetts, Shackbutts, Viols) were used as well. The Chapter were evidently anxious that music should be heard. The organ was played with the Psalms at morning prayer,† as well as with the anthems; and Lugge's contemporary Edward Gibbons, who was choirmaster, has left one example of 'A Prelude upon ye organ as was then usuall before ye Anthem'. But Gibbons was no organ composer, and his prelude, which is a piece of almost unrelieved monotony, chiefly serves to focus attention on the real merits of his colleague's work.

A much clearer foretaste of the Restoration style is provided by the single surviving piece of Orlando Gibbons's pupil Richard Portman. The sole manuscript source‡ is an Organ Book at Wimborne Minster dated 1670, though the two organ pieces it contains

* See p. 83.
† Betty Matthews *The Organs of Exeter Cathedral*, p. 2.
‡ MS u³.

were written before the Commonwealth. Both are fine examples of organ Verses; that by Christopher Gibbons for single organ (see p. 145), that by Portman for double organ. Both fall into clearly defined sections; Portman's piece falls into two, with a clear division at bar 37. Though the material is not quite so well integrated, nor the harmony so original as that of Gibbons's Verse, both pieces finish boldly with left hand scale runs against right hand chords.

In summary, the style adopted by composers of free organ compositions, such as the *Fantasia* or the *Voluntary*, represented a search for that structure of keyboard piece that lay between the monotony of too much repetition of a point, and the inconsistency of too much thematic variety. The homogeneity of the fugue, allied to the rapidly evolving use of tonal relationships, lay in the future.

Meanwhile the other chief structural invention was the breaking up of a long work into shorter, related sections, such as variations on a dance or song.

Keyboard pieces originating from the dance were a secular development, and therefore chiefly suited to the virginal or chamber organ. The dance was an inherent part of Elizabethan life; the commonest were the Pavan, Galliard, La Volta, (which was the ancestor of the waltz); later, in the seventeenth century, the Saraband, Alman, Coranto. Those composers who chiefly captured the earlier style in their keyboard music were Morley, Byrd, Farnaby and Philips, while the later style is represented by Robert Johnson, and those anonymous composers of *Elizabeth Rogers' Virginal Book*.

Composers often linked together Pavans and Galliards by using the same bass-line for each. Two such common bass-lines were as follows:

Bass-line
(numerals indicate degrees of the scale)
Minor mode, 'Passamezzo Antico'   I–VII–I–V ‖ III–VII–I/V–I
Major mode, 'Passamezzo Moderno' I–IV–I–V ‖ I–IV–I/V–I
or Quadran Pavan.

An example of the first type is the 'Passamezzo Pavana' and 'Galiarda Passamezzo' of Philips in the *Fitzwilliam Virginal Book*

(Nos 76, 77); an example of the second is 'The Quadran Paven', and its Galliard, by Byrd, also in the same collection (Nos 133, 134).

Within a set rhythmical and harmonic framework, composers varied widely in their treatment. The delicacy of Farnaby contrasts directly with the broad lines of Byrd; while that subtle rhythmic inter-play and cross-accentuation, so beloved of the Elizabethans, is admirably captured by Weelkes, in his solitary short *Galliard*, and by Morley.

The latter achieves consistency in his pieces by centring each repeat of a section of a pavan or galliard round a particular *motif* or idea; maybe scale runs, maybe canon. The 'Lachrymae' Pavan and Galliard are also closely related in thematic material. In the same way, each variation of '*Go from my window*' is different, though internally consistent. Only one of Morley's keyboard works is patently written for the organ—the *Fantasia*.

Several composers could have written the three Voluntaries in Ed. No. 88, which are fluent examples of early seventeenth-century polyphony; their attribution to Benjamin Cosyn is highly doubtful, particularly in comparison with the pieces in MS k.

If Chaucer was the representative poet of the mediaeval period of 1400 (see p. 19), the equivalent figure two centuries later was without any doubt William Shakespeare. References to dances, which provide strong evidence of their prevalence, occur frequently in his works.

The French ambassador informs King Henry V:*

> *there's nought in France*
> *That can be with a nimble galliard won*

Sir Toby Belch in *Twelfth Night* proves to be an eloquent if unwitting source of information when he says jestingly to Sir Andrew Aguecheek†

* *Henry V* I, II, 252.
† *Twelfth Night* I, III, 120.

Why dost thou not go to church in a galliard, and come home in a coranto?
My very walk should be a jig.

Later, somewhat the worse for wear, his mood better compares
with the more melancholy pavan:*

Sir Toby: *(to Clown) Sot, didst see Dick Surgeon, Sot?*
Clown: *O, he's drunk, Sir Toby, an hour agone; his eyes were set*
            at eight i' th' morning.
Sir Toby: *Then he's a rogue, and a passy-measures pavin: I hate a*
            drunken rogue.

Songs also are as well attested by Shakespeare and his contemporary playwrights as dances. Song variations for keyboard were
a secular extension of the use of plainsong by organ composers.
Popular tunes used in this way included *Mall Sims, Go from my*
window, O mistress mine, Whoop do me no harm, good man,† and
numerous others.

The virginalists did more than merely transcribe; they invented
a new musical form. Their work is a testament, if testament were
needed, to that endemic tradition of English song that had flourished since about the middle of the sixteenth century, and is so
aptly described by Peter Warlock in *The English Ayre.* As with the
music of the dance, so with that of the song, the keyboard composer
could assume a close rapport with his audience—the sure sign of a
vigorous and flourishing tradition.

William Byrd 1543–1623

Conjecture surrounds the early life of the greatest English
composer of the Renaissance. That he was a chorister, either of the
Chapel Royal or of St Paul's Cathedral, seems very probable; also
that he was under Tallis. But the first proven fact is not until his
twentieth year, when he became organist of Lincoln Cathedral on

* *Twelfth Night* V, I, 190.
† See Shakespeare's *Winter's Tale* IV, III, 199.

27th February 1563. Later, on 22nd February 1570, he took Robert
Parsons's place as gentleman of the Chapel Royal, probably on
Tallis's recommendation; but he continued still at Lincoln until
1572, when he joined his teacher as joint organist of the Chapel.

The two composers were extraordinarily close friends and colleagues, in spite of an age difference of nearly forty years. Tallis
was godfather to Byrd's second son, born in 1576, who was named
Thomas after him. Shortly after this Byrd probably went to live
at Harlington, near Hayes in Middlesex, where the name of his
wife Juliana is mentioned among the recusants of that place. Byrd's
own adherence to the Roman Catholic Church, which seems not
to have affected his position in the Chapel Royal, is well known.
Tallis died in 1585, and about then also his own wife Juliana. One
of the principal collections of his keyboard music, *My Ladye
Nevells Booke*, dates from this time (1591), when it was copied
by John Baldwin of nearby Windsor.

In 1593 Byrd left Harlington and went to Stondon in Essex,
with his second wife Ellen, who died in 1605, and was probably
the mother of the last two of his five children, Rachel and Mary.

Byrd was universally respected by his contemporaries as the
greatest English composer. His two best-known pupils were
Thomas Tomkins and Thomas Morley; and the latter speaks of
him as a man 'never without reverence to be named of musicians'.
The Cheque Book, recording his death on 4th July, 1623, refers
to him as 'a Father of Musick'.

It is more than slightly ironical, therefore, that having enjoyed
such acclaim in his lifetime, his music entered a long period of
eclipse after his death. Though his work had been the first to be
published in this country—he and Tallis brought out their first
collection of *Cantiones Sacrae* in 1575 under the terms of their
licence from the Queen—it was not until 1937 that a complete
edition began to appear, edited by E. H. Fellowes.

Byrd's massive output, which takes no account of works lost,
comprises Masses, Services, over two hundred Latin Motets, sixty
English Anthems, Songs and Madrigals. His instrumental pieces
for viols include twelve Fantasias and eight *In Nomine*. He was one
of the first to write for such a consort, calling for any number

between three and seven, and he thus began a development which continued up to Purcell and beyond.

The neglect of a great composer by succeeding generations, and his rediscovery much later by a handful of enlightened musicians, is a process all too familiar in the history of music. In the case of Byrd, his rediscovery in the first half of the twentieth century was one of the chief results of that generally felt desire to uncover the Tudor heritage. Many other scholars than Fellowes were concerned at this time in the transcription and collation of Byrd's manuscripts, and in their publication.* This rediscovery of a past composer, the extent of whose greatness had been lost sight of by subsequent generations, can only call to mind another similar case, that of J. S. Bach.

The Music
Numbers refer to *Musica Britannica*, Vols. XXVII, XXVIII

The publication of the complete keyboard works of Byrd, in two volumes of *Musica Britannica*,† is an event of the greatest importance, since it permits an assessment of the full range of this aspect of his achievement. And although the definitive attribution of certain other pieces to Byrd will continue to be a matter of musicological debate and speculation,‡ the ninety-five pieces in the *Musica Britannica* volumes (which err, if at all, only on the side of caution) represent those keyboard pieces which can be attributed to Byrd beyond dispute.

Among their strongest and most prominent characteristics are his inventive resource, and his discovery and establishment of new musical forms such as, in particular, the Variation and the Fantasia. The most striking feature of Byrd's keyboard style is without doubt his assimilation of secular influences. Far the greater number of the pieces are settings of popular songs or dances; Pavans and Galliards in particular, which are chiefly notable for a freshness of effect within a regular phrase. This regularity does not apply

* R. R. Terry, Hilda Andrews, Margaret Glyn, Charles van den Borren.
† Edited by Alan Brown, Vol. I—1969, Vol. II—1971.
‡ See Oliver Neighbour in *Musical Times*, July 1971.

to the polyphonic keyboard compositions, whose lines are more varied and whose rhythm less marked; which are, in short, more suited to the organ than to the virginal.

Compositions based on Plainchant

Too rigid a distinction between liturgical and non-liturgical, sacred and secular, is an anachronism, and more applicable to the music of the twentieth than of the sixteenth century.* For instance, there are numerous *In Nomine* settings for instruments by various composers; also Byrd several times made use of plainchant melodies in pieces for instrumental groups; while the use of a popular song in an organ piece (No. 58) is not at all incongruous. Transcriptions each way, from instruments to keyboard, and *vice versa*, were commonplace. Indeed it was precisely because the composers of organ music of this time, among whom Byrd is pre-eminent, welcomed and assimilated the fresh styles of secular music, that they so enriched the repertoire, and gave it fresh vitality.

With each type of structure, almost with each piece, Byrd entered fresh musical territory; and nowhere is his exploration of new forms more apparent, with varying success, than in his use of plainchant melodies as the basis of keyboard pieces.

His treatment varies considerably from piece to piece. The simplest, and most primitive form is a two-part one, with the *cantus firmus* in long, equal notes in one hand set against a counter-subject in the other. The first *Salvator Mundi* (No. 68) is an example of this sort. In spite of the change of metre at bar 29 the inherent weakness of such a structure is its tendency to be rhythmically static—a tendency which is only thinly disguised by the addition of a third part, as in the second *Salvator Mundi* setting (No. 69), the second *Miserere* (No. 67), or the second *Clarifica me, Pater* (No. 48), although this piece also employs a change of metre half way through, like No. 68.

---

* It has led one scholar to a very low assessment of Byrd's, and Bull's, merits as a keyboard composer. H. J. Steele *English Organs and Organ Music*, Vol. I, p. 139.

The abandonment of strict note-by-note use of the plainchant led the composer to explore the possibility of a more decorated, varied form of it. According to this principle the plainchant was used as a starting-point, the contrapuntal basis for the composer's free invention.

This technique, known as 'breaking' the plainsong, was described by Thomas Morley,* Byrd's pupil:

... You sing either your first or last note in the same key wherein it standeth, or in his octave.

Otherwise the music moves freely.

Byrd uses this method twice; in the first *Clarifica me, Pater* (No. 47), and in *Gloria Tibi Trinitas* (No. 50). Each setting is in two parts, with the 'broken' plainsong in the lower part, and the other part a counterpoint to it, with some canonic imitation at the entries.

That such a structure can hardly fail to give the impression of a somewhat dry, academic exercise, however much the organist may seek to disguise it by means of two-manual registration, is due to the modal, melodic nature of the plainchant material itself, which no amount of 'breaking' can alter. It is not a case of Byrd's setting a decorated and varied melody against an already existing structure of harmony and rhythm; on the contrary, the counterpoint precedes both harmony and rhythm, which are the result of it. Therefore the original solo-melodic identity of the plainchant is submerged as it assumes this fresh, contrapuntal-harmonic function; but the new structure as yet possesses neither validity, nor tautness. It remains at a somewhat experimental stage. Nevertheless this essential early stage in the use of traditional liturgical melodies was to be the starting point for later German composers in their evolution of the Chorale Prelude. The first composer to continue in this tradition was Samuel Scheidt,† the distinguished pupil of Sweelinck, whose link with, and debt to, Byrd was established by their mutual contact through the Netherland school.

* *A plain and easy introduction* (ed. Harman, 2nd ed. 1962), p. 178.
† Whose *Tabulatura Nova* appeared in 1624.

The origins of that type of liturgical organ composition, of which the Chorale Prelude in its various later manifestations at the hands of Bach was the final development, are found in these few pieces of Byrd. Drawing on the experience of his predecessors, notably Redford, Blitheman and Tallis, he first discovered some of the many various ways of incorporating a traditional sacred melody into an extended polyphonic organ composition, as distinct from the verses of a hymn played antiphonally with the singers, as the mediaeval practice had been. This was the aspect of organ composition that the North German School later developed. Scheidt himself, organist at Halle, saw no relevance in a 'coloured' virtuoso style in the treatment of Chorales, preferring instead the polyphonic style of Byrd. As Schweitzer puts it:* 'This transference of vocal polyphony to the organ by means of Chorale accompaniment was of cardinal significance to the art of organ music.'

One of the most favoured contrapuntal devices was canon; it abounds in Scheidt's *Tabulatura Nova*. Byrd himself was a master of canonic technique, partly no doubt the result of his study under Tallis. Morley says† how he and Ferrabosco each worked forty different canons, two parts in one, on the *Miserere*. These exercises may have been published in 1603, under the title *Medulla Musicke*, but if so they have not survived.

At all events Scheidt would have had easy access in Amsterdam to the work of Byrd and other English composers, whose link with the Netherlands at this time was very close.

In spite of the discovery of many fresh techniques by English keyboard composers, among whom Byrd was first and foremost, they did not pursue the use of liturgical melodies in the same way as the German composers did, who gradually evolved the Chorale Prelude. The reason is plain; the seventeenth century English Church lacked a contemporary repertoire of sacred songs, such as the Lutheran Chorales provided for the German Church. Therefore the only melodies available to English composers were the traditional pre-Reformation Latin hymns, which became gradually more and more outdated. Nevertheless it was by the English

---

J. S. Bach (English edition), p. 36.
† *Op. cit.* p. 202.

School, with Byrd at its head, that the first steps in this newly developing style of organ composition were taken.

In the organ pieces based on plainchant he evidently was inhibited from introducing more freedom of development than the plainchant could assimilate, though occasional variations of metre, such as in *Salvator Mundi* (No. 65) were possible. It is indeed noteworthy that in the one single case where Byrd does allow a certain freedom in the development of the secondary material, the *cantus firmus* tends to disappear from view; the third *Clarifica me, Pater* (No. 49).

This piece in particular among his liturgical keyboard pieces places him in a position of more than merely that of an innovator. The three settings of this melody for the Vigil of the Ascension differ markedly, and use two, three and four parts respectively. It is the third setting, in four parts, which achieves greater structural unity than either of the other two, partly because of the varied points introduced by Byrd with each phrase of the plainchant, from which they are freely derived. The plainchant itself appears in the mean part, note by note up to bar 15, then broken. It is as if Byrd, having started with the exact melody, thereafter leaves the listener to assume the rest. The warmth of this piece derives from the fact that it is a polyphonic composition in which the points, or *motifs*, not the plainchant directly, decide the direction and character of the music, and the composer is not restrained within the intractable limits of a fixed note-pattern.

Free Organ Compositions

If Byrd's pieces based on liturgical plainchant are generally speaking somewhat fettered and inhibited, his free pieces are of a different order altogether; longer and more substantial. No composer covered a wider range than he, who exploited every form of keyboard composition open to him, and also invented new ones.

His free, non-liturgical organ works, of which there are twenty-one, fall under two headings; those nine pieces that are variations based on either a ground-bass, or a hexachord; and the remaining twelve which are freely constructed. He was the pioneer of an extended form, and explored fresh territory. Whereas his predecessors hardly moved at all beyond the use of liturgical plainchant as the basis of their organ pieces, he built free structures, for which he needed to evolve fresh forms. The problems were clear, and had already been demonstrated by his predecessors; for instance in the structural diffuseness of some of Tallis's longer pieces, such as his offertories. Too much repetition leads to monotony, while too much variety can produce inconsistency. Byrd's discovery, brilliantly exemplified in the Fantasias, was the introduction and treatment of secondary material which was in some way related to, or derived from, the original subject.

The restriction imposed by the use of plainchant did not apply to the free pieces, and the composer could allow full rein to his composition, both in style and texture. The most prominent of these works are the seven Fantasias. Each differs in form; only one shows signs of disjointed structure, of which the constituent sections do not form one overall unit; and this piece (No. 13) may well have been an earlier composition than the others.

However the music may develop later, all the Fantasias open with a solemn, polyphonic statement of the main material; invariably the first section uses the duple metre of *tempus imperfectum*, and ends with a cadence onto the key-note of the opening. The use of a 'point', or *motif*, is Byrd's means of building up a sustained polyphonic texture; the music is the instrumental expression of that corporate mediaeval ideal of worship; what matters is not so much the individual character of the subject-material itself, as the sustained effect, over a long span, of an intricate and finely worked polyphony.

After the initial mood has been set, Byrd's treatment varies widely; in those Fantasias that are probably keyboard arrangements of string pieces (Nos. 26, 27) the various sections, though contrasted, are homogeneous, not separate; they form continuous episodes arising from the original material. In No. 27 the development of the musical thought between one episode and the next is very slight, though none the less telling; the rhythmical displacement of a beat; the use of a dotted-note; the new figure is then pursued in each of three parts consecutively with imitation, stretto and so on.

Example 5

No. 27 Fantasia

a) example of dotted rhythm (bars 34-35)   Byrd

b) example of rhythmic displacement (bars 56-57)   (bars 65-66)

In other Fantasias the sections are more defined and separate, each with its own character, like the movements of a suite or later sonata. The two chief means used by Byrd to introduce variety are the contrasted use of homophony and polyphony, and the introduction of different metres and rhythmic patterns.

A brilliant example of the contrast between polyphony and homophony occurs in No. 46, to mark the opening of the first episode. Although the material of the episode is the same as that of the opening, Byrd not only alters the mood; he also alters the tonality. Clearly the organist would ally this also with a change of manual.

Example 6

No. 46 Fantasia   Byrd
(Opening)

(bars 30-31)

(a and a¹ show the rhythmic connection)

The introduction of a section in triple, or compound, metre, like a Galliard or La Volta, was clearly a device that was secular in origin, whose possibilities in an extended composition Byrd was the first to realise. One of the most intricate of these studies in metrical proportion,* so favoured in the sixteenth century, occurs in No. 13 :

Example 7

No. 13 Fantasia
(bars 101-107)

Byrd

However, not all the Fantasias necessarily employ variations of metre.

Another characteristic of Byrd's keyboard style, clearly vocal in origin, is the answering of one phrase by the same one an octave lower, like a dialogue.

Example 8

No. 13 Fantasia
(bars 41-48)

Byrd

* Morley lists the Proportions in *A plain and easy introduction* (ed. Harman, 2nd ed.) p. 57.

The *Voluntary: for my Lady Nevell* (No. 61) is very similar to one of the Fantasias. Indeed, to describe a free composition, not based on a plainchant, the terms are practically interchangeable; the term 'A lesson of Voluntarie' even appears in *My Lady Nevell's Booke* to describe one of the Fantasias (No. 26). The structure of the *Voluntary*, No. 61, is very similar to No. 25; the first section is short, and serves as an introduction to the greater part of the movement which follows. The piece ends with quick scale-passages, against held chords in the other hand.

The *Verse* (No. 28) is little more than a study in two-part invertible counterpoint; this distinguishes it from the three Preludes (Nos. 1, 12, 24), which are simple pieces, short after the manner of *Introits*. Two of them are in the nature of brilliant flourishes; the third is more subdued.

The six pieces made up of variations on a ground-bass contain certain broad similarities with the Fantasias; a very deliberate and measured opening, working towards quicker, more brilliant passage-work as the piece proceeds, with quite frequent changes of metre. The form which Byrd evolved was to be very popular among later seventeenth-century composers; the Division Violist was expected to extemporise variations within the given harmonic framework of a ground-bass, played on the harpsichord.

Byrd's six pieces which use this ground-bass technique all employ a $\frac{3}{2}$ metre, and call for a moderate tempo, like the later Chaconne and Passacaglia, in order to allow room for the runs and flourishes of notes of smaller value. But within this framework the pieces differ markedly. Their bar-lengths are of differing multiples of four. Nos. 9 and 43 use a 4-bar ground; No. 42 a 12-bar, No. 20 a 16-bar, and No. 57 a 24-bar ground—with the result that it only extends to six variations. The extraordinarily colourful piece *The Bells* however, No. 38, has a 1-bar ground consisting of only two notes, repeated 136 times.

Normally Byrd introduces a progressive quickening of the rhythm, and a shortening of the note-values, as the music develops; though in two cases, Nos. 9 and 20, after a gradual diminution of the pulse, he closes with a broad finish. Each variation has a different character, and is based on a different pattern or idea, such as a dotted rhythm, or some other such figure, quaver runs, or canon. He frequently carries the ground into the right hand part.

In many respects the most interesting ground, which is also used in a 5-part string Fantasia, is that of No. 42, since the 12-bar pattern is made up of two 4-bar phrases, each with a 2-bar extension, or 'echo'. Up to the 10th variation Byrd brings the music to rest at the end of the 4th and 10th bars of each variation, and does not continue it over into the following bars; therefore it is possible that he intended these echo bars to be played as such—separated, on another manual where possible. Such an effect would be impossible on a single manual instrument, but there is strong evidence, from the structure of the piece, that some such 'echo' effect is intended. It was a device much exploited by other composers. In the 7th variation, for instance, the metre changes to $\frac{9}{4}$, but reverts to $\frac{3}{2}$ for the 'echo' bars; while in the 11th variation the same principle applies, but with the metres reversed. The ground is carried into the treble after the 12th variation, and the 'echo' bars are given to the bass after the 14th. Some such two-manual treatment would greatly enhance the structural ingenuity of this highly original piece; alternatively it would serve to bring out the invertible nature of the part-writing, in such places as the 8th variation, where quaver runs in one part are set against held chords in the other.

The first of the hexachord variations (No. 58), which is called approvingly by Tomkins[*] 'A good lesson of Mr Byrdes', is a duet; 'The playne-song Breifes to be played by a second person'. Since Byrd treats the six notes of the hexachord both ascending and descending, each variation is twelve bars long. In two of them Byrd introduces popular tunes; 'The Woods so Wild' (bar 25) and 'The shaking of the Sheets' (bar 42). The three sets of variations (Nos. 58, 64, 65) share certain similarities with the ground-bass pieces, except that their metre is duple ($\frac{4}{2}$, $\frac{4}{4}$), and not triple. In each of the two pieces that use hexachords, Byrd builds each variation on the six notes ascending and descending; in No. 58 they begin on C each time; was the second part possibly intended for one of his children? Or a pupil of somewhat limited technique?

[*] In MS g.

The variations in No. 64 vary the starting note, and introduce some considerable chromaticism as a result. The majority of the variations, including the first two and the last three, have G as a key-note; others use D, C, F, A, and B.

The 3-note *motif* of No. 65 is similarly treated both ascending, and descending, in its inverted form, over the octave in each variation. If it may appear that in submitting to the somewhat mechanical scheme of such a form of composition Byrd was simply substituting one strait jacket (plainchant) for another (the haxachord), the purpose in each case was distinct and different. The six notes of the scale represented the first formulation of a tonality, prior to the evolution of the diatonic system. They thus filled a need which was beyond the reach of mediaeval plainchant; namely a harmonic scheme for a large-scale piece.

As the epitome of the ideal of the Renaissance, no keyboard music can serve as a better example than one of Byrd's Fantasias, No. 62. The opening material seems to have been common property; it was used by Peter Philips (Ed. 1, No. 84) and John Bull (Ed. 8, No. 13). In Byrd's piece the range of expression is a wide one, encompassing serenity at the one end, and a brilliance of keyboard effect at the other. The characteristic opening achieves its effect with the bare minimum of stepwise movement; it is only with the sustaining of the polyphonic imitation of the point that the music increases in strength—the very essence of organ music.

Example 9

No. 62 Fantasia
(Opening)   Byrd

[Ornaments omitted, as they are in the version in the Fitzwilliam Virginal Book.]

John Bull *c.* 1563–1628

John Bull stands somewhat apart from his three great contemporaries, partly because of the unorthodox nature of his career, partly because of the strikingly individual style of his compositions. He was, moreover primarily a keyboard composer. Works for organ, virginal or harpsichord make up far the greater part of his output, whereas the keyboard compositions of Byrd, Gibbons and Tomkins can best be seen against the background of their more numerous vocal works.

Bull however wrote comparatively little vocal church music, in spite of ample opportunity, and a position at Court of central importance. He focused his attention instead on keyboard composition, and as a result his surviving vocal works comprise only five full anthems, nine seven-verse anthems—in which it is noteworthy that the use of instruments is prominent. Indeed one, the so-called 'Star' anthem, is suspected of having been originally a *Fantasia* for viols.★ But his works for organ and virginal far outweigh, in number and scope, those of his contemporaries. It is on these that his work as a composer was concentrated.

He entered the Chapel Royal as a chorister at the age of nine, in 1572, when Tallis and Byrd were joint organists, and a certain William Hunnis was Master of the choristers.† Ten years later, on the 24th December, 1582, he was appointed assistant organist at Hereford Cathedral, and the following month he became Master of the children there. In January, 1585, he was sworn a Gentleman of the Chapel Royal, while continuing at Hereford. He was a pupil of Blitheman, who was organist of the Chapel Royal after the death of Tallis, in November, 1585. When Blitheman himself died six years later, Bull succeeded him as organist; William Randoll (or Randall) was his colleague, probably after Byrd had resigned his organistship.

In 1601 Bull made the first of his visits to the Continent, and was away about eighteen months, until Elizabeth recalled him from Brussels. His deputy as organist was Arthur Cocke.‡

In 1596 Bull had also been appointed the first holder of 'Ye place of Readinge ye Lecture of musick' at Sir Thomas Gresham's§

★ See Le Huray *Music & The Reformation in England*, p. 263.
† *Old Cheque-Book*, 15th November, 1566.
‡ *Old Cheque-Book,* 3rd March, 1601.
§ A (much) later holder of the Gresham Professorship of London University, appointed in 1964, was Thurston Dart.

College; so when he went abroad in 1601 he made arrangements that his deputy for this work should be William Byrd's second son Thomas, who was then a young man of twenty-five.

In setting out on his travels, Bull was following the example of several other notable English composers and musicians of the time, such as the recusants Peter Philips and Nicholas Morgan, both organists in Brussels, and the lutenist John Dowland. They helped to make the English style, particularly of keyboard and consort composition, known in Northern Europe, where it had a profound influence.*

Bull was a virtuoso player, with an international outlook and aspirations. How could he not be excited by the possibilities of hearing and playing new organs, to say nothing of capturing new audiences, in France or the Netherlands, from whence the enviable reputation enjoyed by his contemporary Sweelinck had no doubt reached his ears? Moreover what keyboard composer would not be anxious to hear and play the latest harpsichords which Hans Ruckers was building in Antwerp, or Daniel van der Ort in Amsterdam, and to compare them with English instruments?

The year after Bull returned to England Elizabeth died; and the event, and date, 24th March, 1603, was recorded by him with a special Pavan. He enjoyed direct favour at the Court of her successor James I; he was the official teacher of the three royal children, Elizabeth, Henry Prince of Wales, who died in 1612, and Charles. On one occasion, 16th July, 1607, when the King and Prince Henry were entertained at a feast by the Merchant Taylors, Bull:

> played most excellent melodie upon a small payre of Organes placed there for that purpose only.

In a period when music was a necessary part of royal functions, Bull was the chief court musician. He was described as 'Doctor of Musicke to the Kinge' after Prince Henry's death in 1612. That year is also marked by the publication of the first engraved music in England: *Parthenia,* or *the Maydenhead of the first musicke that ever was printed for the virginalls.* It contained virginal pieces by

* Alan Curtis *Sweelinck's keyboard music,* pp. 26–34.

Byrd, Bull and Gibbons. Byrd and Gibbons duly and properly included pavans for the Earl of Salisbury, who had died that year. It is improbable that Bull should have omitted to write a Pavan for Prince Henry, whose 'private music' he had served. 'St Thomas, wake' Pavan is possibly intended as such a tribute.

Several references to Bull, invariably known respectfully as 'Dr Bull', occur in the Cheque Book of the Chapel Royal; on Easter Day, 1593, the Queen came to the Holy Communion, on which occasion it is recorded:

> her Majesties Royal person came moste chearfully, havinge as noble supporters the Right Honorable th Erle of Essex, Master of her Majestes Horse, on the right hande, and the Right Hon. the Lord Admyral on the lefte hand, the Lord Chambrelen to her Majestie (also nexte beffore her Majeste) attendante al the while. Dr Bull was at the organ playinge the Offertorye.

Twenty years later, on 14th February, 1613, when Princess Elizabeth married Frederick Count Palatine of the Rheine, the account of the ceremony includes the following:

> After the Arch Bishopp had ended the Benedic̃on, God the Father, God the Sonne, etc. the Quier sange the same benedic̃on in an Anthem made new for that purpose by Doctor Bull:

Few composers have enjoyed the benefit of greater royal patronage; yet this royal wedding was to be one of Bull's last appearances at a Court ceremony in England; six months later he left the country, on his own account, never to return. The Cheque Book entry is, on this occasion, somewhat more abrupt:

> John Bull, doctor of Musicke, went beyond the seas without licence and was admitted into the Archduke's service, and entered into paie there about Michaelmas, and Peter Hopkins, a Basse from Paules was sworne in his place the 27th of December followinge . . .

Whatever his reason for such a startling departure,★ whether

★ The personal aspect of Bull's private life has been colourfully embroidered by Leigh Henry in his historical novel Dr John Bull (1937).

personal or artistic, or both, Bull went to Brussels, the capital of the Spanish Netherlands, where on the 24th September he entered the service of the Archduke Albert. Among his colleagues was Peter Philips. He remained until the following year, when he began, through many vicissitudes of personal fortune, to seek an appointment as organist in Antwerp. He achieved this in 1617, after the death of Rumold Waelrent, and remained at Antwerp Cathedral until his death in 1628.*

The Music
Numbers refer to *Musica Britannica*, Vol. XIV

Bull's organ works are not only more numerous, but they cover a wider expressive range, and open up more technical possibilities, than those of his contemporaries. The problems of introducing colour, variety and brilliance into an organ style, without thereby destroying the overall structural unity, were triumphantly solved by him in several large-scale pieces.

Not the least of his innovations was his introducing the conception that an organist was a virtuoso solo performer; this, in an age when the public recital did not exist, and the instrument itself was not fully capable of the demands he made of it, places him among those visionary musicians whose work anticipates what future ages were to supply. His technique looks ahead; under the broad headings of rhythm, harmony, texture, structure and registration, he introduced striking innovations.

Rhythm

The ratio between the longest and shortest note-values in Bull's music is 1:32. If the longest note value is the semibreve (○), the shortest is the demisemiquaver, or $\frac{1}{32}$ note (♪). This range is greater than that used by his contemporaries, whose normal

* Shortly after his death Messaus, organist of S. Walburga in Antwerp, copied Bull's works into MS b.

compass is $\downarrow$ – $\eighthnote$ or $\frac{1}{2}$ – $\frac{1}{16}$. Moreover the use of short-note runs in other composers' keyboard works is usually confined to the decoration of an auxiliary, or cadential, figure, as this example from Tomkins shows:

Example 10

From the works of Gibbons, examples such as this are most exceptional:

Example 11

Bull however integrated the short-note run into his passage-work, so that it became an inherent part of his style. Examples of its use are almost too numerous to specify; it may mark the culminating brilliance at the end of a piece, as for instance in the *Fantasia*, No. 11, which is in two-part toccata style, and ends with quick runs, alternating between the hands; it may introduce a piece, with a dramatic flourish, such as the *In nomine*, No. 27; it may be used as melodic decoration and embellishment, as in the *Fantasia*, No. 10, starting at bar 98; he uses it to break a chord, in the *In nomine*, No. 24, starting at bar 50; or to point a rhythm, in the *In nomine*, No. 27, starting at bar 52, L.H. Apart from this use of small note-values, Bull also explored the possibilities of combining parts in different note proportions. The three *Miserere* settings provide a clear illustration of this technique. The simplest is the second piece, No. 35, which straightforwardly sets ♍ against ♪. The first, No. 34, grades the two accompanimental parts, so that they are always in the ratio 1:2; that is to say either ♩: ♪ or ♪: ♫. In the first two sections, with the held *cantus firmus* in the top part, the longer note of the two other parts is always above the shorter; in the third section, with the *cantus firmus* between the other two parts, the longer note appears in the bass, the shorter in the treble. Such an exploration of the possibilities of rhythmic inversion was next to be pursued by Bach.

The third *Miserere* setting is the most intricate. With the *cantus firmus* poised securely between them, the other two parts imitate each other in equal notes, first crotchets then quavers, in phrases of gradually increasing length. The middle bars (31–44) of the piece are freer, and Bull reverts again to the strictness of the opening at bar 45. The parts subdivide, 2 of ♩, 2 of ♪, at bar 56.

This wide range of note-proportions, and the use of different note-proportions, is not the only means whereby Bull achieves rhythmic freedom. Two other devices occur so frequently in his work that they may be considered stylistic hallmarks; one is the changing of metre, or the combination of different metres, which leads to polyrhythm; the other is the displacement of metre, or the repetition of a regular rhythmic pattern on an irregular beat. In this respect Bull was building on the foundations laid by Tallis and Blitheman.

A change from duple to triple metre is commonplace throughout Bull's works: he uses it as a basic technical device, and a means of introducing variety in the overall structure of a long piece. For instance, in the *Fantasia*, No. 3, the change at bar 43 not only leads to rhythmic diminution of the pulse, but alters the very nature of the material, by allowing notes of smaller value. This transformation of the basic idea is further enhanced by a change of manual in performance (see page 95). The triple metre introduced at bar 43 is further subdivided, until at bar 53 it has become $\frac{3}{8} + \frac{3}{8}$. Later still, at bar 83, the main material finally appears itself diminished by half.

In this case rhythmic diminution is the means of achieving both textural variety and thematic unity. Diminution is a rhythmical device much favoured by Bull. Another effective example occurs in the *Fantasia*, No. 14, where diminution of the ground occurs at bar 113, and double diminution at bar 159.

Often, as in the *Fantasia*, No. 12, a change to a simple triple metre is followed by a further change to a compound one. This happens even in such an extreme case of proportional experiment as the *In nomine*, No. 28. Starting with a combination of duple and triple simple time, $\frac{4}{4} + \frac{4}{4} + \frac{3}{4}$, Bull changes at bar 139 to a combination of duple and triple compound, $\frac{6}{4} + \frac{6}{4} + \frac{9}{8}$. But such a conception as this is unique among his keyboard works.

The combination of different metres, producing polyrhythm, is well exemplified in the longest and most complex of the three *Hexachord Fantasias*, No. 18. In this work not only does the metre frequently change, but duple and triple combine, for instance bars 142–147, and 157–162. Another interesting example, combining $\frac{3}{16}$ and $\frac{4}{4}$ metres, occurs in the fifth *In nomine*, No. 24, bars 21–23.

The displacement of a beat, leading to extra rhythmic tautness, is a device which appears in several different forms. It serves as a simple means of introducing variety into one of the episodes of a long *Fantasia*, No. 12, bar 90; it helps the movement of the inner parts in the first *In nomine*, No. 20, bar 44; in the fifth *In nomine* it assumes the nature of a rhythmic *ostinato*, between bars 24–29; it is used canonically between the lower parts in the twelfth *In nomine*, No. 31, bars 39–42, in a passage which is itself a diminution of the opening. The displacement of the beat with which Bull introduces this last of his *In nomine* settings is tantamount to polyrhythm, as it transforms the metre of the left hand into $\frac{3}{8} + \frac{3}{8}$, against the $\frac{3}{4}$ of the right hand.

Harmony

The use of the chromatic fourth was, according to Thomas Morley, writing in his *A Plaine and easie introduction to practicall musicke*,* a commonplace, and a well established practice among organists. It was an aspect of the Italian madrigal style† that English keyboard and instrumental composers took and stamped with their own personal characteristics, which in turn had a great effect on later composers. It can be detected, in a mild form, in certain places in the work of Tallis, but it took a much firmer hold in the later years of the sixteenth century, until composers had eventually accommodated chromaticism along with tonality as an inherent part of their idiom. The chromatic fourth, in keyboard and instrumental composition, was used mainly as an expressive accompanimental figure, often as a ground-bass; as such it was to survive until the eighteenth century. Two, to us, very familiar instances of its use by later composers, are *Dido's Lament*, from Purcell's *Dido and Aeneas*, and the *Crucifixus* from Bach's *B minor Mass*.

Bull was one of the chief exponents of its early use.‡ The *Fantasia on a theme by Sweelinck*, No. 4, uses it in the repetition—style of a Hexachord Fantasia, while the *Chromatic Fantasia*, No. 5, is freer in its construction. It was perhaps inevitable that a composer of an experimental and innovating turn of mind such as Bull should concern himself with the assimilation of chromaticism into his style; and the most patently experimental of his organ pieces is without doubt the first of the three *Hexachord Fantasias*, No. 17, in which the six-note figure (G–E) is introduced on each of the twelve degrees of the chromatic scale. Though this piece is clearly a study in chromaticism, involving the composer in awkward modulations and enharmonic changes, he tries to bring some artistic

---

* pp. 101–103 (1962 edition, ed. Harman; first edition 1597). The chromatic fourth consists of the six notes, ascending or descending, making up the five semitones of a perfect fourth.

† Such as that of Marenzio, Cipriano de Rore & Gesualdo.

‡ Dowland was another, whose *Lachrymae*, based on a falling fourth, was published in 1605. See Alan Curtis *Sweelinck's keyboard Music*, p. 134 for further discussion.

cohesion to it by moving up in whole tones at each variation, by beginning and ending the piece on G, and by allowing a short coda at the end. In spite of this however, Bull was clearly in this piece preoccupied with chromaticism at the expense of other factors. Numerous instances of his use of the chromatic fourth are also seen in the virginal pieces; for instance in the *Chromatic Pavan*, No. 87, at bar 34 it occurs in each hand, in contrary motion; it is inherent in the melodic line of numerous such passages as this, which is representative of the English style of this time:

Example 12

The combination of natural and sharp inflection of the leading note at a cadence, apparent in the C♮–C♯ of this example, is another English characteristic, inherent in Bull's style, which he sometimes uses in a surprising way. This play on C♮–C♯ originates from the chromatic fourth:

Example 13

Another example in the same vein occurs a few bars further on:

Example 14

Further still Bull develops a chromatic melodic line against a sustained left hand part:

Example 15

No. 4 Fantasia on a theme by Sweelinck
(bars 49-52)

Bull

This form of chromatic cadence is much favoured by Bull, and occurs throughout his work; for instance it appears, casually almost, in No. 20, bar 6. Moreover, he is often discontented with the conventional plagal cadence, as this example shows:

Example 16

No. 5 Fantasia
(bars 42 - end)

Bull

Another instance of this chromatic plagal harmony occurs in No. 1, bars 72–73:

Example 17

No. 1 Fantasia
(bars 69-76)

Bull

A comparison of Bull's cadences with those of the earlier Tudor composers gives one clear indication of his style; Preston, Redford and Blitheman favoured the plagal form of cadence, and the feminine ending, which followed on naturally from their use of plainsong melodic material. Bull's cadences however are altogether freer and bolder, often with an unexpected twist. For instance, No. 32 is in the fifth tone (C); its final cadence is into A.

Frequently the cadence-pattern is emphasised with bold splashes of colour; for instance in the *Fantasia* No. 13, bar 91; No. 12, bars 109–111; No. 11, bars 77–78.

Nevertheless, the pieces based on plainchant usually have the expected plagal cadences. All twelve *In nomine* settings do, however much it may be disguised, as in No. 24, bar 55. Of some fourteen Latin hymns, perfect cadences are used only for certain verses of *Salve Regina*, Nos. 40 and 41, and *Telluris ingens conditor*.

Texture

Bull's invention of organ keyboard textures is in many ways his chief claim on our attention. They range from the brilliant toccata style in two parts of the *Fantasia* (No. 11), to the intricate 4-part polyphony of the *Hexachord Fantasia* (No. 19), in which Bull distributes the hexachord in free rhythm, not in even notes as is usually the case; the manuscript shows the six notes in red ink, as they interweave with the parts. It is the most complex of all this composer's polyphonic works.

The twelve *In nomine* settings all exploit different textures, largely decided by the position of the *cantus firmus*. In six of them it is in the treble, or highest part; in three of them it is in the tenor, and in three in the bass. All the settings use three parts, except No. 27, after bar 10, and No. 28 which is the most elaborate of the set and is an essay in the very exceptional metre of $\frac{11}{4}$. Throughout the twelve settings, the texture of the two accompanying parts varies widely; they make two equal melody parts (No. 23), brilliant runs and *roulades* (No. 24), or a dotted rhythm *ostinato* (No. 29). The parts often derive their figurations from the *cantus firmus*, and imitate each other, whether in canon or not; No. 26 contains examples of both these features, at bars 35 and 44.

Bull was the first English composer to make extensive use of broken chord figurations, arpeggios and repeated notes. The fifth *In nomine* (No. 24), combines numerous examples of all these, which were to become so innate a part of later keyboard technique, and which also appear extensively in the works of his Dutch contemporary Sweelinck. The repeated note style occurs for instance in Bull's *Fantasia* No. 7, bar 77, in the middle section of the *Fantasia* No. 9, starting at bar 26, and in the first of the three *Miserere* settings (No. 34). Sometimes Bull achieves brilliance by the progressive accumulation of a complex texture, perhaps finishing with virtuoso scales in thirds, as in No. 10, bar 118, or much more prolonged, in No. 18, bars 130–140; a startlingly novel conception.

Again, variety of texture between the episodes of a *Fantasia* may be the chief means whereby the composer maintains the interest over a long span. Such a case occurs in No. 12, where runs in one hand against held chords in the other (bars 42–51) are followed by more homogeneous part-writing, which in turn is succeeded by a 'displaced-beat' texture, starting at bar 90.

Ornaments form a small but integral part of Bull's style, as indeed they do in that of most keyboard composers of this period; though he, like Gibbons, suffered at the hands of Benjamin Cosyn in this respect. Ornaments are more necessary and more suited to the virginal or harpsichord than to the organ, and Cosyn has over-ornamented Bull's scores in several instances; No. 12 is a particularly blatant example.

But an example of the musical use of an ornament for a specific purpose by the composer, as distinct from the editor, can be seen in No. 13 at bar 92, where the introduction of secondary material in a lower part, in canon at the fifth, is reinforced by means of an ornament, without which it might pass unnoticed.

Another point where the ornament is part of the fabric of the musical idea, occurs in No. 37 at bar 72. Bull's addition of the ornament on the first quaver of every beat greatly increases the vigour and the brilliance of the left hand accompanimental figure, and makes a characteristic keyboard effect out of what would, without the ornaments, be quite ordinary and unremarkable octaves.

Structure

As far as the structure of his organ works is concerned, Bull achieved unity in three principal ways—by building a work round a plainchant, or other liturgical melody; by building a ternary structure (A–B–A); or by making continuous use of the same material, figure, or 'point'.

Something of the construction of the twelve *In nomine* has been mentioned already. Among the Latin hymns, the first of the two settings of *Salve Regina* (No. 40) is far the most elaborate; it is more of a polyphonic elaboration of the hymn than a statement of the tune; and the five verses, if played consecutively, represent variations in the way of treating a melody, without that melody being explicitly stated. Motifs and 'points' arise from the fabric of the counterpoint, for instance in verse 5, bar 12.

Nothing illustrates the flexibility of Bull's approach to musical structure better than his three settings of *Salvator mundi*. These range from the long and elaborate first piece (No. 37), finishing with a brilliant flourish, to the short and simple third piece (No. 39), in the simpler style of a prelude. In a piece built round a hymn-tune a composer can well afford to introduce variety in the surrounding parts; the underlying melody will ensure the unity of the structure. Bull may well begin such a piece simply, and finish brilliantly; *Veni Redemptor Gentium* (No. 42) is a case in point.

Many of the pieces use a ternary structure, A–B–A. This may be built round a metrical scheme, with the middle section making use of a different time-signature, or 'proportion', from the first and third sections. Nos. 3 and 10 are examples of such a procedure. The change of pulse-rate may be written-in, without any explicit change of time-signature; this is the case in No. 9, in which the middle section begins at bar 26, the third section at 53. In the preceding piece, which is another setting of the same tune, the middle section, bars 24–43, is polyphonic, preceded and followed by more straightforward writing in free *fantasia* style.

The use of consistent thematic material, a technique followed by most composers of this tradition, gives a work like the *Fantasia* (No. 13) the unique, overall, sustained power of true organ music. No composer better captures the character and sheer sonority of the instrument. Bull achieves unity of mood, along with unity of tone and subject, and builds a large-scale structure with the greatest apparent simplicity of means, though secondary material is admitted at bar 92, and a 'third subject' at bar 160.

But the clearest examples of Bull's achieving structural unity by the repetition of a figure are the *Hexachord Fantasias*, in which the music is overtly built round the repetition of the 6-note *motif*. In the first piece, (No. 17), the figure is repeated on a different starting-note each time (as already mentioned), while in No. 18 it occurs twenty-three times, always starting on the same note (G), and always in the right hand, but with varying metre, and, it goes without saying, registration varied by means of manual changes.

A very simple 'ground', a four-bar *motif* which occurs no fewer than thirty-three times, is the basis of Bull's greatest tour-de-force of keyboard virtuosity, the *God save the King* variations (No. 32).

The basis of this piece is nothing more complicated than ut-sol-fa-mi (C G F E); but within this framework the composer indulges in elaborate flights of technical fancy.

Registration

It may safely be assumed that colourful registration, apt for the texture and structure of the music, is a *sine qua non* of the satisfactory performance of Bull's organ music. Indeed, with no other composer of this period is one more aware that he is stretching the resources of the organ in all directions—including the use of stops. It is even a tenable hypothesis that Bull saw beyond the physical limitations of the instrument with which he was acquainted, and visualised in his imagination the fuller tonal range, the more integrated divisions, to say nothing of the equal temperament, of the organ as it was later to develop in Northern Europe—and wrote accordingly.

Yet in this respect the performer advances into uncharted and somewhat uncertain waters, with only three markings by Bull in one of his pieces to tantalise and mock him, if not to spur him on; these consist of the indications *Cornet, Cromhorne* and *Voll Register* ('Full organ') in bars 37–48 of the Dutch carol *Een kindeken is ons geboren* (No. 55). This was written during the composer's time at Antwerp, and it will be noticed from the Dutch organs mentioned on p. 137, that each of these three stop requirements were standard in the instruments at this time. The 5–6 rank Cornet was a composite solo stop whose ranks normally included 8^1, 4^1, $2\frac{2}{3}^1$, 2^1 and Tierce $1\frac{3}{5}^1$. It operated from d upwards, so that the left hand accompanying part, which in Bull's piece never goes above c, could be played on the same manual as the right hand solo. Such a stop was perfectly normal in the organs that Bull knew; even in a small, one-manual instrument, the Tierce was included, which would allow a Cornet to be built up rank by rank.

The Crumhorn was also a standard continental reed stop, secondary to the Trumpet, and normally found on a manual other than the Great. The term *Voll Register* meant the full Principal chorus, usually 4–6 stops.

But for the majority of Bull's work, the organist can only decide registration partly on the internal evidence of the music itself, and partly on the evidence of the organs which the composer himself played—though even this, as has already been suggested, may not prove to be adequate for music of such bold and imaginative resource. Clearly the choice of stops should match the nature of the music. In a piece of moderate length, built throughout on the same subject-material, such as No. 4, too much change of registration may militate against this effect of unity. The runs are not intended as Cornet solos, since they go below c; the texture therefore is homogeneous, and played on one manual. But the simplest effective way to realise the change of mood at bar 54 is by means of a change of manual.

Repeated-note passages, such as No. 7, bar 77, are realised more clearly with light, bell-like registration, and are correspondingly less effective with a full chorus. On the other hand certain pieces, such as No. 6, strongly indicate that the composer had in mind a full, rich sound; he was writing, perhaps, for a ceremonial occasion, and in that case the registration needs to be correspondingly large-scale. It is reasonable to suppose that Bull would have introduced some change at bar 34; the sudden reversion to scale-runs in bar 62 is effective and dramatic if they are interpreted as a return to the full tone of the opening. But it goes without saying that a piece may be registered equally well in several different ways.

There are moreover many examples of two-part writing, where the composer's musical thought is greatly enhanced if it is matched by two-manual treatment on the part of the player. The long *Fantasia* (No. 10) is a case in point; moreover the construction of a three-part *In nomine* can be characteristically emphasised if the *cantus firmus* and one of the accompanimental parts is played on one manual, the second accompanimental part on another manual, with equal, contrasted, perhaps overlapping registration.* The separate melodic lines of Nos. 23 and 30 benefit from some such individual treatment.

In certain pieces, of which the *In nomine* (No. 25) is an example, Bull seems to anticipate the texture and style of the later German

* See example 18.

Chorale Prelude, in which the chorale melody might be allocated to a 4¹ pedal reed, which the manual parts accompany with imitative counterpoint. Were it not that it would have been impossible on the organ as Bull knew it, the registration of No. 25, in accordance with the later Chorale Prelude principles would be:

Example 18

Whereas for Bull's organ a possible registration would be:

Example 19

Orlando Gibbons 1583–1625

Orlando Gibbons was born into a musical family. His father William came of East Anglian stock, and was one of the town waits of Cambridge; his elder brother Edward, b. 1567, was Master of the Choristers at King's College, when he himself entered the choir as a chorister in 1596. Eight years later, on the 21st March, 1604, he was appointed organist of the Chapel Royal, after the death of Arthur Cocke, Bull's former deputy. Thus his outstanding talents as a keyboard player were recognised early. When Bull left the country in 1613, Gibbons was the recipient of part of the elder composer's salary; he was awarded, according to the Cheque Book,

£3.6.8. By 1615 his fellow organist was Edmund Hooper; and after the latter's death on the 14th July, 1621, Tomkins became his assistant in the organistship.

In addition to his Chapel Royal duties, Gibbons was also appointed in 1619, to succeed Walter Earle as Organist and Virginal player in the King's Private Musick—he was to be one of the 'Musicians for the virginalles to attend in his Highnes privie chamber'. He thus filled something of the vacancy left after Bull's departure.

In 1623 he succeeded John Parsons as organist of Westminster Abbey, where two short years later he was called on to officiate at the funeral of King James I. And his twenty-one-year period of service with the Chapel Royal was to be of almost the same duration as his monarch's reign. That same year, 1625, he attended with the Chapel Royal, at Canterbury, on James's son Charles, now Charles I, who was awaiting his French bride Henrietta Maria. It was in such festive surroundings that on the 5th June, Whitsunday, Gibbons died, at the early age of forty-one, 'to the great reluctancy of the Court'. He was buried at Canterbury, where a monument was put up to his memory.

Gibbons's whole life and work was carried on within the circle of the Court, at Whitehall or Westminster. His wife Elizabeth was the daughter of John Patten, Yeoman of the Vestry of the Royal Chapel. Their seven children included three boys and four girls; the youngest child Orlando was born in 1623, while the second son Christopher was destined to follow a course remarkably similar to his father's; he too became organist of the Chapel Royal and Westminster Abbey, as well as private organist to Charles II, after the Restoration. But his wife did not long survive the composer's death in 1625; she died the following year.

The Music
Numbers refer to *Musica Britannica* Vol. XX

Gibbons's surviving church works number some twenty verse anthems, ten full anthems, as well as service settings and hymns.

Of his keyboard works, some are unquestionably organ works, such as the *Fantasias*; some are unquestionably for virginal, such as the *Earl of Salisbury's Pavan and Galliard*; stylistically such dances clearly originate in the King's privy chamber, not in his royal chapel; not so much because speed and virtuosity are necessarily un-organistic, but because irregular rhythmic inflection and subtlety are inconsistent with the sustained, even nature of organ tone. Moreover, pavans and galliards call for a fall-away of tone at the cadence-points, marking the divisions of the dances; these cadence-points are very often characterised by a plagal, ornamental figure; and such a feature is intrinsically unsuited to the organ.

Moreover an excess of ornamentation is more obtrusive in organ than in virginal or harpsichord music. Many of the ornaments in the Fantasias of Gibbons choke the melodic line, because the auxiliary notes sound with exactly equal stress and volume to the others. These ornaments clearly originate in Benjamin Cosyn's editing. A particularly blatant example of excessive ornamentation is that of the *Fantasia for Double Organ*,* for which the sole source is Cosyn's Virginal Book.

Example 20

No 7. Fantasia for Double Organ   Gibbons
(bars 65-67)

This proliferation of ornaments by Cosyn, who may or may not have known the composer, is in direct contrast to the brilliant, but simpler, organ piece *Prelude*, No. 2, for which the chief source is Gibbons's own edition, as it appears in *Parthenia*. An ornament which, in the case of a piece played on the virginal, fulfils a definite and necessary purpose by prolonging the duration of a note, or by reinforcing the thin and evanescent tone-quality for a

* Double organ = Organ with two manuals. See p. 133.

rhythmical or metrical reason, is unnecessary, obtrusive even, in the case of the organ, whose tone is bolder and more sustained.

The other piece in *Parthenia* which is clearly an organ piece is the *Fantasia of foure parts*, No. 12. It is likely that Gibbons first wrote a version of this for organ, which he later re-wrote in a slightly more lively style, with more ornaments and rhythmic subtleties, inappropriate to the organ, for inclusion among the virginal pieces of *Parthenia*. Two of the manuscript sources appear to refer back to this original, simpler version.

If the core of Gibbons's work for virginal lies in his dances— though his song-variations *The wood soe wilde* (or *wander ye woods*) compare favourably with similar works by Byrd or Bull—the core of his organ works lies without question in his Fantasias. The three short ones, Nos. 5, 6 and 49, differ from short preludes only in so far as they use imitative entries; the nine substantial Fantasias, Nos. 7–14 and 48, include the *Fantasia for Double Organ*, and the *Plainsong Fantasia*.

All the Fantasias and Preludes might be called 'Voluntaries'; indeed some of the manuscript sources do so describe them; they are non-liturgical, and they are not based on plainsong melodies. This is true even of the *Plainsong Fantasia*, whose 'plainchant' basis, in the inner of the three parts, has not been identified. Probably Gibbons deliberately sought to imitate the pre-Reformation liturgical style with a melodic inner part of his own invention. Certainly the recurring held-notes of this *cantus firmus* style act as something of a restriction on the composer's free invention, and this sets the piece somewhat apart from the other Fantasias.

These are all substantial polyphonic compositions, akin to the *ricercare* of the Italian and German composers of this time, and the direct ancestors of the fugue. Gibbons's Fantasias however are not based on a theme or subject, but on a number of short figures, or points. His commonest device is that of canon, with or without a displacement of the metre, to give the music an additional rhythmical tautness. This technique, which is closely akin to *stretto* entries of the subject in later fugal technique, is a keyboard reproduction of a device which Gibbons frequently used in his vocal writing. Indeed it is not difficult to imagine words set to the entries of the parts in his organ Fantasias. Such entries may be regularly spaced:

Example 21

or they may overlap:

Example 22

Overlapping may even occur at the very beginning, like a vocal composition:

Example 23

Gibbons's *Preludes* and *Fantasias* reveal the incipient tonal sense that was so characteristic at this time. Each piece begins and ends on the same tone. Yet the composer does not yet possess that overall sense of key-unity, covering a long span, with subsidiary modulations, that was to develop later.

Moreover all his organ works make use of the dignified duple metre of *Tempus imperfectum*. Gibbons reserves the use of triple metre for virginal pieces, which are based on quicker dance movements, such as the Galliard. This also serves to emphasise the generally subdued, restrained character of his organ style. Only occasionally, for instance in the toccata style of the Preludes, Nos. 1 and 2, does there appear the brilliance of that virtuoso keyboard player and that polished executant that we know him to have been.

Thomas Tomkins 1572–1656

Like Gibbons, Tomkins was born into a musically talented family, who originally were of Cornish stock, from the town of Lostwithiel. His father (also Thomas) was Master of the choristers and organist at St David's Cathedral, Pembrokeshire;* subsequently, in the early 1590s, the family moved to Gloucester, where Thomas (senior) became a minor canon and precentor of the Cathedral.

The composer's elder brother (yet another Thomas), who was born in 1567, became a Vicar Choral at St David's, until he was expelled in 1586 for having 'grossly misbehaved'. He then joined the navy, only to lose his life in 1591 in the *Revenge*, during Sir Richard Grenville's famous action against the Spanish.

The composer however showed nothing of his elder brother's dashing temperament. He was, on the contrary, a 'quiet peaceable man', ready to assist the poor and those in need. His musical training began when he was a chorister at St David's, and later continued under Byrd. This necessitated his travelling to London, which probably occupied his early twenties, about the years 1594–6. In 1596 he was appointed Master of the choristers and organist at Worcester Cathedral, a position which he retained for the rest

* He is so mentioned on 12th July, 1571.

of his life. He succeeded Nathaniel Patrick, whose widow Alice became his wife in 1597. They had two children, Nathaniel (b. 1599) and Ursula.

Nathaniel, probably named after his mother's former husband,* became a canon of Worcester Cathedral in 1629, after his initial training as a chorister and organist. He later became an important figure in Worcester, a staunch Royalist; but chiefly he is remembered as the compiler and editor of his father's church compositions, under the title of *Musica Deo Sacra*, in 1668. In 1654 he married Isabella, the daughter of Guthlake Folliott, one of the chapter clerks of the Cathedral. She inherited the manor house at Martin Hussingtree, a few miles north of the city; and so this was where Nathaniel and his wife took care of the ageing composer for the last years of his life. The *Lady Folliott's Galliard* (No. 59), is almost certainly a musical tribute from Thomas to his daughter-in-law.

After 1600 the composer's reputation gradually spread. He contributed to Thomas Morley's collection of madrigals *The Triumphs of Oriana* in 1601, but not to his teacher's *Parthenia* in 1612. Clearly Tomkins was chiefly first known as a composer of vocal music, not so much of keyboard works; these were to come later in his life, though Tregian included five pieces in the *Fitzwilliam Virginal Book* (1609–19).†

Tomkins was admitted to an Oxford degree in July 1607, at Magdalen College. Some time later he became a Gentleman of the Chapel Royal; perhaps by 1612, when he wrote a funeral anthem on the death of Prince Henry, 'Know you not'. In 1621, he succeeded Edmund Hooper as one of the organists of the Chapel, with Orlando Gibbons as his colleague.

Tomkins divided his time between Worcester and London—or wherever else the Royal Chapel might be required to travel. Although the journey from Worcester took about a week, and thus involved long absences, his appointment to the Chapel Royal greatly enhanced his position in that city, where he was already a man of some substance. But it also included numerous responsi-

* Though Nathaniel was a very common name at this time.
† Nos. 39, 56, 58, 62, 65 of *Musica Britannica* V.

bilities; particularly the funeral of James I in 1625, and the corona-
tion of his son Charles the following year; the latter event indeed
was made the more onerous by the sudden death of his much
respected friend and colleague Orlando Gibbons in June, 1625.
Tomkins himself died, as already mentioned, at Martin Hussingtree, where he was buried on 9th June, 1656.

Two events of his lifetime are of specific concern to the organist.
The first is the building of a new organ at Worcester Cathedral in
1613–14 by the renowned organ-builder Thomas Dallam. The
specification, which has survived,* was probably drawn up in con-
sultation with Tomkins, who was certainly active in the instigation
of the organ's being built. Though most of his organ compositions
were written later, the instrument formed an integral part in the
verse anthems, or 'Songs to the organ' which were becoming
increasingly popular, and of which there are many examples in
Musica Deo Sacra.

An account of the new organ's visual aspect, as it appeared about
1639, is quoted by Atkins:†

> At the west end and highest ascent into the Quire is mounted
> alofte a most faire and excellent organ adorned with imperiall
> crownes, red roses, includinge the white flowredeluses, pomgran-
> ades, being all Royall badges. Towardes the topp are towe stars, with
> the one, W. Parry, Episcopus; with the other, A. Lake, Decanus;
> and written aboute the Organ, By the meditation and mediation of
> Thomas Tomkins, Organist heere unto the Righte reverend Bishop
> and venerable Deane, who gave theise munificent gviftes and invited
> their fryndes by the industry of the said Thomas Tomkins.

The 'meditation and mediation' of Tomkins must have included
the persuasion of potential benefactors to pay for its cost, which
amounted to £211 for the organ itself, £170 for the gallery and
case. It seems that 112 contributions were received, and the arms
of 57 'honourable and worshipful gentlemen' appeared embossed
on the organ-case.

* See p. 134.
† In *The early occupants of the office of Organist . . . Worcester*, p. 46 (referring
to Habington's *Survey of Worcestershire*).

The second event, which had a direct bearing on the work of the composer, was the Cromwellian revolution of the 1640s, leading to the Commonwealth. All musical services were suspended in Worcester Cathedral on 23rd July, 1646, and Dallam's organ was removed, after its life of thirty two years.* Choral music was not to be resumed for fourteen years, until the Restoration of 1660; and so after more than a century since the former monastery was re-founded in 1541 as a Cathedral of the New Foundation by Henry VIII, its foremost organist was to see its services silenced, its music proscribed, and the organ which he himself had taken such pride in seeing built, removed.

It is however somewhat ironic to notice that, so far as keyboard composition is concerned, the last ten years of Tomkins's life were extremely rich. He turned necessity to advantage. Since choral works were no longer called for in the Cathedral, he could now devote his time to solo works for organ or virginal, as well as to copying and editing.

It is quite possible that the seventy-year-old composer had a small chamber organ in his house, as his son Nathaniel did;† probably also a harpsichord or virginal; and that in such conditions of private music-making he wrote, or re-wrote, many of his organ compositions; he had time for reflection, for correction; and he was the most conscientious editor. 'There is scarcely a page' says Professor Tuttle, in his introduction to *Musica Britannica* Vol. V, referring to the Paris autograph manuscript, 'on which he has not made corrections, revisions or sketches'.

The Music
Numbers refer to *Musica Britannica* Vol. V.

Tomkins contributed substantially to the repertoire of both vocal and instrumental music. As well as secular songs, his vocal works were for the church; forty-two verse anthems, sixty-two

* It was replaced in 1666, after the Restoration, by Dallam's son-in-law Thomas Harris.
† See Atkins, *op. cit.*, p. 52.

full anthems. His consort music comprised nineteen pieces labelled *Fantasia*, nine *Pavan*, two *In nomine*, and some others.

In considering his organ compositions it is a mistake to attempt to read too much into the differences between what was liturgical and what was not; whether a piece was based on an out-of-date *cantus firmus*, or whether it was not. If Tomkins had confined himself to writing only those organ pieces for which there was an immediate need, or an obvious liturgical justification, he would hardly have put pen to paper. But by the seventeenth century, organ music was a thing in its own right; accordingly he adopted for his pieces those forms that by then had become generally and independently established. Nevertheless, like the organ works of other composers, his may be divided between those based on a plainchant, Nos. 4–20, and those that are of free invention Nos. 1–3 and 21–40. For the first category Tomkins writes mainly in three parts; for the other he uses four; and though his style shows no conscious striving after novelty, a certain virtuoso brilliance of execution is implicit in it. The harmony is coloured by an individual chromaticism. It is quite plain that he was fully acquainted with the works of his predecessors, particularly those of his teacher Byrd, and of John Bull; indeed the first 71 pages of that manuscript which is the chief source of his own keyboard works,* is given over to sixteen works of these two other composers—six by Byrd, ten by Bull. Another manuscript which he possessed† is heavily annotated with his comments. He was a musician of wide knowledge, who respected technical excellence in the work of others. Particularly he admired imitative and canonic treatment of the inner parts, and this was something which he himself frequently used; quite arbitrary instances, out of many, are No. 7, bars 9, 15 and 27 and No. 8 bar 22 foll. It is easy to understand Tomkins's instinctive pursuance of such a unifying device, for from such a development of a 'point', and its treatment between the parts, frequently in canon, was later to grow the fugue.

Tomkins's organ work based on the established plainchant forms comprises eight settings of the *In nomine*, eight of the

* MS g.
† MS t.

Miserere, and one of *Clarifica me Pater*. This small gem No. 4, immediately stamps Tomkins as a sure craftsman of the organ; not only are the accompanimental parts a diminished form of the *cantus firmus*, but the pulse-rate is graded throughout the piece; starting with a quaver pulse, changing to a semiquaver pulse at bar 10, and a demisemiquaver one in bar 19. This progressive diminution of the metrical unit lends an urgency to the music which is matched by the ascending scale, the chief characteristic feature of the first two 'points', in bars 1 and 10 respectively.

Example 24

a) No. 4   Clarifica me pater   Tomkins
(Opening)

b) (bars 10-11)

Was Tomkins writing an ascending phrase to represent that feast for which the plainsong melody was originally intended? *Clarifica me Pater* was the antiphon sung on the vigil of the Ascension.

Naturally, as already mentioned, plainchant melodies lean towards the plagal cadence; it is no surprise therefore that each of Tomkins's eight *In nomine* ends plagally; moreover in each case the penultimate chord is a minor one, and the ending is on A, except in the case of Nos. 10 and 11, which end on D. As has been said, Tomkins was very fond of revising and re-writing, and in this set of eight pieces, he provides two pairs of alternatives. No. 11 is another version of No. 10, while No. 6 is an alternative to No. 5. In the case of No. 6, the composer evidently had several second thoughts about the ending, for which he supplied no fewer than six versions. It is a big piece, the phrasing spacious. The composer's indebtedness to Bull, is very plain; in No. 5 he introduces short-note runs (at bar 55), thereby increasing the note ratio to the wide one of 1:32 (or ○: ♪), while in No. 6, at the corresponding place, he makes use of repeated notes.

Technical devices which in Bull's work were innovations, in Tomkins's work are inherent. Of these the most noteworthy are the use of repeated notes. Apart from the example just mentioned, another may be seen in No. 7 (bar 20); Broken figures are used in No. 7 (bar 30), and a decorated bass line in No. 10, (bars 23 and 32). The derivation of a point from a *cantus firmus* occurs in many other pieces than *Clarifica me Pater*. The first *In nomine*, (No. 5), opens with a particularly brilliant example; the fifth is another (No. 9), in which both points are derived from the shape of the original melody:

Example 25

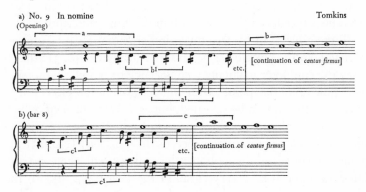

a) No. 9 In nomine   Tomkins
(Opening)

b) (bar 8)

All the *Miserere* settings exploit the use of canon between the accompanimental parts; all except one (No. 15) end, expectedly, with a plagal cadence. Two of the settings are multiple; No. 16 contains three, and No. 18 contains two, which are intended to be played consecutively. All exploit the same mood and tonality, G; all are built on scale movement, and the first five settings (up to the second of No. 16) begin with a prominent falling figure. There is strong evidence that Tomkins intended the pieces to be played like suites, in the following distribution:*

> First suite   :   17, 13, 18 (2 settings)
> Second suite :   15, 14, 19, 20
> Third suite   :   16 (3 settings)

It will be noticed that settings using the falling phrase, feature in each of the three suites.

To those pieces of free invention that were not based on any plainchant, Tomkins gave the title Verse, Fancy or Voluntary. They are interchangeable terms, and the difference between the three categories is negligible. They are written mainly in four parts, except No. 26, which the composer specifies particularly as *A verse of three parts*. This in no way means, however, that they are therefore intended for virginal, or are transcriptions of string pieces. Only one of these pieces is a transcription from a composition for viols, the *Fancy* (No. 33), and it is interesting to note that though it is called in the composer's index a *Fancy for five viols*, Tomkins has reduced the parts to four for this transcription.

All these pieces of his free invention are attempts by Tomkins to 'maintayn the poynte', as he says specifically of No. 31; that is to say the composer maintains a consistency of mood, texture and key, while using the 'point', with which he opens the piece, not so much as a 'ground' to be repeated, but as a thematic *motif*, which he treats by imitation, or by canon, and which may give rise to subsidiary *motifs* as the piece proceeds. In the *Fancy* (No. 23) the 'point' is maintained throughout; the analogy with the construction of a fugue is here very close. In the *Fancy* (No. 25) on the other hand, fresh material is introduced about half way, at bar 17. The word *Voluntary* however was used for the simple pieces that he wrote for his friend (and pupil?) Edward Thornbrough, Archdeacon of Worcester, who died in 1645.

One small piece stands apart from the rest, the *Fancy for two*, No. 32. Tomkins's friend Nicholas Carleton wrote a similar piece, 'a verse for two to play on one virginall or organs', which appears

* See Dart in *Musica Britannica* V, p. 173.

in the same manuscript* as this one. Whether for organ or virginals, Tomkins succeeded in writing a very light-hearted piece; an instrumental equivalent of one of the ballets of his old friend Thomas Morley. Indeed from bar 25 to the end, one can almost hear the entry of a 'fa la la' refrain. Pieces such as this clearly illustrate the development of the chamber organ as a secular and domestic instrument, apart from any connection with the church or Cathedral environment.†

Tomkins's *Offertory* No. 21 is a flexing of his technical muscles, very much in Bull's manner; it is not altogether surprising therefore that this piece, and the two *Grounds* (Nos. 39 and 40), which are similar, should dwell on such proven feats of virtuosity as repeated notes, short-note runs, displaced-note rhythms, and scales in thirds. The progressive increase of brilliance, and the introduction of polyrhythm in No. 21 (bar 105) are also standard keyboard practice; but in his freedom of tonality, and the switching from minor to major, major to minor, quite freely, Tomkins anticipates the later style of Purcell.

A piece such as Purcell's *Fantasia: three parts upon a ground*,‡ for three violins, violoncello and harpsichord, is harmonically and structurally in direct line of descent from Tomkins's keyboard variations, and the tradition they represent.

This characteristically free use of tonality is particularly marked at an important junction-point between the sections that make up this work, when Tomkins introduces a fresh 'point' derived from the *Cantus firmus*.

Example 26

No. 21 Offertory   Tomkins
(bars 141-145)

The piece is built on the repetition of a simple 'ground' in the third tone, and is marked by various section-divisions, all with cadences into A, (at 118–119, 140–141, 207–208, 239–240,* 251–252), which strongly indicate changes of manual.

The hexachord variations (No. 35), are very similar, and in this case the composer consoles and encourages the aspiring performer with the instruction:

> Use as many or as few as you will of these many wayes upon this playnesong.

The six-note figure, which Tomkins describes as a 'playnesong', appears 32 times; as before, there is an alternative ending, and Nos. 36 and 37 contain various 'bitts and morcells', which clearly also represent his second and third thoughts about the same piece. The composer looked on this work as something of a technical study, which he constructed section by section, somewhat piecemeal. So with its performance. Far the greater number of the appearances of the hexachord start on G, as this diagram shows:

Musica Britannica V:	No. 35 ——————————————→	No. 35a ——→
Number of Variation:	1–24 25–27 28–29 30 31	33 34–38
Compass of Hexachord:	G/E C/A G/E C/A G/E	D/B G/E

Other variations include the use of a broken hexachord (No. 38), and the two 'grounds' (Nos. 39 and 40). On the manuscript of No. 40 appears the name of Arthur Phillips; it may perhaps be that this musician, who received an Oxford degree in 1640, either

---

* Not 231–232, where there is a ⌒ in the manuscript. See the textual commentary in *Musica Britannica* V, p. 175 (3c would seem to be the case here!) Stevens, *Thomas Tomkins*, p. 140, astonishingly says of this piece that the ground 'moves freely . . . without any pre-arranged plan or system of tonality'; an unfortunate assessment.

supplied the theme of the 'ground' (no very exacting task), which he then gave to Tomkins, or for some other reason was made the dedicatee of the variations. Each of the two 'Variations on a ground' is in compound time, and uses a seven-note figure.

As far as the registration of his organ works is concerned, Tomkins gives no indication. Dallam's instrument, however, was a simple one, with just three choruses; two of diapason, the other of flute quality. Tomkins therefore probably requires a simpler approach than Bull. It is noticeable that the prevailing style of his melodic lines is one of breadth, simplicity and dignity, rather than one of violent contrasts or extremes of colour. Moreover his organ pieces are remarkably free from ornaments, which occur much more frequently in the secular keyboard pieces. Every note is composed, and is structurally and polyphonically important; and with just the basic manual choruses that Dallam had provided for him, Tomkins built pieces of varying sizes and textures. The Great Diapason choruses must have been firm and full, lacking only the brilliance of the Mixture. The Choir was also reasonably complete. Both manuals could be used in solo. Indeed, many places seem to call for two-manual treatment; the same principles apply to Tomkins as to Bull, as far as the performance of a three-part *In nomine* is concerned. Very often the use of a second manual can effectively emphasise the nature of the music; if the counterpoint is canonic this is even more true. Parts of No. 7, for instance, might well benefit from such performance. A possible registration on the Worcester organ might be:

Bar 16	R H	Choir: 8, 4, 2
(eighth crotchet)	L H	Great: 8

COMPOSERS AND EXTANT REPERTOIRE UP TO 1656
William Byrd—Keyboard Works (I)
Musica Britannica Volume XXVII

		MS Source	Other Editions
	Pieces with G final (Minor)		
1	Prelude	nn, mm, d	2, 67–9
2	Passamezzo Pavan & Galliard	rr, tt, n, p, vv	10
3	Pavan: Sir William Petre; Galliard	j, tt, vv, n, nn	2, 10, 67–9
4	Pavan & Galliard	p	1
5	Pavan (delight) & Galliard: Johnson	n, p	1
6	Fortune	n, p, r	1
7	Rowland or Lord Willoughby's Welcome Home	hh, tt, p, n, d, i	1, 10
8	Walsingham	tt, n, p, vv	10, 1
9	Ground	n	83
10	The Queen's Alman	p, i, hh	1
11	Alman	p	1
	Pieces with A final (Minor)		
12	Prelude	d, p	1
13	Fantasia (to follow Prelude No 12?)	g, p	1
14	Pavan & Galliard	d, tt, ss, j, p	10, 1
15	Pavan & two Galliards (The Earl of Salisbury)	nn, j, l	2, 67–9, 75
16	Pavan & Galliard	ss	83
17	Pavan	tt	10
18	The Galliard Jig	tt	10
19	Qui Passe: for my Lady Nevell	n, tt	10
20	Hugh Aston's Ground or Tregian's Ground	d, n, p, tt	1, 10
21	French Coranto I–III	n, p	1, 83 (II, III)
22	Jig	p	1
	Pieces with B flat final (Major)		
23	Pavan & Galliard	d, j	83
	Pieces with C final Major and (Minor)		
24	Prelude	b, p	1, 2, 67–9
25	Fantasia	p, tt	1, 10, 42
26	Fantasia (A lesson of voluntarie)	g, k, nn, tt, t	10
27	Fantasia (Voluntary)	q, t, tt, mm	10, 83
28	Verse	g	83
29	Pavan & Galliard	j, p, tt	1, 10
30	Pavan & Galliard	d, tt	10
31	Pavan & Galliard	ss, j, tt	10
32	Pavan (Kinborough Good) & Galliard	d, ss, tt	10
33	Pavan & Galliard	j, n	83
34	Galliard, Mistress Mary Brownlow	—	2, 67–9
35	Callins Casturame	d, p	1
36	Tha Carman's Whistle	vv, d, p, r, a, n, tt	1, 10
37	Wilson's Wild	p	1
38	The Bells	p	1
39	Hornpipe	d, n	83
40	The Hunt's up (I)	uu, p, tt	1, 10
41	The Hunt's up (II)	hh, i	83

William Byrd—Keyboard Works (I)—*contd.*

		MS Source	Other Editions
42	Ground	tt	10
43	Ground	n	83
44	Alman	p	1
45	Coranto	j, p	1

End of Musica Britannica Volume XXVII

William Byrd—Keyboard Works (II)
Musica Britannica Volume XXVIII
Pieces with D final (Minor)

		MS Source	Other Editions
46	Fantasia	d, tt	10
47	Clarifica me, Pater, (I)	d	83
48	Clarifica me, Pater (II)	d, p	1, 42
49	Clarifica me, Pater (III)	d, p	1, 42
50	Gloria tibi Trinitas	g	83, 42
51	In nomine (Parsons, set by Byrd)	n, p	1, 83
52	Pavan & Galliard	p	1
53	Galliard	p	1
54	Lachrymae Pavan (Dowland set by Byrd)	n, p	1
55	Galliard (Harding set by Byrd)	n, p, vv	1
56	All in a garden green	tt, p	1, 10
57	My Lady Nevell's Ground	tt	10

Pieces with F final (Major)

58	Ut re mi fa sol la	g	83, 42
59	Pavan: Bray, and Galliard	p	1
60	Pavan: Ph. Tregian, and Galliard	uu, j, p, n	1

Pieces with G final (Major)

61	Voluntary: for my Lady Nevell	tt	10
62	Fantasia	d, p, k, nn	1
63	Fantasia	p	
64	Ut re mi fa sol la	tt, p	1, 10
65	Ut mi re	p	1
66	Miserere (I)	u	
67	Miserere (II)	u	83
68	Salvator Mundi (I)	d	83, 42
69	Salvator Mundi (II)	d	83, 42
70	Quadran Pavan & Galliard	d, n, p	1
71	Pavan & Galliard	d, tt, n, p	1, 10
72	Pavan & Galliard	d, j	83
73	Pavan & Galliard	d	83
74	Pavan: Canon 2 in 1	p, tt	1, 10
75	Lady Monteagle's Pavan	p	1
76	Pavan	n	83
77	Galliard	n	83
78	The Ghost	p, r	1
79	Go from my Window	n, e	83
80	Gypsies' Round	p	1
81	John Come Kiss me now	p	1
82	The maiden's song	p, tt	1, 10
83	O Mistress Mine	p	1

William Byrd—Keyboard Works (II)—*contd.*

		MS Source	Other Editions
84	Sellinger's Round	p, tt	1, 10
85	The Woods so wild	hh, f, p, tt,	
		n, d, a	1, 10
86	Ground	n	83
87	Monsieur's Alman (I)	n, r, p	1
88	Monsieur's Alman (II)	n, d, p, tt	1, 10
89	Alman	n, p	1
90	Lavolta: Lady Morley	p	1
91	Lavolta	n, p	1
92	The Barley break	tt	10
93	The March before the Battle or The Earl of		
	Oxford's March	hh, p, tt	1, 10
94	The Battle	l, tt, f, oo, s	10
95	The Galliard for the Victory	f, hh, tt	10

Appendix: Spurious, doubtful or misattributed works
(incipit only, but printed in full in other ed. where shown)

96	Prelude	n, p	1, 83
97	Prelude★	a, f	83
98	Pavan & Galliard	j	83
99	Pavan (x 2) and Galliard	p, f, hh	1
100	Pavan & Galliard	d	83
101	Pavan	p	1
102	Pavan	p, j	1, 83
103	Galliard: If my complaints	l	83
104	Sir John Gray's Galliard	p	1
105	Untitled piece (Galliard)	n	83
106	Bonny sweet Robin	b, p, h, j, nn	1, 83
107	Malt's come down	p	1
108	Alman	f, pp	83
109	Alman	n	83
110	Lullaby	d, j	83
111	Medley	n	83
112	Medley	p	1
113	Pieces from *The Battle*		
	a The burying of the dead	s, oo, f, s	10, 83
	b The Morris		
	c The soldiers' Dance		

Postscript

114	Echo Pavan & Galliard	n

End of Musica Britannica Volume XXVIII

John Bull—Keyboard Works
Musica Britannica Volume XIV—(Organ works)

1	Prelude and Fantasia	o
2	Prelude and Fantasia in the 8th mode on 'Sol, ut,	
	mi fa sol la'	a, b
3	Fantasia on a theme from 'La Guamina'	b
4	Fantasia on a theme by Sweelinck (15th Dec. 1621)	b
5	Fantasia (chromatic)	o

★ Ascribed to Gibbons. See *Musica Britannica* Vol. XX Nos 46, 47.

John Bull—*Keyboard Works—contd.*

		MS Source	Other Editions
6	Fantasia in the 5th mode	b	2, 67–9
7	Fantasia in the 6th mode on 'A Leona'	b	
8	Fantasia (I) on Vestiva i colli	b	
9	Fantasia (II) on Vestiva i colli	b	
10	Fantasia (Duo)	a, h, p	1
11	Fantasia (Duo)	c	
12	Fantasia	e	
13	Fantasia in the 6th mode	b	
14	Fantasia in the 8th mode on 'Re re re sol ut mi fa sol'	b	
15	Fantasia	k	
16	Fantasia (Prelude?)	o	
17	Ut re mi fa sol la (I chromatic)	o, p	1
18	Ut re mi fa sol la (II treble ostinato)	g, h, p	1
19	Ut re mi fa sol la (III 5 parts)	b	
20–31	In Nomine I–XII ('Gloria tibi Trinitas')	g, h, k, p	1
32	God save the King		4
33	Christe Redemptor omnium	p	1
34	Miserere I (3 settings)	i, j, k, h, p, q	1
35	Miserere II	o	
36	Miserere III (ascr. 'anon')	h	
37	Salvator mundi I (3 settings)	h, p	1
38	Salvator mundi II	a, h, j, i	
39	Salvator mundi III	b	
40	Salve Regina I (5 verses)	o	
41	Salve Regina II (2 verses)	o	
42	Veni Redemptor gentium I	j, k, h, e, p	1
43	Veni Redemptor gentium II and Prelude	p	1
44	Vexilla regis prodeunt (4 verses)	b	
45	Jam lucis orto sidere (2 verses)	b	
46	Te lucis ante terminum	b	
47	Telluris ingens conditor (7 verses)	b	
48	Alleluia I	b	
49	Alleluia II (canon 2 in 1 at the 5th between inner parts)	b	
50	Canon 4 in 2 (at the 4th between two upper and two lower parts)	a	
51	Canon 2 in 1 (at the 5th between upper parts)	a, d	
52	The Merry May (30th May 1622) ('Den lustelijcken Meij')	b	
53–55	Unto us a son is born I–III ('Ein Kindeken ist uns geboren')	b	
56	'Laet ons met herten reijne' and Prelude	b	75, 78
57	Dorick music 3 parts	h, k	
57a	Fantasia attributed to Orlando Gibbons	e	
58	Dorick music 4 parts	h, k	
58a	Dorick music 4 parts (for consort)		
59–61	Dorick Prelude (Cosyn?) I–III	e, h, p	1

End of *Musica Britannica Volume XIV*

John Bull—Other Keyboard Works
Musica Britannica Volume XIX

		MS Source	Other Editions
	In the first tone D		
62–4	Why ask you? I–III	d, f, h, j	5 (II)
65	Bonny sweet Robin (Farnaby?)	b, h, j, p	1, 5
66	(a) Pavan		
	(b) Galliard	e, h, j, p, n	1
67	(a) Melancholy Pavan		
	(b) Melancholy Galliard	e, h	
68	(a) Pavan 'Symphony'		
	(b) Galliard 'Symphony'	b	70
69	Pavan (incomplete ascr. ('anon.')	h	
70	Galliard	—	2, 67–9
71	Galliard	p	1, 2, 67–9
72	Lady Lucy's Galliard	e, h	
73	Galliard (Charlotte de la Haye?)	p (*et al.*)	1
74	Coranto 'Brigante'	b	5
	In the second tone G		
75	Bonny Peg of Ramsey	f, h, r	5
76	The Spanish Pavan	p	1
77	Pavan in the second Tone	b	
78	Galliard	e, h	
79	Coranto	f, j	5
80	Coranto 'Alarm'	b	5, 70
81	Coranto 'Kinston'	b	6
	In the third tone A		
82–4	Prelude I–III	d, k, p	1
85	Walsingham	e, h, p, k	5, 76
86	(a) Fantastic Pavan		
	(b) Fantastic Galliard	e, h, j, p	1
87	(a) Chromatic Pavan		
	(b) Chromatic Galliard	e, h, k	
88	(a) Pavan		
	(b) Galliard	e, h, k, j	
89	Piper's Galliard I, II (Dowland/Bull)	p	1
90	Vaulting Galliard	c, e, h, j, p	1, 7
91	Air (see critical commentary)		
92	Italian Galliard (ascr. 'anon.')	h	
93	Duke of Brunswick's Alman	e, h, j, l, p	1, 5, 6
94	Germain's Alman	h, k, m	5, 6
95	French Alman	h, k	6
96	English Toy	h, k	5
97	Duchess of Brunswick's Toy		
	('Most sweet and fair')	f, h, j, k, p	1, 5, 6
98	The Prince's Coranto	b	5
99	Dutch Dance (ascr. 'anon.')	h	5
	In the fifth tone C		
100	Revenant	o	
101	Les Buffons (on ground 'John come kiss me now')	b	5
102	Dr Bull's Ground I, II (see critical commentary)		

John Bull—Other Keyboard Works—*contd.*

		MS Source	Other Editions
103	Galliard (ascr. 'anon.')	h	
104	Dallying Alman	h, k, p	1, 5, 6
105	French Cortanto (ascr. 'anon.')	h	5
106	Coranto 'Battle'	b	
107	Welsh Dance (ascr. 'anon.')	f, h, l	5

In the sixth tone F

108	A Battle, and no Battle (ascr. 'anon.')	h	
109	(a) Battle Pavan		
	(b) Battle Galliard (Richardson?)	h	
110	Ionic Alman	h, k, m	5
111	Country Dance	b	5
112	Irish Toy (ascr. 'anon.')	h	5

In the seventh tone D

113	The Prince's Galliard	j, o	
114	Alman	k	6
115	Alman	k, m	6
116	What care you? (ascr. 'anon.')	h	5

In the eighth tone G

117–121	Prelude I–V	a, e, k, h, j, p	1, 2 (I), 7, 67–9
122	Rosasolis (Farnaby?)	b, p	1
123	Go from my window	e, i, j	5, 7
124	The New Bergomask	b	5
125	The King's Hunt	h, o, p	1
126	(a) Pavan 'St Thomas, Wake!'		2, 6, 67–9
	(b) Galliard 'St Thomas, Wake!' I, II	d, e, l, p	1, 2, 6, 67–9
127	(a–c) The Quadran Pavan I–III	e, h, j, n, p	1
	(d–f) The Quadran Galliard I–III	e, h, p	1
128	(a) Trumpet Pavan		
	(b) Trumpet Galliard	e, h, j, p	1, 7
129	(a) Lord Lumley's Pavan		
	(b) Lord Lumley's Galliard	e, h, j, p	1
130	(a) Pavan		
	(b) Galliard (ascr. 'anon.')	h	
131	(a) Pavan		
	(b) Galliard		2, 67–9
132	(a–c) Regina Galliard I–III	h, j, p	1
133	Lord Hunsdon's Galliard	e, h	
134	Alman Fantasia (Farnaby?)	h, k, m, p	1, 5
135	Alman	h, k	5
136	Coranto 'joyeuse'	b	
137	Coranto 'a round'	b	
138	My self	h, p	1, 5
139	My Grief	e, h, p	1, 5, 6, 7
140	My Choice (24th August, 1612)	r	
141	My Jewel I (four versions)	b, e, h, p	1, 5, 6
142	My Jewel II (12th December, 1621)	b	70
143	Bull's Goodnight	h	5

End of *Musica Britannica Volume XIX*

Orlando Gibbons—Keyboard Works
Musica Britannica Volume XX—(Organ works)

		MS Source	Other Editions
1	Prelude (Tone 3) A Runing fantasia	i, e, y, bb, w	14^5, 19
2	Prelude (Tone 8) Voluntary	nn, mm, kk, a y, z, j, ii, b	2, 14^4, 67–9, 19
3	Short Prelude (Tone 1) a short Voluntary	e, a	14^4, 15, 19
4	Short Prelude (Tone 3)	x	
5	Fantasia (Tone 1) a short prelude of 4 parts	c, dd	14^4, 19
6	Fantasia (Tone 1)	e, i	14^4, 15, 19
7	Fantasia for double organ (Tone 1)	e	43,* 14^5, 15, 19
8	Fantasia (Tone 2 transposed)	e	14^5, 15
9	Fantasia (Tone 2)	e	14^5, 15
10	Fantasia (Tone 3)	a, e, k	14^4, 15, 19, 77
11	Fantasia (Tone 3) a Voluntary	a, e, k, dd	14^4, 15, 19, 43
12	Fantasia (Tone 3) Fantasia of foure parts	a, h, k	2, 14^5, 67–9, 43
13	Fantasia (Tone 5) Voluntary of foure parts	a, e, y, ee	14^4, 15
14	Fantasia (Tone 5) A Voluntary (of 4 parts)	a, e, c, dd	14^4, 15

Musica Britannica Volume XX—(Other keyboard works)

		MS Source	Other Editions
15	Pavan (Tone 1) Allmaine	t, e, h, dd	14^3, 33
16	Pavan (Tone 2)	j	14^3
17	Pavan (Tone 3) A Voluntary?		14^4
18	Pavan, Lord Salisbury (Tone 3)	j, nn, i, p	1, 2, 14^3, 67–9
19	Galliard, Lord Salisbury (Tone 3)	j, l, nn	2, 14^3, 67–9
20	Galliard, Lady Hatton (Tone 1)	e, j, k	14^1
21	Galliard (Tone 1)	e, nn	14^3
22	Galliard (Tone 1)	e	14^3
23	Galliard (Tone 1)	nn	
24	Galliard (Tone 3)	c, e, j	14^3
25	Galliard (Tone 5)	j, nn	2, 14^3, 67–9
26	Ground† (Tone 3)	j	14^2
27	The Italian Ground† (Tone 5) Allmaine	c, s, h, hh, j, k	14^1
28	The Queen's Command (Tone 5)	ll, e, y, j, w, nn	2, 14^2, 67–9, 75
29	The woods so wild (Tone 6/8)	c	14^2
30	Peascod time, or The Hunt's up (Tone 8)	nn, e, j	14^2
31	Whoop, do me no harm good man (Tone 8) Ground	l, y, nn, oo, i	14^2
32	French Air (Tone 1/6)	c	14^1
33	Alman (Tone 1)	j	14^1, 16
34	Alman (Tone 3) An Air	h, i, j, aa k, m, oo	14^1, 16
35	Alman (Tone 5)	e, j	14^1, 16
36	Alman, The King's jewel (Tone 8)	e, c	14^1
37	Alman (Tone 8)	e, nn	14^1
38	French Coranto (Tone 1)	c	14^1, 16

* Ed. 43 is unreliable.
† Prob. intended primary for the organ.

Orlando Gibbons—Keyboard Works—*contd.*

		MS Source	Other Editions
39	Coranto Two versions (Tone 1) A maske	h, c	14[1], 16
40	Coranto (Tone 3) A Toy	b, e, j, p	1, 14[1]
41	Nann's Mask, or French Alman (Tone 1)	s, e, hh, j	14[1], 16
42	Mask, Welcome home (Tone 1) Allmaine	oo, h, cc	14[1], 16
43	Mask, The fairest nymph (tone 3)	c, f, cc, hh,	
	Grayes Inn Maske	oo, s	14[1]
44	Lincoln's Inn Mask (Tone 5)	h, aa, j	14[1]
45	The Temple Mask (Tone 5)	e, h, j	14[1]

Appendix—doubtful works

46	Prelude★ A Voluntarie (Tone 8)	a, f, hh	14[4]
47	Prelude★ (Tone 8)	a, f, hh	14[4]
48	Plainsong Fantasia★ (Tone 3)	c, e, f, k, i, g	14[4]
49	Fantasia★ (Tone 5)	dd	19
50	Galliard (Tone 3)	e	14[3]

End of *Musica Britannica Volume XX*

Probable attribution

Fantasia (Voluntary) for Double organ (Tone 3)		108[1]

Thomas Tomkins—Keyboard Works
Musica Britannica Volume V—(Organ Works)

1	Prelude	g	
2	Piece of a Prelude (9th July, 1647)	g	
3	Prelude	g	
4	Clarifica me Pater (September, 1650)	g	
5	In nomine Version I (20th–28th Jan. 1647)	g	
6	In nomine Version II		
	(20th Jan., 1647–2nd Aug., 1650)	g	
7	In nomine (May, 1648)	g	
8	In nomine (16th June, 1648)	g	
9	In nomine (27th October, 1648)	g	
10	In nomine Version I (Feb. 1650)	g	
11	In nomine Version II (14th Feb., 1650)	g	
12	In nomine (28th June, 1652)	g	
13	Miserere† (15th Sept., 1648)	g	
14	Miserere (7th Oct., 1648)	g	
15	Miserere (26th May, 1651)	g	
16	Miserere (3rd–4th Feb., 1652)	g	
17	Miserere	g	
18	Miserere	g	
19	Miserere	g	
20	Miserere	g	
21	Offertory (1637)	v	
22	Fancy (9th Sept., 1646)	g	
23	Fancy (8th July, 1647)	g	17

★ Prob. intended primarily for the organ.

† The *Miserere* settings seem to have been planned by the composer in a definitive order: Nos. 17, 13, 18 to form a suite, in that order. He may have planned possibly also a second suite, consisting of Nos. 15, 14, 19, 20 (*From a note by the editor*).

Thomas Tomkins—Keyboard Works—*contd.*

		MS Source	Other Editions
24	Voluntary (or Fancy) (10th Aug.–10th Sept., 1647)	g	17
25	Fancy (24th October, 1648)	g	17
26	A verse of three parts (12th Aug., 1650)	g	17
27	A short verse	t	17, 33
28	Voluntary	w	17
29	Fancy	k	
30	Voluntary	w	17
31	A substantial verse maintaining the point	g	17
32	Fancy; for two to play	t	32
33	Fancy (for viols)	g	
34	Ut re mi fa sol la (for a beginner)	g	
35	Ut re mi fa sol la	g, v	
36	Ut re mi fa sol la	g	
37	Ut re mi fa sol la	g	
38	Ut re mi	v	
39	Ground	p	1
40	Ground	t	33

Musica Britannica Volume V—(Other keyboard works)

41	Pavan: Earl Strafford (29th Sept., 1647) short version	g	
42	Galliard: Earl Strafford short version	g	
43	Pavan: Earl Strafford (2nd Oct., 1647) long version	g	
44	Galliard: Earl Strafford long version	g	
45	Pavan (April, 1650)	g	
46	Galliard (1st Oct., 1650)	g	
47	Pavan (4th Sept., 1654)	g	
48	Galliard (7th Sept., 1654)	g	
49	Pavan of three parts	g	
50	Galliard of three parts	g	
51	Pavan (10th Sept., 1647)	g	
52	Pavan (14th Sept., 1647)	g	
53	A sad pavan, for these distracted times* (14th Feb. 1649)	g	
54	Pavan (20th Aug., 1650)	g	
55	Short Pavan (19th July, 1654)	g	
56	Pavan	p	1
57	Pavan, Lord Canterbury (1647)	t	33
58	The hunting Galliard	j, p	1
59	The Lady Folliott's Galliard	j	
60	Galliard	j	
61	Fortune my foe (4th July, 1654)	g	
62	Barafostus' dream	p	1, 13
63	Robin Hood (ascr. 'anon.')	n	
64	What if a day	j	13
65	Worcester brawls	p	1, 13
66	The perpetual round (7th–8th Sept., 1654)	g	

★ i.e. Two weeks after the execution of Charles I.

Thomas Tomkins—*Keyboard Works—contd.*

		MS Source	Other Editions
67	Toy, made at Poole Court	g	
68	(On a plainsong)	k	

Appendix

		MS Source	Other Editions
69	Toy, Mr Curch (or Almaine)	k, j, p	13
70	Ut re mi fa sol la (fragment)	g	
71	Ut re mi fa sol la (fragment) (30th June, 1654)	g	
72	Go from my window (fragment)	g	
73	Bitts or morcells (fragments)	g	

End of *Musica Britannica Volume V*

Additional organ works:

	MS Source	Other Editions
Voluntary for Edward Thornbrough	v	31
Voluntary for Mr. Archdeacon Thornbrough	v	31
Another Voluntary	v	31

Other Composers' Extant Works

Composer	Work	MS Source	Printed Editions
ANONYMOUS			
An easy one for a new beginer		c	
An Introduction	Unnamed piece		
'The first Maske'	'The second maske'		
A toy	The solitary widdow		
'The King's Morick'	The Mallinchol's Loss		
Unnamed piece	Pavan		
Unnamed piece	Martir's tune		
O God that art, unnamed piece			
Yee children which doe serve			
Unnamed piece			
Blessed (are the undefiled)			
Unnamed piece (variations)		a	
A Ground	Verse in A minor		
Voluntary in A minor	Prelude in E minor		
Suite in G minor (Prelude, Allemande, Courante, Saraband)			
Piece for the Trumpet stop in G			
Prelude in G minor	Overture in G minor		
Piece in G			
Suite in D minor (mov. as above)			
Ground & Jigg in D minor			
'Francis Forcer'	Allemande, Gavotte, Gigue		
	Prelude, Courante, Gavotte, Gigue		
Allemande in A, D	Prelude in A minor		
Prelude in D minor	Prelude in C		
Verses I–VII	Voluntary		
Two Verses			
Shall I despair	Quadron peven & Galliard	d	

Composer	Work	MS Source	Printed Editions
ANONYMOUS–*contd.*			
(Kinlonghe) Pavan & Galliard		d	
Unnamed piece			
(Philip van Wilder?)	'Las que ferra'		
Si je me plaine	Pavan (Bickerll.)		
Fancy 'Renold'			
The Queenes new year's gifte			
(James Harding) Fancy, I, II			
Wakefield on a greene			
Two Pavans	Lacrimae		
Prelude	Pavan & Galliard		
Pavan & Galliard	Ground		
Unnamed piece	4 unnamed pieces		
2 unnamed pieces	(incl. *Eterne Rex*		
	Altissime, Miserere)		
'O neighboure Robert'	Unnamed piece, gigg		
Unnamed piece	A Gigge	vv	33
Mall Sims	Hoope doune		33
Tomboy	Wanton season		33
Goe no more a-rushing			33
Corranto			
Elizabeth Rogers' Virginal Book			
'Sir Thos. Fairfax' Marche'		s	
Allemande	'The Scots' Marche'		
'The ffairest Nymphes the valleys or mountaines ever bred'.			
'Prince Rupert's Martch'			
'One of ye Symphonies'			
'Nann's Maske'	Selebrand		33
'When the king enjoyes his own again'			
Allemande	Trumpet tune		
'Essex' last good night'			
(Thos. Strengthfeild)	Allemande and Courante		
Rupert's Retraite			
(Thos. Strengthfeild)	Allemande & Courante		
Beare ⎧ Courante & Saraband ⎨ Courante ⎩ Two Courantes			
'The Nightingale'	A Maske'		33
'The Chesnut'	Courante		33
Allemande	'Mock-Nightingale'		33
Saraband	Courante		
Saraband	Unnamed piece		
Phill. Porter's Lamentation			33
Allemande	Courante		
'The Souldier's delight'			
Courante & Saraband	Courante & Sarabande		

Composer	Work	MS Source	Printed Editions
ANONYMOUS–*contd.*			
★'Ly still, my Deare'		s	
★'Cloris sight'	'Now ye spring is comme'★		
★'Oh Jesu meeke'	Courante I, II		
Maske	'The King's complaint'		
★'Could thine incomparable eye'			
'What if the King should come to yᵉ city'			
Allemande and Courante			
'My delyght'	'The faithfull Brothers'		
'The Finnex'	'The Spaynard'		
'An Irish Toy'	Allemande		
'A Scotts tuen'	Hornpipe		
Allemande	Allemande & Courante		
(Thos Strengthfeild)	Courante & Saraband		
Allemande	'I wish noe more'		
(Thos. Strengthfeild)	Allemande (?) and Saraband		
'Love is strange'	Glorye of ye North		
	Two Courantes		
Alman I–VIII	Can shee	p	I
Corranto I–XI	Daunce I–II		
Galiarda I–II	The Irish Dumpe		
The Irish Ho-Hoane	The King's Morisco		
Martin sayd to his man			
Muscadin	Pakington's Pownde		
Prelude I–VI	A Toy I, II		
Veni	Watkins Ale		
Why aske you			
BEVIN, Elway	Fancy	c	
	Canon on 'Miserere'	a	
	Canon	a	
	Double Canon	a	
	Duo, I and II	a	
	Preludes, I and II	a	
	(Study: 'Twenty parts in one')	t	
CARLETON, Nicholas	A verse of four parts	t	33
	A verse upon the 'sharpe'	t	33
	A verse for two to play on one virginall or organs (*In nomine*)	t	32
	Praeludium	t	33
COLEMAN, Charles	Fantasia	p¹	
COOPER, John	24 untitled pieces (Fantasias?)	s¹	
	Fantasias I–V	p¹	
	Fantasias I–XV	v¹	
	Fanceys of 5 parts I–XV	s¹	
COSYN, Benjamin	8 pieces for Virginals	e	
	Three Voluntaries†		88

★ With words.

† Doubtful attribution.

Composer	Work	MS Source	Printed Editions
DERING, Richard	Fantasia	p^1	
ELLIS, William	Fantasia	k	
FACY, Hugh	A Galyard	c	
	Two unnamed pieces (Fancy?)	c	
	Voluntary	w	
	Ave Maris Stella	w	
FERRABOSCO, Alfonso	Fantasias I–XI	p^1	
	In nomine I, II	p^1	
	Hexachord Fantasia	t	
	Fancies I, II	d	
	6 unnamed pieces (Fantasias?)	s^1	
CALEAZZO, ?	Praeludium	p	I
GIBBONS, Edward	Prelude	t^1	
HOLMES, Thomas	Fantazia	k	
HOOPER, Edmund	Alman	p	I
INGLOTT, William	A Galliard Ground	p	I
	The leaves bee greene	p	I
	Unnamed piece	n	
JENKINS, John	Fantasias I, II	p^1	
	Pavan	p^1	
JOHNSON, (i) Edward	Johnson's Medley	p	I
(ii) Robert	The Prince's Almayne	c, p	I
	Mr Johnsonn's Almayne 1629	c	
	Mr Johnson's Flatt Pavin	c	
	Flat Paven	d	
	Allemande	j, k, s, cc	
	Alman	p	I
	Almaygne	s	
LAWES, William	Allemande 'The Golden Grove'	m	
	Keyboard suite—Allmaine, Coranto, Sellabrand	h	
LOOSEMORE, Henry	Courant	gg	
LUGGE, John	Gloria tibi Trinitas I–VI	q^1	
	In nomine	q^1	
	Miserere	q^1	
	Hexachord Fantasia	q^1	
	Voluntaries I–III	q^1	34
	Christe qui lux es	q^1	
	Mr Luggs Jigg for harpsichord	l	
LUPO, Thomas	Air	s	
	Fantasias I–X	p^1	
	Seven unnamed pieces (Fantasias?)	s^1	

Composer	Work	MS Source	Printed Editions
MARCHANT,	Allemanda	p	1
?	Pavan and Galliard	d	
MERCURE,	Almaine, Corant, Sarabrand for		
John	harpsichord	gg	
	Allemande	s	
	Unnamed piece	s	
MICO,	Two Pavens	s[1]	
Richard			
MORLEY,	Pavan and Galliard	p	1, 21
Thomas	Quadro Pavan	n	21
	'Pasmeasz' Pavan	u[1]	21
	'Lachrimae' Pavan and Galliard	p	1, 21
	Galliard	n	21
	Pavan and Galliard	u[1]	21
	Alman	n, p	1, 21
	Nancy	p	1, 21
	Fantasia	p	1, 21
	Go from my window (see Mundy)★	p	1, 21
MUDD,	A lesson of Voluntarie of 3 parts	i	
Thomas	The answer to ye former lesson	i	
MUNDY,	Fantasias I, II	p	1
John	Go from my window (see Morley)★	p	1
	Munday's Joy	p	1
	Robin	p	1
OLDFIELD,	Praeludium	p	1
Thomas			
OYSTERMAYRE,	Galiarda	p	1
John			
PARSONS,			
(i) Robert	In nomine	t	
(ii) John(?)	In nomine	p	1
PEERSON,	Alman	p	1
Martin	The Fall of the Leafe	p	1
	Pipers Paven	p	1
	The Primerose	p	1
PHILIPS,	(a) *Vocal arrangements*		
Peter	Deggio dunque partire	k	
	Io partirò, ma il core	k	
	Ma voi	k	
	Cosi moriro ⎫	p	1
	Freno ⎬(arr. of Marenzio)	p	1
	Tirsi ⎭	p	1
	Le Rossignol	k, p	1
	Bon jour, man coeur	p	1
	Margott laborez (arr. of Lassus)	p	1
	Amarilli (arr. of Caccini)	p	1
	Chi fare fede al Cielo		
	(arr. of Striggio)	p	1

★ Two settings occur in the *Fitzwilliam Virginal Book* (Nos. 9, 42) The second is attributed to Mundy by Tregian.

Composer	Work	MS Source	Printed Editions
PHILIPS	Fece da voi partita	k, p	I
Peter	Benedicam Dominum	k	
—contd.	Veni Creator Spiritus	z	
	(b) *Instrumental works*		
	Almande	k, m	
	Fantasia I, II	p	I
	Galliard I, II	p	I
	Pavann dolorosa; Galiarda dolorosa		
	(Tregian)	p	I
	Pavana (Pagget)	p	I
	Pavana passamezzo; Galiarda		
	passamezzo	p	I
	Pavana	p	I
PICHI,	Toccata	p	I
Giovanni			
PORTMAN,	Verse for Double Organ	u³	
Richard			
PRICE,	Voluntary	i, ee, t³	
John			
RICHARDSON,	Pavan & Galliard I, II	d	
Ferdinando	Allemande	d	
	Pavan & Variation ⎫ I, II	p	I
	Galliard & Variation ⎭		
SIMMES,	Fantasia a 5	o¹	
William			
SONCINO,	Prelude (1633)	a	
Emanuel	Cromatica	c	
STROWGER,	In nomine I, II	u	
Nicholas	Fantasia 'upon ut re my fa soul la'	u	
	Fantasia	p	I
	Unfinished In nomine	u	
TISDALL,	Almand	p	I, 39
William	Pavana Chromatica		
	(Mrs Katherin Tregian's Pavan)	p	I, 39
	Pavana, Clement Cotton	p	I, 39
	Pavana	p	I, 39
	Coranto, Jig	u¹	39
	Galiarda	p	I, 39
WARWICK,	Pavane and Galliard	p	I
Thomas			
WEELKES,	Galliard	d	
Thomas	Voluntary	j, mm	
	Voluntary	j, mm	
WHITE,	Ut re mi fa sol la	u	
(i) Robert?	Fantasias I, II	p¹	
(ii) W.?	Unnamed piece (Fantasia?)	s¹	

BIOGRAPHICAL NOTES ON THE COMPOSERS

AMNER, John.
?–1641. 1610–1641 Organist at Ely Cathedral. (8 Verses on a psalm tune appear in MS j.)

BEVIN, Elway (Edward?) (or Ab Evan?).
155?–1637. 1575–84 Vicar Choral, Wells—Pupil of Tallis. 1589–1637 Organist Bristol Cathedral (Chapel Royal?). 1605, (3rd June) Gentleman extraordinary of Chapel Royal. 1631 Published *Briefe and Short Instruction of the Art of Musicke* (see in MS a for treatment of ornaments).

CARLETON, Nicholas.
?–1630. Several musicians of this name make exact identification difficult. The composer of the duet in MS t was a friend of Tomkins, and lived in Worcestershire. Another Carleton appears in the *Mulliner Book*, while Richard Carleton, Vicar and choirmaster in Norwich, appears as a madrigalist in Morley's *Triumphs of Oriana* (1601).

COLEMAN, Charles.
?–1664. Violist to Charles I. 1628 Musician for the Lutes and voices. Songs, Fantasias for viols. 1656 Entr'actes for *Siege of Rhodes*.

COOPER, John (alias Coperario, Giovanni).
1575–1626. A visit to Italy introduced him to the newly-developing opera. Member of the Private Musick. Composer to James I, and Charles I. Teacher of Prince Charles & Prince Henry; also of Henry & William Lawes. Fancies for strings and organ; lute songs, masques.

COSYN, Benjamin.
?—?. 1622–4 Organist Dulwich College. 1626–43 Charterhouse. Edited MS e, though not all pieces with his name are necessarily his.

DERING, Richard.
c. 1580–1630. Illegitimate, Catholic son of old Kent family sent to Italy. c. 1610? returned. 1617 Organist in Brussels. 1625 Musician for the lute and viols to Charles I. 1630 Place taken by Giles Tomkins.

ELLIS, William
?—?. Copyist (eg MS k) and friend of Cosyn (q.v.). 1639 Succeeded Robert Lugge as organist of St John's College Oxford. Arranged musical evenings during the Commonwealth.

FACY, Hugh.
Fl. Early seventeenth century. Assistant (or pupil?) to John Lugge at Exeter Cathedral c. 1618.

FARNABY, (i) Giles *c.* 1565–1640, (ii) Richard *c.* 1590–1640.

(i) Virginalist; of Cornish descent, like Francis Tregian, whom he knew. Cousin Nicholas 'a joiner and virginal maker'—Perhaps Giles also lived in London; married at St Helen's Bishopsgate, 1587. (ii) Son Richard also a virginalist (see *Fitzwilliam Virginal Book*).

FERRABOSCO, Alfonso (II)

c. 1575–1627. His father, Alfonso (I) had been in service of Queen Elizabeth. Lutenist to Earl of Pembroke. 1603 Private Musick, Teacher of Prince Henry & Charles. Exponent of the viol, compositions include Fantasias, Songs, Masques. 1625 Composer in ordinary to the King.

GIBBONS, Edward.

1568–1650. Elder brother of Orlando Gibbons. 1593–8 Master of the choristers, King's College, Cambridge, 1598–? Exeter Cathedral (Lay-clerk?). 1609 Priest-vicar. 1608–44 (25th June) Choirmaster. 1611 'Custos of ye College of Lay Vicars.' 1615 Succentor.

HOLMES (i) John ?–1629, (ii) Thomas 1606(?)–1638.

(i) 1615–21 Organist Winchester Cathedral. 1621–29 Master of Choristers, Salisbury Cathedral. (ii) Son of (i). 1631–38 Organist Winchester Cathedral, succeeded by Christopher Gibbons. 1633 (17th Sept.) Gentleman of Chapel Royal.

HOOPER, Edmund.

?–1621. Born in Devon; chorister at Exeter Cathedral. 1588 Organist & Master of the children at Westminster Abbey. 1603 (1st March) Gentleman of the Chapel Royal. Later organist with Orlando Gibbons.

INGLOTT, William.

1554–1621. Son of Edmund Inglott, organist of Norwich Cathedral (1560–1593). 1568 Chorister at Norwich Cathedral. 1576 Layclerk. 1579 Master of the children. 1608–21 Organist at Norwich Cathedral.

JENKINS, John.

1652–1678. 1660–6 Lived with Lord North, and taught his sons. Later with Sir Philip Wodehouse. Exponent of viol music, especially fantasias. Friend of William Lawes (q.v.). 1660 (16th June) Musician for the lute in the Private Musick.

JOHNSON, (i) Robert 1569(?)–1633. (ii) Edward?

(i) Son of John J., one of Queen Elizabeth's musicians 1586. 1604 One of King's Private Musick. 1611 Lutenist to Prince Henry. 1625 Lute in the Consorte. Largely vocal, theatre compositions; equally spoken of with Dowland. (ii) Madrigalist.

LAWES, William.

1602–1645. Pupil of Cooper (q.v.). 1635 'Musician in ordinary' in Charles I's Private Musick. Compositions include viol sonatas, fantasias, masques. Killed at Chester during the civil war.

LOOSEMORE, Henry.

?–1670. 1627–1670 Organist King's College, Cambridge.

LUGGE, (i) John ? (ii) Peter ? (iii) Robert ?

(i) 1634 Vicar Choral at Exeter Cathedral. 1602–c. 1645 Organist at Exeter Cathedral. (see Edward Gibbons) 1618, (24th Jan.) Suspected of Roman Catholic sympathies and 'examined'. Seven children (see Robert below). (ii) Brother of (i), and like him involved in religious controversy and intrigue. (iii) Son of (i), Organist St John's College, Oxford 1635–1639.

LUPO, Thomas (i) ?–c1627, (ii) ?–c1637, (iii) ?–c1642.

Active between 1593–163?. 1621 Composer of the violins to James I. Three musicians of this name; exact identification practically impossible.* Musical family extends over several generations.

MARCHANT, ?

?–1611. Nothing known.

MERCURE, John.

?–165?. 1641 Musician for lutes and voices to Charles I.

MICO, Richard.

Sixteenth/seventeenth century. Nothing known.

MORLEY, Thomas.

c. 1557–1603. Pupil of Byrd, and Westcote (St Paul's, d.1582). 1583–87 Master of the Choristers Norwich Cathedral. 1589 Organist St Giles's, Cripplegate (?). 1589–92 Organist St Paul's Cathedral. 1592, (24th July) Gentleman of Chapel Royal. 1596–1601, in parish of Little St Helen's Bishopsgate. 1597 Published *Plaine and Easie Intro-duction to Practical Musicke*. 1602 Resigned or retired from Chapel Royal, perhaps for health reasons. Compositions chiefly vocal, incl. stage lyrics, ballets, madrigals, canzonets.

MUDD, Thomas.

c. 1560–1632. ?–1632 Organist Peterborough Cathedral.

MUNDY or MUNDAY (i) William 1529–1591, (ii) John 156?–1630.

(i) Vicar Choral, St Paul's. 1563, (21st Feb.), Gentleman of Chapel Royal. (ii) Son of above. Gentleman of Chapel Royal. Organist at Eton College. 1585 (?) succeeded Marbeck at St George's Chapel, Windsor.

* See Pulver, *A Biographical dictionary of old English Music*.

PARSONS, (i) Robert ?–1569, (ii) John ?–1623, (iii) Robert ?

(i) Born at Exeter. 1563 (17th Oct.) Gentleman of Chapel Royal. 1569, (25th Jan.) Drowned at Newark. Succeeded by Byrd. (ii) Son of above. 1616 Organist St Margaret's Westminster. 1621 Organist Westminster Abbey, in succession to Hooper. On his death in 1623, he was succeeded by Orlando Gibbons. (iii) Another Robert Parsons was Vicar Choral at Exeter in 1634.

PEERSON, Martin.

1572–1650. 1613 Master of the Choristers at St Paul's Cathedral. 1626 Almoner. Compositions largely vocal, sacred music, and instrumental fantasias.

PHILIPS, Peter.

c. 1560–c. 1638. Chorister at St Paul's Cathedral under Westcote. (c.f. Morley). 1590 Left England for Low Countries. 1595 travelled to Rome (?). 1598 Organist to Archduke Albert in Brussels. Lived in Netherlands, music published in Antwerp. Compositions mainly vocal, madrigals, motets. Organ works include transcriptions (Marenzio, Lassus etc.).

PORTMAN, Richard.

?–1659. Pupil of Orlando Gibbons. 1633–44 Organist Westminster Abbey. 1638 (27th Sept.) Gentleman of Chapel Royal. Teacher, composer of anthems and services.

PRICE, John.

?–1641. Player on tabor, cornett and other instruments. Settled on the Continent after 1605 (Stuttgart, Dresden, Vienna).

RICHARDSON, Ferdinando.

1558 (?)–1618 (alias Heybourne). Pupil of Tallis. 1587 Groom of the Privy Chamber.

SIMMES, William.

Nothing known.

SONCINO, Emanuel.

Nothing known.

STROWGER (or STROGERS), Nicholas.

fl. late sixteenth/early seventeenth century. Son of E. Strowger? (see Chapter II) Nothing otherwise known.

TISDALL, William.

1570 (?)–? Nothing otherwise known.

WARWICK, Thomas.

156?–164?. Cumberland family. Son Philip W. Treasury Secretary after Restoration. 1586–89 Organist at Hereford Cathedral in succes-

sion to John Bull. 1625 Musician for the lute in the Private Musick.
Gentleman of Chapel Royal. 1625 Succeeded Gibbons as organist at
Chapel Royal. 1630 Reprimanded for his 'insufficiency' as organist.
1641 'Musician for the Virginall' in Private Musick.

WEELKES, Thomas.
?–1623. 1603–23 Organist of Chichester Cathedral after Winchester
College. Chiefly known as madrigalist. Works also include anthems,
services & some pieces for viols.

WHITE, (i) Robert ?–1574 or (ii) W. ?
1561–66 Succeeded Tye as Master of the Choristers Ely Cathedral.
Married Ellen Tye (Composer's daughter?). 1567(?)–1569(?). Organist
at Chester. 1570–4. Master of the choristers, Westminster Abbey.
(ii) W. White is mentioned in MS s[1].

The following composers, represented by a single work in The
Fitzwilliam Virginal Book are otherwise unknown: GALEAZZO,
OLDFIELD, OYSTERMAYRE, PICHI.

THE ORGAN OF THE PERIOD 1558–1656

From the accession of Elizabeth can be traced the beginning of that insularity which was to be the most conspicuous feature of English history for the next four hundred years.

As far as organ-building is concerned, the divergence between the instruments built in England and those built on the continent, can largely be traced from this period. The use and manufacture of organs was discouraged in the later sixteenth century, probably due very largely, as Sumner suggests, to their being associated with the pre-Reformation Latin rite. By the same token rood-lofts were removed, and crucifixes destroyed; the prevailing Puritan mood was one of anti-clericalism. The placing of organs in the rood-loft dates from this post-Reformation period, when roods were removed or destroyed. And so correspondingly greater importance came to be laid on domestic music-making in the Elizabethan period; and this trend affected not only the organ itself, but its music.

Hitherto the Regal had been the only form of organ used for private, or 'Chamber' music. This, with its nasal, non-resonating reeds, could only be of limited use, though it was used in some churches, and Henry VIII possessed several. The characteristic tone of the Regal was produced by a beating reed in a very short wooden tube. The word was applied either to the reed stop itself, which might be incorporated into an organ; or to the small instrument, which was the oldest of portative organs, and much in demand for court entertainments. It was used for dance music, such as the Galliard, and later for the dramatic music of the Masque.

In the later sixteenth century, however, and more particularly after the accession of James I, who himself possessed one, the chamber organ, portable as need be, began to be used for banquets and official entertainments. In this way organ music became secularised; and this was a trend which continued right up to the time of Samuel Wesley.

The most prominent name among organ-builders of the late sixteenth century was that of the Devonshire family of Chappington; in particular John Chappington, who died in 1606 and whose work included the organs of Westminster Abbey (159?), Magdalen College, Oxford (1597), and many other churches. Beyond this, unfortunately, nothing is known of his instruments, and none of his specifications survives.

The first half of the seventeenth century was dominated by the Dallam family. Thomas Dallam (*c.* 1575–*c.* 1632), organ-builder to Queen Elizabeth, was the most renowned builder of his day. His son Robert (1602–1665) succeeded him. He was also the grandfather of the later-famous Renatus Harris.

Thomas Dallam built organs all over the country; at King's College, Cambridge (1606); at Hatfield House (1611); at Holyrood Palace, Edinburgh (1616); at St Margarets, Westminster (1617). Far the most interesting however, because its original specification has survived, is the instrument he built at Worcester Cathedral for Tomkins in 1613–14.

Dallam had built an organ for St John's College, Oxford a few years before; also for King's College, Cambridge in 1605–6, the very year in which John Tomkins (1586–1638) became organist there. John was the composer's half-brother;* as well as an organist and harpsichordist, he soon became well known in Court circles, doubtless through his elder brother, whom he frequently met in London; and it is highly probable that when the question of a new organ at Worcester was being considered, it was he who recommended Dallam as the best organ-builder in the country. Perhaps he even persuaded Thomas to come to Cambridge and judge for himself. Naturally the latter, with his connection with the Chapel Royal, would be predisposed towards the organ-builder who held the royal warrant. The Worcester instrument cost (with its case) some £385; The Cambridge instrument cost about £370. Both were 'double organs', that is to say they had two manuals, a 'Greate' and 'Chayre'. Clearly the two instruments were

---

* Thomas senior had three children by his first wife, Margaret Pore, of whom the composer was the youngest. He married again, and by his second wife, Anne Hargest, had seven more children, 5 boys and 2 girls, of whom John was the eldest. In 1619 the latter was organist of St Paul's, in 1625 a gentleman of the Chapel Royal. His branch of the family is shown in Stevens, *op. cit.* p. 12.

comparable, though the specification of that at King's has not survived, and only one stop is known; 'the shaking stoppe', or tremolo.

But the specification of the Worcester organ* was as follows:

Great		Choir	
Probable compass GG–c²		*Probable compass GG–a²*	
1 Open Diapason I	metal (8)	9 (stopt?) Diapason	wood (8)
2 Open Diapason II	metal (8)	10 Principal	metal (4)
3 Principal I	metal (4)	11 Small principal or	
4 Principal II	metal (4)	fifteenth	metal (2)
5 Twelfth	metal (2⅔)	12 Two-and-twentieth	metal (1)
6 Small principal, or		13 Flute	wood (4)
fifteenth I	metal (2)		
7 Small principal, or			
fifteenth II	metal (2)		
8 Recorder–a stopt pipe metal (2)			

Bracketed numbers indicate the corresponding pipe-lengths today. The lowest pipe, the Open Diapason, was described as 'CC fa ut—a pipe of 10 feet long', as it was in Duddyngton's organ of a hundred years previously. The lower limit of the compass was therefore GG.

Dallam's instrument uses the customary double pipes; indeed such duplication was the standard practice. The Great has two separate Diapason choruses, of different scales. One might almost say three choruses, if instead of one of the fifteenths is added the Recorder, which was a *Blockflute*, of 2' pitch, and which would therefore lend flute colour to the chorus-tone.

If a solo mutation was used in one hand, the accompaniment would require the use of the second manual. Dallam's Chayre organ, which could be played from the same position as the Great, though the pipe-work was behind the player, also contains a reasonably complete Diapason chorus. The term 'small' is used to refer to a pipe one octave above the normal; thus 'small principal' means the fifteenth; 'small twelfth' means the nineteenth.

Still no pedals are mentioned, though by this time they are a

* See Bodleian Library Add. C 304a, f. 141. (letter from Nathaniel Tomkins). We know also from this source that the organ at St John's College, Oxford, was the same as that at Worcester.

commonplace on the Continent. This is related to the fact that the English compass, which extended down to GG, differed from the continental, which stopped at CC. This discrepancy remained until the nineteenth century.

Strangely, 'pedals' are mentioned in connection with an organ that Robert Dallam built for Jesus College, Cambridge, in 1634. He was paid £12 the following year *for the addition of pedals*. But the word 'pedals' does not necessarily mean pedal keys, or 'pull-downs',* which were a later addition; they were probably pedals for some other purpose, such as blowing the organ. This is most likely, in view of the difficulty that seems to have been found in supplying air to the instrument.†

No 'shaking stoppe' is mentioned on the Worcester organ, although this was a commonplace from a very early date, and was one of Thomas Dallam's specialities. He included one on a smaller one-manual organ, of just five stops, that he built at Eton College in the same year (1613). His Worcester specification was very similar to that of John Chappington's organ at Magdalen College, Oxford, built in 1597. Indeed this kind of specification was to remain standard for the double organ of the first half of the seventeenth century. His son Robert built a slightly larger instrument in York Minster in 1632–4, at a cost of £297; but the overall tonal scheme is the same:

Great Organ		Choire Organ	
51 notes, probable compass GG–c^2		*51 notes, probable compass* GG–c^2	
Open Diapason I	tin (8)	Diapason	wood (8)
Open Diapason II	tin (8)	Principal	tin (4)
Stopt Diapason	wood (8)	Flute	wood (4)
Principal I	tin (4)	Small principal fifteenth	tin (2)
Principal II	tin (4)	Recorder	tin (2)
Twelfth	tin (2⅔)	('unison to the voice')	
Small principal fifteenth	tin (2)		
Recorder	(2)		
('unison to the said principall')			
Two and twentieth	(1)		

* See pp. 194–5.
† See F. Brittain *A History of Jesus College, Cambridge* p. 76.

The description of the Recorder stop as 'unison to the voice' means that it was not a mutation. The Recorder stop on the Great manual is described as 'unison to the said principall', which signifies the *small principal*, or fifteenth.

By the early seventeenth century two-manual organs were common; the 'Double organ', consisting of a 'Great' and 'Chayre' or 'Choyre', was the normally accepted standard. The Great organ had developed from the earlier Positive; the Chayre organ pipe-work was now placed behind the player's seat.[*] The upper manual (Great) is referred to as *Double* or *Bass*; the lower manual (Chayre) is called *Single, Little* or *Tenor*. This is reflected from now on in the *Double Verse* or *Double Voluntary* of post-Restoration composers. An interesting sidelight is thrown onto the prevalence of this general attitude by the addition of a second manual. Trinity College, Cambridge, acquired a new Chayre organ in 1610[†], and the same addition was later made to the organ of one of the Royal Chapels by Edward Norgate, keeper of the organs to Charles I.[‡]

February 3rd, 1636

Warrant to the signet, for a privy seal of £140, to be impressed unto M[r] Edward Norgate, to be employed for the altering and reparation of the organ in the Chappell at Hampton Court and for the making of a new Chayre organ there conformable to those already made in the Chappells at Whitehall and Greenwich.

In compositions specifically intended for two manuals, the upper, right hand, parts were generally played on the Chair Organ throughout, while the bass, or left hand part alternated between the Chair and the Great. Portman and Hingston, however, specify both hands on the Great for the final sections of their pieces for Double organ.

A comparison of the instruments of Thomas and Robert Dallam with those of their contemporaries in Europe, is highly instructive. When Bull became organist at Antwerp, this was the instrument, built by Brebos (1565–7) that he played in the Cathedral:[§]

[*] French *Positif de dos*; German *Rückpositiv*.
[†] See Cobb, H. F. *op. cit.*
[‡] Lafontaine *op. cit.* p. 94.
[§] Quoted from Vente *Die Brabanter Orgel.*

Great

(Diapasons)		(Flutes)	
1. Bourdon	16	7. Hohl Flute	8
2. Open Diapason	8	8. Open Flute	8
3. Principal	4	9. Stopt flute	4
4. Fifteenth	2	10. Gemshorn	2
5. Mixture I	IV	11. Larigot	$1\frac{1}{3}$
6. Mixture II	VI	12. Twenty second	1
		13. Cornett (d^l upwards)	V–VI

(Reeds)		Bovenwerk	
14. Trumpet	8	17. Quintadena	8
15. Shawm	4	18. Piccolo	2
16. Cornett (reed)	4	19. Cymbal	
		20. Crumhorn	8
		21. Regal	8 or 4

Manual compass C—a^{ll}. Pull-down pedals, coupler, tremulant. Also: 'Harp, nightingale, birdsong(?) throughout the whole manual'. (the names have been anglicised)

The Cathedral also possessed a second instrument of similar specification. And in 1627 yet a third organ, a smaller Positive, with Bull's specification, was provided:

1. Hohl flute	8	6. Mixture	?
2. Principal (c^l upwards)	4	7. Nachthorn	?
3. Flute	4	8. Tierce	$1\frac{3}{5}$
4. Fifteenth	2	9. Trumpet	8
5. Larigot	$1\frac{1}{3}$	10. Shawm	4

Compass: C—c^{ll}, 45 notes. Also 'nightingale', tremulant.

In comparison with the organs of the Dallams, these Antwerp instruments had more completeness of chorus-work, greater brilliance without duplication, and above all they possessed reeds. The only reed used in England, occasionally, was the Regal, which for many reasons (not least its tone-quality) was unsatisfactory, and could not compare with the Dutch Trumpet or Crumhorn. Moreover the absence of mixtures in the Dallam instruments at Worcester and York, robbed the full Diapason chorus of brilliance. The Tierce, or seventeenth, is nowhere to be seen in the English specifications; yet it is interesting to note that, even in a small one-manual organ, Bull evidently felt this rank to be necessary—as well as a mixture and two reeds. Clearly therefore it is with both a sense of brilliance of tone, and of range of colour, that his organ compositions must be approached, while those of Byrd, Gibbons and Tomkins call for more sober registration, without reeds and mixtures.

The divergence between the British and continental instruments, already noticeable in the sixteenth century, was clearly apparent by the time of the Dallams. It was a trend which progressively increased, and to which many factors contributed. The extreme anti-ecclesiasticism of the Commonwealth marked the culmination of a process which had already begun under Elizabeth; it represents the moment of greatest disparity, since the removal of organs and the banning of music was confined to Puritan England.*

Yet the existence and survival of more advanced organs in Northern Europe was due to many other reasons. Compared with those in England, churches on the continent were, generally speaking, larger, and therefore could more easily accommodate an organ, and its bellows, which in an English church would need extra space.

Again, continental churches were usually the property of the town or community, and therefore not so open to the spoiling hands of a predatory ruler or political party. The organs, like other church property, were a communal possession, the organ builders were respected craftsmen, whose skill was handed on to succeeding generations—usually of the same family. Moreover the continental aristocracy were zealous patrons, and helped to further this process; and while certain of the English nobility, such as the Earl of Salisbury and Sir Henry Fanshawe, were lovers of music, the great English houses of this period did not possess organs which could compare with those on the continent, such as some French *châteaux*.

* An interesting comparison between the English and French valuation of the organ, and attitude to its music, can be seen in the revolutions of the two countries. During the English revolution of 1640 the Parliamentarians removed organs, and anything else of value, from churches and cathedrals. During the French revolution of 1789 a Commission was set up (1793) who inspected the churches and cathedrals of Paris to make sure that the organs were not damaged in the fighting. (See Paul Brunold, *Le grand orgue de St. Gervais de Paris*, Paris Oiseau-Lyre, 1934.)

4

1656–1759

THE RESTORATION

The period that came to an end with Thomas Tomkins, and that was marked with such monuments of organ and other keyboard composition as the works of Byrd and Bull, was the high noon of the Renaissance in this country. It was a time of greatness; not necessarily merely because great composers happened to live then, but because the mood and the ethos of the age were susceptible of greatness. It was one which admitted, encouraged, demanded excellence, and this spirit of confidence gave rise to a wide range of contrasting art-works—even within the apparently circumscribed field of organ music. A period which could support such divergent composers as Bull & Byrd, Gibbons & Tomkins, could only do so if it was both secure in its past tradition, and optimistic about its future. These composers represent the full flowering of that tradition whose roots can be traced back to the early Tudor school of Redford and beyond.

It may seem that the organ music of the post-Restoration period offers but meagre fare indeed in comparison with the incomparable riches of the preceding one. Certainly the additions to the repertoire cannot seriously measure up in range or diversity to the great work of the four composers mentioned. No doubt this can partly be ascribed to the fact that the hundred years up to the death of Handel witnessed a progressive shift in the centre of gravity of music in this country. Handel, who was far the most dominant figure of his or indeed of any age, and was an organist of the highest repute—and therefore might have been expected to expand the repertoire materially—worked in the theatre rather than the church. His organ compositions focused on his concertos, and his pieces for solo organ form but a minor part of his overall output.

So whereas, with their ever-enlarging and ambitious reach, the composers at the beginning of the seventeenth century included organ compositions within their grasp, and broadened the scope of organ music in the process, those at the end of the century sought their chief outlet elsewhere. Moreover the confidence of the former age was replaced by questioning and experiment by the later composers, and excessive reliance on other traditions, such as the Italian or the French. Again, whereas the earlier composers displayed great diversity of style, their successors (the more so as the eighteenth century proceeded) tended rather towards a stylistic similarity; a sameness, which is an unmistakable pointer to an insecure tradition. It is only when the creative tradition within which a composer works is stable and secure that he can expand his style within it; failing that, the search for a fresh idiom means that composers are preoccupied with means rather than ends, and that their individual style will be submerged until such an idiom is discovered which finds general acceptance. It is only to be expected that a period of security, and great musical achievement, should be followed by one of comparative uncertainty and experiment.

Yet the Restoration was a period of great activity; and the character of this most colourful period is amply recorded in the work of the two great contemporary diarists, John Evelyn and Samuel Pepys. Both these writers clearly show the importance placed on music in Court circles, by the educated, and in the private gatherings of the nobility. Pepys's diary, which started on 1st January, 1660 and lasted ten years, is full of just those details of daily life and apparently trivial events, which enable us to bring the style and mood of these years into focus. He sang in a consort with Matthew Locke and Henry Purcell senior;* he went with Christopher Gibbons, organist of Westminster Abbey, to inspect a chamber organ in the Dean's lodgings, but decided that it would be too big for his room; his house-boy was a chorister at the Chapel

* Uncle of the composer.

Royal, sent to him by his friend Captain Cooke, the master of the
Children; his love of music was rivalled only, so he tells us, by his
love of a pretty woman; and ample evidence of each pursuit fills
a large part of his diary; he was an enthusiastic amateur, who could
compose passable songs, sing, play the flageolet; his harpsichord
was one of the finest in London, while his private concerts were the
envy of Society, at which even temperamental Italian singers agreed
to appear—the very height of social distinction.

But Pepys was more than merely a dilettante; as President of
the Royal Society and friend, among many others, of Sir Isaac
Newton and Sir Christopher Wren, he respected those ideals of
order and beauty which this age sought to enshrine, in music as
much as in science or architecture; indeed at this time one without
the other would have been unthinkable.

As far as a contrast with a preceding period of great achievement is concerned, there are parallels to be drawn between the
later seventeenth and the early twentieth centuries. The period of
fulfilment of the Renaissance which ended, in this country, with
the death of Tomkins, was followed inevitably by a period of
comparative musical instability; in just the same way the period of
greatest achievement in German music, which was terminated by
the death of Brahms, was also followed by a period of uncertainty
and experiment. It seems to be an inexorable law of aesthetics that
a traditional idiom, which is based on general acceptance, and
within which a composer develops his own style, cannot for long
outlive the period and the circumstances that gave rise to it in the
first place. Thereafter it progressively loses validity. No doubt this
is partly due to the unique cultural requirements of each succeeding period, and society. Yet paradoxically mere newness and
experiment are no substitute.

If this is the case, the application of this principle to the gradually evolving pattern of organ music of this time becomes clear.
The earlier composers worked within an expanding and vital
tradition, and drew for their material partly on the traditional
Hymns and Antiphons of the mediaeval liturgy, partly on their own
developments of keyboard technique. Both were equally sources
of strength.

But this period, once ended, could not be prolonged. The later composers built afresh, and their music was not so much an expansion of traditional procedures as an attempt to meet the requirements of a new age; to please the senses of a society that was replacing the former spirit of optimism with one of rationalism, cynicism. Whereas the characteristic voice of Byrd's age was the heaven-aspiring music of a mature, overflowing, sacred tradition, the characteristic form of musical expression of Purcell's was secular; opera and instrumental music in particular.

The requirements of opera, and the replacement of polyphony with monody, required and invited the clear, expressive, dramatic inflection of words, in a style quite remote from their former polyphonic treatment, in which syllabic stress was subservient to the musical metre, and in which individual words were submerged in the overall texture. The new instrumental style also pursued harmony rather than counterpoint, and developed such new inventions as the thorough-bass.

All these developments diverted attention from the composition of sacred works; and although, with the Restoration, the Chapel Royal resumed its earlier form and function, and composers continued to write functional liturgical music, nevertheless the direction of music was changing.[*]

Though most composers were organists, fewer wrote for the organ than in the pre-Commonwealth period. Moreover it will become apparent that two of the most interesting composers, Handel and Roseingrave, were not connected with the official duties of the Chapel Royal—the first time this occurs—and they had travelled in Europe, thus adding a dimension of freshness to their work.

But at the close of the seventeenth century the central figure was John Blow. He acted as a focus for activity, much as Redford did 150 years earlier. He centred his work round church music; tradition was his starting-point; he was also a most active teacher, and his numerous pupils included Croft, Daniel and Henry Purcell,

* It is interesting that the same year (1656) which witnessed the close of the great Renaissance period should also see the first British opera; Davenant's *The Siege of Rhodes.*

Clarke, Barrett, Reading, Daniel Roseingrave, the copyist George
Holmes,* and many others.

The Music

Those composers whose work spanned the Commonwealth
years continued to pursue traditional models. The four whose
organ works have survived are John Hingston, Benjamin Rogers,
Christopher Gibbons and Matthew Locke.

Hingston and Rogers are minor figures, each represented by a
single voluntary. Hingston's is well-sustained, with a built-up
climax at the end. Rogers was known by his string Fancies, which
were much played; but his single organ Voluntary, which was
written in 1664, when he was *informator* at Magdalen College,
Oxford, does not sustain the polyphonic texture. The piece is 55
bars in length, but after bar 34 the musical argument switches from
a contrapuntal to a harmonic one, and the right hand part degener-
ates into sustained chords.

A much more important composer was Christopher Gibbons,
second son of Orlando Gibbons. During the Commonwealth he
was in the Royalist army. He also taught, performed and composed; *Cupid and Death* was produced in 1653. He was connected
with Oxford during the Commonwealth, and in 1654 (12th July)
the diarist, John Evelyn, heard 'Mr Gibbons, that famous musician,
giving us a taste of his skill and tallent' on the double organ in
Magdalen College which was not removed.†

Gibbons's Double Voluntary in A minor is a substantial work,
111 bars, and larger than Purcell's, which follows it in the same
manuscript.‡ Its brilliance derives from great rhythmic articula-
tion, and integrated passage work; the secondary, more lyrical
material flows naturally from the preceding section. Unfortunately
the manuscripts are not precise in the directions 'Great Organ' and

---

* He copied MS z¹.
† There were two organs in Magdalen College; one of them was removed
during the Commonwealth to Hampton Court. It was returned in 1660.
‡ MS a².

'Little Organ', which disappear for the last pages, after being most exact for the opening section.

The Great Organ is used by Gibbons, as it was also by Purcell, to point the theme when it occurs in the left hand part. Moreover the novel registration (Cornet, Sesquialtera, Trumpet) is highly characteristic of both period and composer.

Two versions of the Voluntary appear; that for single organ (MS b²) forms the first 49 bars of the other version for double organ (MS z¹). Indeed it seems to have been the regular practice of late seventeenth-century composers, to write two versions of the same piece, one more extended and elaborate than the other.* Purcell's D minor Voluntary is another example.

Gibbons's D minor Voluntary also develops considerable momentum during the working out of the subsidiary material, after bar 36; the wide-ranging arpeggio figure is in total contrast with the solemn, stepwise opening subject. Gibbons combines in a single-movement piece something of the balance of contrasting themes; and again he wrote an extended version of this piece for Double Organ. The whole of the Single Voluntary forms the opening of the Double Voluntary, virtually note for note.

The longer version calls for a similar registration as the A minor Double Voluntary. After the alternating use of 'Double' and 'Single', Gibbons then requires a solo Cornet. Probably an assistant would be needed to make this stop-change. Later he uses the Sesquialtera, for a brisker fugal section based on the opening subject, and follows this with a Trumpet fanfare. The work ends with a brilliant section for 'Double Organ'.

The short Verse, in MS b², is a gem of condensation (only 24 bars) and demonstrates that Gibbons was as technically skilled in a short piece as he was structurally adventurous in a larger one. The same piece also appears in an extended version in MS ee, where it is attributed to Orlando Gibbons. The theme is a remarkable one, unfolding in triple sequences, which are followed by a rest before the entry of the next voice. Moreover the triple rhythm of the

---

* The same procedure was later followed by Bach in setting the Catechism Hymns of his *Clavierübung*.

phrases, within an *alla breve* metre, ensures great metrical variety, as the pulse falls on a different beat of the bar at each occurrence. At the entry of the third voice (bar 6) Gibbons introduces canon at the twelfth, echoing the subject, and binding the texture closely together. This technique is used again at the repeat (bar 14) in the tonic key, but this time fifths in the top part, instead of thirds before, lead the music up to a higher point of climax from which the composer can drop to the final cadence.

The final three bars correspond with the middle bars of the piece, (bars 9–13) which serve as a link between the two halves, and consist of a descending figure based on sequences, made up of notes 2–4 of the main theme. Thus the rising tension of the subject, made more marked by contrapuntal elaboration, is answered on each appearance by a descending cadence-figure; this is cut short in the concluding bars, and the harmony varied to form a plagal conclusion; direct repetition is thus avoided. In this short piece Gibbons's artistry is consummated.

The early D minor Verse in the Wimborne manuscript is an unusual threefold structure; it uses the same material in three contrasted, expressive sections. The first (bars 1–22) focuses interest onto the reversed dot rhythm; the middle section (bars 23–39) consists of even-note scales in canon between the hands; the third section (bars 40–49) is a pedal point, and concludes with gradually quickening scales.

In the few organ pieces of his that have survived, Gibbons expanded the structure of the single movement Voluntary until it became a thing of dramatically contrasted sections, each making use of a characteristic tone-quality of the organ of his day. In this way he anticipated the two-movement form that was soon to become established. He was evidently more interested in the structure of a composition, than in its registration. For instance, in writing for the Cornet stop, he did not quite achieve the brilliance of a solo melodic line, that is in the very nature of this stop, and that was to be such a feature of the eighteenth century; instead he writes for the Cornet in more than one part, where the effect is less characteristic, since the major third interval (in the Tierce) leads to some harsh harmonic clashes. Blow was in this respect much more successful in capturing the true nature of the Cornet, in such a piece as his Voluntary No. 28 (Ed.90). Gibbons however was much more adventurous than Blow in his attempts to develop the structure of the Voluntary, whose seams he occasionally stretched practically to bursting point. And his adventurous enquiry into many different sorts of organ sonorities clearly anticipates the work of later composers, such as Greene and Handel. Moreover his harmonic sense is daring and unorthodox.

Matthew Locke 1630–1677

By contrast, Matthew Locke, who was acquainted with Gibbons at Exeter, though fifteen years his junior, wrote only slight pieces for the organ. The seven numbered works at the end of *Melothesia* (1673) are called simply 'for the organ', thus differentiating them from the earlier pieces of that collection, which are for harpsichord. They represent 'lessons' in the late seventeenth century style, and the sort of organ that Locke seems to have had in mind was the double organ of Dallam, consisting of Great and Chair, without reeds and mixtures, rather than that of post-Restoration builders such as Smith or Harris.

Six out of the seven pieces open with a fugato, as was customary for the Verse or Voluntary of this period. They are all short, single-movement pieces; studies rather than significant compositions; the longest is 42 bars in length, and they are intended to introduce the aspiring organist to some of the expressive possibilities of the double organ; though only one piece expressly uses both manuals, and then somewhat hesitantly. In style they hark back to the earlier seventeenth century; harmonically to Tomkins, rhythmically to Bull.

The plentiful array of ornaments is another characteristic of keyboard composition of the earlier period, derived as it is from the virginal or harpsichord style. It is noticeable that Blow, whose feeling for the innate character of the organ was more instinctive than Locke's, and whose organ works are much more substantial, is more sparing in his use of ornaments. Later in the eighteenth century, as organ music and harpsichord music follow separate and independent paths, the use of ornaments by organ composers progressively diminishes, until they virtually disappear by the time of John Stanley. One organist, indeed, Philip Hart, was taken to task by the historian Hawkins for his excessive use of the shake.

John Blow 1649–1708

The thirty-three Verses and Voluntaries that make up Blow's organ output are the most fully representative collection of organ pieces of this period. They epitomise the musical situation that had been reached by composers at the turn of the century; they sum up past styles and forms of composition, and also take into account the fresh resources of the post-Restoration instrument. Their prevailing overall impression is of a sombre gravity, workmanlike and dignified. Not one of the pieces, for instance, uses a triple metre; they tend to be somewhat four-square, and they are best suited to a moderate tempo. None of them is of great length, though the pieces for Double Organ (Nos. 25–30)* are more extended than those for single manual (Nos. 1–24). Of the latter, the longest is 79 bars (No. 16).

All overtly liturgical composition for the organ, such as the use of a plainchant melody, disappeared after the Restoration. Tomkins was the last composer to make use of this basis as an integral structure of organ music. Yet some of Blow's thematic material derives from a plainchant ancestry. As an example of this, the material of his Verse in F has affinities with the hymn 'Bina coelestis'.

But the absence of liturgical plainchant as a structural basis for organ composition obliged the composer to rely on his powers of invention of original material, and on his ability to exploit the latent possibilities of the post-Restoration instrument. Far the greater number of Blow's pieces open with imitative entries; a chordal opening is rare. Such a one occurs in No. 2, which has the appearance of an improvisation, whose harmonic direction is undecided, veering now this way, now that.

* Numbers refer to Ed. 90.

Blow's harmonic sense is occasionally ambiguous, while the small note runs are more important for the colour and sheer dexterity they add to the texture than for any sense of overall development or harmonic direction they impart to the architecture of the music. The frequent contradiction of implied modulation impedes and frustrates the flow of the musical argument. The opening section of the Double Verse No. 29 is a case in point.

Example 27

No. 29   A Double Verse   Blow
(Opening)

By the time of the first change to the second manual, no harmonic norm has been established, from which the music can develop. It seems the composer was aware of this, as the right hand is soon allotted held chords, as if in a search for just such a sense of harmonic stability and certainty; but from the listener's point of view it is already too late, and the moment has passed.

This feature of Blow's style occurs also in several other pieces, and weakens his otherwise highly polished work. His treatment of the double organ is generally to use the hands on different manuals simultaneously, not to use one manual as an echo to the other. Normally therefore the Great Organ and the Chair (or Little) Organ would have been set at an approximately equal dynamic level, each with contrasting timbre. Only in one case is one part treated as a solo against the accompaniment of the other. That is No. 28, in which the Little Organ provides the accompaniment to the Great Cornet. Starting with the opening point, the right hand solo soon moves off with a free development of its own. The entries of the solo are interspersed with sections on the other manual; moreover each solo section is contrasted and distinctive. This highly original piece was to be the pattern of later eighteenth-century developments in the use of solo stops. In the Echo Voluntary (No. 32), the left hand accompaniment remains on the Chair manual, while the right hand alternates between the Great and the Echo. This technique was also used by his pupil John Barrett, in both his extant pieces.

The effectiveness of some of Blow's pieces lies not so much in his thematic or structural invention, in which he is not so adventurous or original as Christopher Gibbons, as in his use of the material and exploitation of the instrument. Occasionally he achieves, over a short span, great impetus and homogeneity; as in No. 23, in which by diminution (in bar 18) of the opening left hand part, and by its treatment in sequences, the composer at one stroke brilliantly imparts to the music both variety and unity. It is noteworthy that this piece, without recourse to any virtuoso devices, and within a restricted expressive range, is the more successful for these very reasons; the introduction of novel elements (such as small-note runs, or changes of manual) would have broken the unity of the structure without necessarily increasing the effectiveness of the sound.

Another piece which maintains the impetus of the opening, this time more melodically expressive than rhythmically motive, is No. 18. Blow here combines the chromatic fourth with a characteristic cadence-figure, to form a theme of great expressiveness, whose polyphonic elaboration flows naturally from the moment of its initial statement. This falling phrase, which was frequently used by composers of this time, also occurs to a more limited extent in Nos. 7 and 8.

If Blow's treatment of chromaticism occasionally weakens the structure of his organ works, this is no doubt due to an incomplete assimilation of tonality by church composers; his material still has a certain modal flavour, as the opening of No. 8 shows:

Example 28

Yet Blow's use of tonality is quite specific. He favours a G final, either major or minor, in thirteen out of the thirty-three pieces; no doubt because G was the lowest note of the instrument.

Henry Purcell 1659–1695

As for his illustrious pupil Purcell, only six organ pieces may be ascribed to him without hesitation; and of these two overlap, and make use of the same material, while three are in the nature of short, rather undistinguished *pièces d'occasion*. Which leaves just two works of substance; hardly a significant output from the most prolific and inventive composer of his generation.

The first three pieces★ are short simple preludes; 'Verses' after the manner of Tomkins; quiet, respectable music, but hardly suggesting the composer of the string Fantasias, let alone of the dramatic works. Indeed one of the short pieces, the Voluntary in C, is in the nature of improvised, aimless sequences, of the sort to which organists are sometimes all too prone.

The remaining three pieces are larger, more characteristic of Purcell, and make fuller use of the instrument. The Double Voluntary is a longer, more elaborate version of the preceding Voluntary in D minor; the first nineteen bars of each are identical, and suggest a transcription of a vocal work. Indeed the subject is reminiscent of the Verse Anthem 'Lord, how long wilt thou be angry?'

Example 29

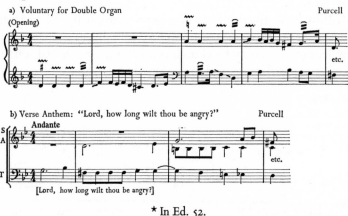

a) Voluntary for Double Organ   Purcell
(Opening)

b) Verse Anthem: "Lord, how long wilt thou be angry?"   Purcell
Andante

[Lord, how long wilt thou be angry?]

★ In Ed. 52.

The Single Voluntary develops lyrically, with comparatively simple three-part polyphony; the Double Voluntary uses the characteristic 'solo and accompaniment' feature of the double organ. Purcell uses the Great Organ in the same way that Christopher Gibbons did, to mark the entries of the subject-material, accompanied by chords on the Chair organ. These entries are then pursued and developed into runs and passages of great brilliance— the origins of the later eighteenth century Cornet Voluntary, though Purcell requires only the simple Diapason chorus on the Great (8^1, 4^1, $2\frac{2}{3}^1$, 2^1), not the Cornet stop.

The Voluntary in G is also characteristic; slow expressive music, containing certain melodic, rhythmic and harmonic *motifs* which only he could have written:

Example 30

Voluntary in G
(bars 24-28)   Purcell

etc.

The concluding fugato, bolder, but based on the shape of the opening melody, suggests the use of another manual.

Purcell's 'Rules for Graces' were printed at the front of *A Choice Collection of Lessons for the Harpsichord or Spinnet*, which the composer's widow Frances had published in 1696. Although the organist is more sparing in the use of ornaments than other keyboard players, these guide-lines cannot fail to be of the closest concern to the performer of keyboard music of this period.

Purcell's rules are as follows:

Shake   Marked   Explained

Beat

'Observe that you allways shake from the note above and beat from ye note or half note below, according to the key you play in; and for ye plain note and shake, if it be a note without a point +, you are to hold half the quantity of it plain, and that upon ye note above that which is mark'd, and shake the other half; but if it be a note with a point ++ to it, you are to hold all the note plain, and shake only the point.'

+ i.e. ♩   ++ i.e. ♩.   Standard modern notation is shown in brackets [ ].

Anonymous Works

Among the numerous anonymous works of this time, one particularly colourful Double Voluntary★ demands pride of place; the pronounced dotted rhythm, the unexpected yet controlled modulations, the melodic patterns, the use of chromatic movement (particularly in the secondary material after bar 56), the sustained and consistent development of the material, the bold use of scale passages covering the entire range of the keyboard, the powerful dominant pedal (bars 62–67)—all these features point strongly to one composer: Purcell.

★ Ed. 86.

The theme is a bold one:

Example 31

And capable of melodic variation:

Example 32

The runs have a sense of harmonic direction and are not empty display, or filling in:

Example 33

The same manuscript (MS z¹) contains several other pieces of comparable interest, and similar in style. Though it is tempting to allot them to one or other of the three chief organ composers, Gibbons, Blow or Purcell, it is possible that they are not necessarily the work of an English composer at all. The field of speculation is large, and not necessarily rewarding.

Most of the pieces, which are single movements, open with the usual imitative entries. An exception such as No. 17* differs

★ The numbering used on p. 175.

markedly in style and technical polish from the others; a slightly different title, such as Prelude, seems therefore fitting.

The Voluntaries at the end of the manuscript however are fine examples of organ music of this time. They are all substantial works, which well sustain the mood and texture after the introduction of the secondary material.

The opening D minor Voluntary, No. 1, is a long, closely-knit musical argument, clearly the work of a composer of the front rank. The sharing of the answers between different parts (in bar 3), the use of canon, and the widely spaced secondary theme set against the stepwise movement of the opening, immediately suggest this to be the work of Christopher Gibbons.

In the same way, the theme of the Voluntary in D no. 8, is very similar to that of Blow's Verse in A.* Are these two pieces therefore by the same composer? It seems not unreasonable. The following Voluntary in D, No. 9, which is the only one of this fine collection not to open imitatively in single parts, is a most brilliant, fanfare-like piece, built round a figure of rising fourths, and culminating in scale-passages, which positively invite performance on full organ.

Generally, as these and other contemporary pieces amply show, the Voluntary at this time was not a virtuoso piece. Gibbons, Purcell and Blow avoided empty display, and were much more concerned with the structural evolution of the single-movement organ piece, and with the exploitation of the stops newly available.

An equally characteristic collection of Verses is found in another manuscript of *c.* 1700.† Generally not so elaborate, nor so contrapuntally close-knit as the Voluntaries, these were the pieces used by an organist on those numerous occasions when he was required to play during a moment in the liturgy of movement of some kind, or of silence. The heading of one of the Verses in this collection betrays both its origin and something of its nature: 'A verse to play after prayer.'

The verse therefore needed to be short, subdued, and more of an improvisation, of variable duration, than a fixed structure. The

---

* No. 14, Ed. 90.
† MS a.

exception that proves the rule in this set is No. 7 in A minor, which is a remarkable and most exciting *alla breve*, a study in brilliant chromaticism, marked by dotted-note scales in alternate hands. Clearly the piece can only adequately be played on full organ.

Composers became progressively less inclined to the Verse as a form, since it was in conception contrary to the chief trends of this period, which were towards an expansion and diversification of the single-movement piece, and towards the full and more varied use of the instrument. Moreover as the comprehension of the diatonic system gained ground, and compositions evolved which took it into account, this further accelerated the trend. The Verse therefore died out as the eighteenth century advanced, and became incorporated into the Voluntary.

THE EIGHTEENTH-CENTURY VOLUNTARY (I)

The marked change in organ music styles between the seventeenth and eighteenth centuries may be considered from various viewpoints.

Primarily, the last vestiges of all reference to liturgical material are done away with. Even Blow's oblique references to a modal idiom, or such anachronisms as the Blow/Purcell exercise on the *Old 100th Psalm* tune, are henceforward relegated irretrievably to the past. Eighteenth-century organ music became as firmly diatonic as all other music. It aimed to delight the listener in a direct way, such as his reason would admit; it abandoned all attempt to decorate or illustrate an already-accepted ritual.

Next, organ music became in the eighteenth century fully separate from other forms of keyboard music. The use of variation form, one of the chief glories of the Tudor period, disappeared. Various aspects of style, such as ornamentation, that had previously been derived from the style appropriate to other secular instruments, also practically disappeared from editions of organ music, which from now on came to be printed.

Third, whereas the seventeenth century organ normally consisted of two manuals, Great and Chair, that of the eighteenth often had also a third, the Echo. This was a short-compass manual, tonally a reproduction of the Great, but with the pipes enclosed in a box: the prototype of the later Swell organ.*

The disappearance of liturgical organ composition in England after 1660 is what chiefly distinguishes the eighteenth century English organ school from its German counterpart. Whereas the continental composers developed and perfected the long tradition of the Chorale Prelude, to which they gave a place of central importance, equally with such purely instrumental forms as Preludes, Fantasias, Fugues, Ricercare and so on, the English composers focused their attention on just two forms of solo organ composition, the Fugue and the Voluntary. Moreover they took full advantage (as Bull and Byrd had done before) of the newly-evolving structures and styles of secular keyboard composition, which they translated into organ terms. Brilliant runs and passage-work became standard practice after Handel, while the newly discovered tone-colours of the instrument were incorporated into the music itself.

In turning away from the liturgical repertoire as a source of organ composition, the eighteenth century composer denied himself a potent and unique source of musical expression. In the event, the Voluntary flourished and grew as something unique from other keyboard styles, and the accompanied solo sonata; and it only declined in the early nineteenth century, when it lost its original impetus, and keyboard composition became focused on the newly invented pianoforte.

Two factors chiefly affected the eighteenth century Voluntary, and determined its character. The first is that the organ, unlike the harpsichord, combines in itself the effects of a sustained sonority and of a brilliant velocity. In this respect it is unique among keyboard instruments, and eighteenth century composers were quick to seize on both these features of the innate quality of organ music as an integral part of their style.

The second factor is that the eighteenth century organ possessed certain clearly differentiated and characteristic tone-colours, which

* See p. 188.

again set it apart as a keyboard instrument. The chief of these were the Diapason, which was the foundation-tone of the full Diapason chorus, up to Sesquialtera and Mixture; the Flute, or Stopped Diapason; the solo five-rank Cornet (8^1, 4^1, $2\frac{2}{3}^1$, 2^1, $1\frac{3}{5}^1$); the solo Trumpet, and other reeds.

So the composers of the Voluntary based their conception of the form round these tonal characteristics of the instrument at their disposal. For the first time to any marked degree, composers wrote organ music largely in terms of particular tonal effects.*

The chief composers of the first half of the century were Rose-ingrave, Travers, Greene, Handel and Stanley, in whose hands the Voluntary and the Fugue assumed fresh stature and characteristics.

Roseingrave's first set of Voluntaries were printed in 1728 by Walsh; the same publisher also brought out Handel's Six Fugues (Op. 3) seven years later. These two publications marked the direction of organ music of the eighteenth century. Moreover the confidence and sureness of touch which mark such a piece as the G major Voluntary (Ed. 108, No. 4), probably the work of Maurice Greene, when compared with Blow's Double Voluntary already mentioned, is due not so much to Greene's superiority as a composer, as to the security of idiom, and freshness of approach to the keyboard, that was the inheritance of the eighteenth century.

There is very little doubt where the origin of this freshness lay— in the influence of the Italians. Both Handel and Roseingrave were much-travelled composers, whose musical horizon thus extended beyond the confines of this country. Their debt to the Italian composers, particularly Scarlatti, is quite overt. The Italian baroque school provided just that fresh source of vitality that the English organ and keyboard composers needed; more specifically in their task of enlarging the scope of the Voluntary.

By the mid-eighteenth century the Voluntary was established as consisting, in the main, of two movements; a slow movement followed by a quicker movement. That this scheme may have owed something to the old dance suite in which a Pavan was followed by a Galliard, an Allemande by a Courante, detracts nothing

---

* Though John Bull had been the pioneer in this respect (see p. 94).

from the importance of this development. The two-movement Voluntary grew out of the single-movement pieces of the seventeenth century. Occasional examples occur of four movements; an exceptional case is that of William Hine, whose sole surviving Voluntary is in six movements, alternating slow and fast.

The introductory movement was usually homophonic, slow-moving, and registered 'Diapason', or 'Full Organ'. Firm, uncomplicated music. The following movement was quicker, and introduced some characteristic brilliance of the organ, such as the Trumpet, the Cornet, or Full Organ. It might well be a fugal movement, though Handel and Roseingrave reserved most of their contrapuntal elaboration for their fugues, not their voluntaries. It is not unreasonable to detect a certain similarity between the construction of the two-movement Voluntary, and that of the Prelude & Fugue of the German school.

The Music

The gap between the styles of the seventeenth and eighteenth centuries is bridged by the transitional and somewhat unequal composer William Croft. His pieces are occasionally little more than improvisations, the exploratory use of certain stops; for instance the short movement in MS h^2, marked 'Full Organ or Diapason', is little more than a sequence of chords, without thematic cohesion.

One of the twelve voluntaries listed in MS g^2, No. 4, is a short single movement, after the seventeenth-century manner; others are more extended single movements, for instance Nos. 5, 6, 7, 8, 9, 11; others again (Nos. 1, 2) attempt to combine within a single movement some of the contrasted features of the two-movement form shortly to come, with the directions 'slow', 'faster'.

Nos. 3, 10 and 12 alone fall into two separate movements. No. 10 is a Cornet Voluntary, No. 3 a Trumpet Voluntary, changing to the Cremona (Cromorne). What these pieces, and the single movements, unfortunately lack is the impetus of distinctive thematic writing. The most substantial piece of the set is reserved for the end. No. 12 is a double fugue, whose material is built from the slow chords that make up the introductory movement.

Thomas Roseingrave 1690–1766

But the first important organ composer of the eighteenth century was without doubt Thomas Roseingrave, whose first set of
pieces (1728) contained fifteen Voluntaries and (single) Fugues. The
Voluntary in his hands remains a single-movement piece, but within this traditional framework Roseingrave built a highly original
structure. His Voluntaries, which are homogeneous in texture and
call for only a single manual, are chiefly concerned with the discovery and development of new harmonic progressions. They are
therefore homophonic and chordal, which distinguishes them from
the fugues, which are polyphonic and contrapuntal. He evidently
had no use for the Double Voluntary or the exploration of solo
stops.

Roseingrave's most favoured device is the harmonic suspension,
which he uses to increase the nervous tension of the music, and to
explore chromatic progressions, with occasional 5-part writing.
Naturally such uses occur more in the Voluntaries than in the
Fugues of this collection. A characteristic example occurs in the G
minor Voluntary No. 4:

Example 34

In the fourth bar of this piece the two parts are inverted, with
the right hand part taking over the second subject. All movements
are fugal, whether called so or not, except for the second and
fourth; but the second Voluntary is clearly intended to be followed
immediately by the third, as it finishes on a half-close. The twelfth
Voluntary is a double fugue in invertible counterpoint.

But Roseingrave was much more than merely an innovator.
His pieces have a consistency and brilliance which singles them out
from the average. And although he confined his organ works to

single-movement pieces, nevertheless in every other way his music belongs unquestionably to the style and mood of the eighteenth rather than the seventeenth century. The style of the G major Voluntary, No. 14, which was clearly derived from the *spiccato* style of string writing, and the perky subject of the D minor fugue, No. 5, are a far cry indeed from the subdued gravity of Blow.

Roseingrave's Six Double Fugues place their composer among the chief contrapuntists of this time in England. His counterpoint is much more complex than that of most of his contemporaries. Both the subjects of the Double Fugues are pursued with equal thoroughness; they are immediately treated in invertible counterpoint, and occasionally one of the subjects itself is inverted, as in the first Fugue.

Example 35

Double Fugue No. 1 in B flat   Roseingrave
(Opening)

The second subject usually starts on a weak beat, in quavers. The vitality and interest in Roseingrave's fugues derives not so much from the subjects themselves, which are for the most part quite ordinary and unremarkable, as from their intricate, subtle treatment, and from the elaboration and development of *motifs* derived from them. In the first Fugue the dotted note *motif* that first appears in bar 3 is later pursued with great effectiveness. An example of such development, which also leads to some highly original harmonic progressions, may be seen in the second Fugue:

Example 36

Double Fugue No. 2 in G minor   Roseingrave
(bars 47-49)

The material in each part is derived from the subject. Frequently the first entry of the two subjects expands into three real parts, before the answer. This occurs in the 2nd, 3rd, 4th and 5th Fugues. Nowhere does the composer write in more than four parts. As usual with fugues of this period, their texture is entirely homogeneous and unified; they are without episodes. The registration can therefore be made to match this, and the entire piece be played on the same manual. Since their nature and character is forthright, a bold sound quality (Diapason, Principal, Fifteenth) is the most appropriate, if not full organ.

John Travers 1703(?)–1758

The Voluntaries of John Travers typify the eighteenth century style in much the same way as those of Blow did that of the seventeenth. His style never falls below an enviable level of workmanship, if his music rarely rises above it.

His pieces were not published until after his death. Registration directions therefore may not be those of the composer; moreover it is not possible to identify exactly which of those Voluntaries in Ed. 105 are by him. His undisputed works are therefore best confined to Ed. 106.

Eleven out of the twelve Voluntaries make use of the normal two-movement structure. The exception is the first piece, in which the opening slow section is longer than usual, and is followed by two quick movements, one in D minor for the Cornet stop, the other in D major for the Trumpet. No doubt the composer wished to balance the dimensions of the long opening Adagio, which is a fine example of sustained writing for the Flutes, using only the upper half of the keyboard. In this case the first movement serves a much greater purpose than merely to act, as it usually did, as an introduction to the second. Travers has successfully captured something of the capacity of the organ for sustained, expressive quietness.

In seven out of his twelve Voluntaries (Nos. 1–7) the second movements exploit the instrument's solo stops, such as the Cornet, Trumpet, 'Full Chair Organ', Flute; the remaining five

Voluntaries (Nos. 8–12) end with a substantial fugue. Travers' style is broad enough to accommodate these complementary demands made on it; on the one hand, colour and brilliance, on the other the cumulative growth of a sustained polyphonic structure. The Cornet movements are made up of long melodic passages in semi-quavers, often sequential, whose harmonic progressions are uncomplicated, and whose figurations lie naturally under the hands, which facilitates velocity. Trumpet movements on the other hand, like those of Handel or Greene, consist of fanfare-like phrases, usually in the key of D, and built, somewhat obviously, round arpeggios, or a dotted rhythm. Only in Voluntary 5 does Travers introduce contrasting episodes, using the Flute stop with more melodic material. With the exception of the first Voluntary, all the slow first movements of Voluntaries 1–7 are registered 'Diapasons'; 8^1 tone only, acting as a short, subdued prelude and in total contrast to the colourful movement which follows.

The first movements of the last five Voluntaries on the other hand, whose final movements are fugal, are registered 'Full Organ'. The texture is fuller, richer than in the earlier pieces; the harmonic movement more enhanced by pointed, rhythmic figures such as dotted notes, syncopation, or small note decorations. These contrast markedly with the fugue subjects, which are usually in notes of longer value. The exception to this general principle is the twelfth Voluntary, in which the introduction is an extraordinarily powerful, chromatic Adagio in F minor, using even minims over 15 bars; the fugue on the other hand uses considerable rhythmic resource, and consists largely of crotchets and quavers.

Three of the Fugues are Double Fugues (Nos. 9, 10, 11), and normally Travers chooses a subject whose outline is simple and clear, and whose movement is conjunct. He has a marked preference for writing the second note a tone or semitone above the first, producing an effect of increased tension at the start.

Example 37

Fugue subjects   Travers
a) No. 10

b) No. 11

c) No. 12

One of these fugues uses the sort of angular, jagged subject so favoured by Handel. In this case the second note instead of being a semitone above the first, is merely displaced an octave lower:

Example 38

Voluntary No. 9 in C/G minor   Travers
(Fugue subject)

Travers occasionally weakens the structure by a certain metrical laxity at an important point in the exposition of a movement. At the opening of the Cornet Voluntary (No. 2) the structural strength of the otherwise highly colourful phrase is impaired by the metrical imbalance of its two constituent parts:

Example 39

Voluntary No. 2 in F
(Opening of second movement)   Travers
Cornet

The same characteristic imbalance occurs, with disturbing effect, in Voluntary No. 8.

Example 40

Voluntary No. 8 in C/G   Travers
(Opening)

Full organ

Harmonic fluidity and rhythmical laxity mark this fugue as a result; but this is not the case in the remaining fugues, in which the composer amply explores the potential of the organ for sustained power.

Maurice Greene 1695–1755

Greene's style is similar to that of Handel only in outward appearance. As in the case of Travers, the twelve Voluntaries that make up Ed. 112, were published posthumously, and contain no registration directions. Each piece is in two-movement form, even if in one case (No. 9) the introductory slow section is only four bars in length. The quicker second movement is often fugal, with a double or single subject; but some of Greene's most characteristic second movements, including that of the well-known Voluntary No. 8 in C minor, are homophonic.

The absence of registration directions imposes on the organist the decision of which organ colour to use. There is strong evidence that this set of Voluntaries, all of which make use of a different key, was carefully polished by the composer, and is probably a late work; there is hardly a superfluous note, and the harmonic movement is extremely fluent. Greene must have devoted much thought to achieve the mood and characteristic quality associated with the different keys. Moreover not only are the two movements of each Voluntary contrasted; they are also unified by their use of the same thematic material.

An instance of this can be seen in the second Voluntary, in which the descending scale of the first movement is inverted to become the ascending scale of the second:

Example 41

a) Voluntary No. 2 (Ed. 112) in F minor   Greene
(Opening of first movement)

b) (Opening of second movement)

[a¹ and b¹ are the inversions of a and b respectively]

In Voluntary 3 the bass notes of the first movement provide the pattern for the theme of the second:

Example 42

a) Voluntary No. 3 in A minor   Greene
(Opening of first movement)

b) (Opening of second movement)

[a and b provide the pattern for a¹ and b¹]

In Voluntary 5 it is the rhythms that form the connecting link; while in Voluntary 8 the link is rhythmic, melodic and harmonic to such an extent that the two movements may be seen as twin aspects of the same musical thought. Greene often exploits chromaticism and syncopation, but he invariably reintroduces the original theme, in the key of the tonic, as the final and concluding stage of a long movement. Occasionally, as in Voluntary 10, in which the subject is a long, chromatic one, such a recapitulation is both logical and brilliant.

An interesting case, in which two different fugal movements are derived from the same introduction, occurs in the Dulwich College manuscript (MS l²). Even when full allowance has been made for the possibility that the copyist John Reading may have been responsible for the repetition, nevertheless each of the Voluntaries in

F makes a satisfactory unity, and is thematically related between the two movements.

Another Voluntary (in C minor/major) in that collection is unusual for various reasons; first, because a minor key in the first movement is followed by a major key in the second—an early instance of a practice that was later to become quite common; next, because it approaches as near as any eighteenth century composer ever did to introducing independent episodes. The subject lends itself admirably to brilliant semiquaver runs, and broken-chord passages, which Greene fully exploits; the only link between such passages and the fugue subject is a rhythmic one in the accompanying part.

Generally speaking chromatic writing such as Greene uses in Voluntary 2 and 10 (of Ed. 112) is better realised with a subdued registration, such as the Flutes; if a chromatic movement is juxtaposed with a diatonic one, as is the case in Voluntary 3, this provides an additional opportunity for the organist to underline this contrast with a difference in registration during a movement. But some of the movements might well benefit from two manual treatment, or from an occasional change of manual; for instance the first section of Voluntary 7. In this case the introduction ends with the cadence at the last bar but two. The final two bars constitute a lead-in, in the conventional eighteenth century manner, to the following movement; they might for this reason be played on another manual, perhaps very quietly.

In certain movements the appropriate registration is evident from the nature of the music itself. In Voluntary 1 for instance, the somewhat subdued, feminine writing of the first movement suggests the Flutes; this is balanced by the bolder, more masculine nature of the second movement, which is best interpreted with a Diapason chorus. Again, the opening of Voluntary 5 would lose effectiveness if played on anything less than full organ. On the other hand, whereas the opening of Voluntary 7 may reasonably be played with a full registration, too loud a volume impedes the velocity and vivacity of the ensuing movement. Whereas one may be treated as full and slow, the other may well be registered in total contrast, and played quick and light.

Two manual treatment greatly enhances the second movement
of Voluntary 8; for instance the repeat of the subject at bar 11 is
by this means given not only an octave transposition by the composer, but a change of tonal quality by the performer.

Among the other pieces, the first of the Voluntaries in Ed. 104
is much more Handelian in spirit and style. For this reason we may
guess that it was written earlier than the set of twelve (Ed. 112).
Indeed, the third movement of this piece of Greene's, which is a
slow and short 4-bar link between two different fast movements, is
identical to the equivalent movement in Handel's A minor Voluntary (Ed. 95, No. 3). Moreover Greene's trumpet tune, with its
connecting episodes allotted to the Echo organ, is highly reminiscent of Handel's in style, texture and rhythm (in Ed. 109). If such
pieces were improvised, as they probably were, when Handel and
Greene played to each other in St Paul's, and subsequently written
down, who could say precisely who had written which piece? But
this certainly does not apply to Greene's later, and more mature
work.

Two pieces in the same set (Ed. 104) by a minor figure, John
Reading, are noteworthy, though lacking the completeness of
Greene's style. The Voluntary in D minor alternates full organ
(Great) with Diapason and Principal (Chair);* an interesting conception, but one that unfortunately neither in this voluntary, nor
in that in G, is quite balanced by the composer's inventive powers,
which never reach beyond the ordinary. His own compositions in
the Dulwich College manuscript (MS l²) also show that his style
was compounded from that of other composers, ranging from
Handel to his own pupil John Stanley. Occasionally the phrase-
endings are awkward; the main Cornet theme of this Voluntary in
C is a case in point.

Both the voluntaries in Ed. 105 (Nos. 1 and 10) may confidently
be ascribed to Greene on grounds of style alone. The three movements which, unusually, make up the first Voluntary are all based
on a falling minor third (C–A) in the left hand; while the tenth

---

* The omission of the direction *Chair Organ* after the second full organ passage
  is obviously a misprint, of the sort that were very common in eighteenth-
  century editions.

Voluntary bears Greene's fingerprints in several important respects. The opening Largo effectively finishes two bars before the end; this cadence is followed by a preparatory phrase leading into the next movement, which can best be played on another manual. The Fugue is highly characteristic of Greene, with its chromatic melodic shape, its use of syncopation, and its dramatic reprise towards the end, after the second Echo section.

Handel 1685–1759

Handel brought fresh life to English organ music. He was a man of the theatre, not so much of the church, and he owed nothing to the ecclesiastical English tradition; so his works refer not at all to the liturgical aspect of the instrument, and instead they exploit almost exclusively its secular aspect. Despite the comparatively small number of his organ compositions, he dominated the first half of the eighteenth century in the style and form of organ composition (as indeed in most other matters) and in his hands organ music developed in the three directions already mentioned, which were subsequently pursued by his successors:

(a) The single-movement contrapuntal piece was henceforward called what it was: a Fugue.
(b) The Voluntary; a sequence of contrasted movements, usually two, instead of the single-movement piece it had been up to the time of Croft and Roseingrave (c. 1730).
(c) The Organ Concerto; the descendant of the earlier seventeenth century concerted piece, such as the Fantasia.

Handel's fugal technique

The six Fugues Op. 3 (1735) are masterly, polished compositions; finished, not improvised, and followed through with a consistent stream of counterpoint. Each Fugue is built on a subject substantial enough to sustain the entire piece. Handel does not introduce contrasting, independent episodes, as he does in the concertos, although occasionally the subject-materials overlap. For instance the second half of the subject of the second Fugue in G is remarkably reminiscent of the fugal finale of the concerto in F, Op. 4, No. 4; indeed the repeated note, and the subsequent intervals, exactly correspond:

Example 43

Overlapping themes in Handel's work are not hard to come by; but whereas in the Concerto the subject, with its rising tetrachord, is used to punctuate various colourful episodes in the organ part, in the fugue it is developed contrapuntally, and never ceases to form an integral part of the structure. So whereas the one piece gives the effect of brilliance and colour, the other gives the effect of sustained power.

The Organ Fugues are the keyboard equivalent of the great contrapuntal choruses. Indeed the first half of the subject quoted above is the same as the choral fugue 'Let all the servants of the Lord' in the sixth Chandos anthem.* The same monumental quality characterises each.

All six organ fugues are homogeneous, substantial, sustained, dignified; all use duple or common time, never triple. Their performance is therefore best confined to one manual, with the same stops maintained throughout. But as far as registration is concerned they are by no means all equally effective if played loudly. Indeed the anguished chromaticism of the fifth fugue is much more expressive if this music is played at a quiet dynamic level; which means, on the eighteenth century organ, the Flutes, or Stopped Diapason.

Of the two fugues edited by Diettenhofer (Ed. 103), the first in

* 'O praise the Lord with one consent.'

B minor was originally in two voices; the third voice is editorial. It is a comparatively slight work, similar to the fugal fourth movement of the third Voluntary. The other Fugue in C minor is much more substantial, largely in two parts. Its wedge-like chromatic subject makes this composition comparable with the other Fugues of Op. 3.

The Voluntaries

Unlike the Fugues, the Voluntaries were published posthumously. There is no reason however to doubt their authenticity. Handel, or the publisher, invariably specifies the registration required; and sometimes the simplest directions produce startingly effective results. An instance of this is shown in the first Voluntary, which requires just two stops, (Ed. 95, No. 1). For the opening slow movement an 8¹ Diapason; to this is added the 4¹ Principal for the ensuing Allegro.* But the feature that Handel brings to the music, that was not generally speaking shown by Blow or Purcell, is a keyboard virtuosity; the same quality that marks his organ concertos is also present in the solo organ pieces.

Of the thirteen Voluntaries listed, only one is a single-movement piece (Ed. 95, No. 7), in which *Full organ* (Great Organ) alternates with *Horn or Diapason* (Choir Organ); this resembles the alternation of *tutti* and *solo* in a concerto. One is arranged by the publisher in four sections (Ed. 95, No. 3), but it may also be considered as two Voluntaries juxtaposed. The first two movements make up a Cornet Voluntary in A minor; the last two movements are a Fugue, to which the publisher may have seen fit to add a short, somewhat nondescript slow section, which also occurs in one of Greene's works, published thirteen years before.

All the other Voluntaries follow the two-movement structure; a slow first movement, usually for the Diapasons, followed by a quick second movement. It is the second, larger movement, that decides the character of the Voluntary. Handel's fall into the categories of Cornet, Trumpet, Full Organ or Fugal. A fugue may well be registered 'Full Organ', as in the case of Nos. 3, 8, 9, 10, 11,

---

* This has been misunderstood by the editor of Ed. 55.

12; the characteristic Full Organ piece is splendidly demonstrated by No. 8. The slow movement (*Grave, alla breve*), rich in harmonic movement and chromaticism; the quick movement (Allegro) is a free double Fugue, largely in just two parts; its construction is similar to that of the first Voluntary—indeed the left hand part begins in the same way—but the 'answer' in bar 4 is still in the tonic key (C), with the counterpoint inverted.

Nos. 9, 10 and 11 are Full Organ Voluntaries in which a chordal slow movement is followed with more fluid counterpoint in the finale. Naturally, where the texture of the music remains homogeneous, as in No. 9, the piece is best realised on a single manual. But where Handel introduces episodes of related material, these invite a contrasted registration. No. 10, bars 36 and 67, are a case in point.

Of the solo Voluntaries, those for the Trumpet are sometimes the most stereotyped. The Trumpet Voluntary in Ed. 109, if indeed it is by Handel, is somewhat threadbare in invention; like Ed. 95, No. 5 it leans heavily on the chord of D major, and relies for its effect on the sound-quality of the individual Trumpet stop. In two cases Handel ventures beyond the key of D. In Ed. 95 No. 2, an otherwise ordinary composition is rescued by a more lyrical middle section for the Flute stop; while the material of Voluntary No. 6 makes use of longer phrases for the Trumpet Stop, repeated on the Echo Organ, as well as a long central Flute episode.

The Cornet Voluntaries (Nos. 3 and 4) are characterised by a broad sweep of melody, and a brilliance of figuration, marked by that sense of keyboard dexterity that was Handel's main contribution to the organ style of this period.

There are occasional moments in some of the Voluntaries, of which No. 4 provides a clear example, when the score represents a characteristically Handelian shorthand, during which the organist would be expected to play freely and extemporarily within the framework prescribed by the composer. The last six bars of the Diapason movement of Voluntary No. 4 are a case in point, where the dotted minim chords are merely the scaffolding round which the performer builds. Bars 57–8 of the Cornet movement are similarly incomplete as they stand. Chords were not suitable for the Cornet stop, and in this case the major third interval in the Tierce would lead to a violent clash A♮/A♯, and B♭/B♮. The chords written are in effect a background for the player's own invention and improvisation. The end of Voluntaries Nos. 6 and 11 may also be considered in this light.

John Stanley 1713–1786

Although Stanley lived until 1786, his three principal sets of Voluntaries, which gained him a wide notoriety, were first published in 1748–52. His work therefore belongs to the first, rather than the second half of the eighteenth century. Indeed Stanley's style summarises the state of organ music up to 1759.

Most of his Voluntaries are in two movements,★ and make their effect with the greatest economy of means. The solo Voluntaries are normally in two parts; that is to say a solo part, with an accompanimental-bass part for the left hand. The exception to this is Op. 6, No. 6, in which the French Horn solo consists of two parts. But each movement is built round a single, consistent effect; and Stanley clearly differentiates between the characters of the different solo stops.

Secondary material is either contrasted, on another manual such as the Echo, or else derived from the main material, and retained on the solo stop. His Trumpet voluntaries usually introduce secondary material, such as flute scale passages, as a contrast on another manual; in the case of the Cornet stop on the other hand, the composer enjoyed inventing scale sequences or arpeggio figurations. In one case, Op. 6, No. 2, he introduces the Echo manual while using the same material.

Stanley is fond of contrasting loud with soft of the same tone quality; this is particularly the case with the Voluntaries of Op. 6 and Op. 7; not so much in Op. 5. The exception to this is Op. 5 No. 8, which is set in the three-movement form of a concerto. Indeed this particular piece gives a strong impression of being a transcription of a String Concerto, and lacks something of the sense of direction that the composer shows elsewhere.

★ The exceptions are Op. 5, No. 1 & 8, Op. 6 No 5 & 6, Op. 7 No. 8.

If the solo movements make use of just two parts, the slow, Diapason, movements and the fugues are generally in three. The last three Voluntaries of each set, and the last four of Op. 6, are fugal, for full organ. Stanley was not a great contrapuntist, like Handel, or Roseingrave, and in his fugues interest focuses much more on the colour and melodic vitality of his subject-material than on its working out. His fugues therefore consist of a strong melodic part, against which the others fit and supply the harmonic movement in a subsidiary accompanimental role, rather than of the working-through of independent subject and counter-subject in one homogeneous texture.

The introductory Diapason movements are invariably sustained by harmonic direction, and never meander. Stanley's style is also marked by a controlled use of chromaticism and of melodic sequences; these can so easily deteriorate into mechanical formulae. Phrase answers phrase, which gives the music a melodic, horizontal continuity; while chordally, or vertically, the harmony anticipates the quick movement that is to follow.

Clearly this connecting of the two sections of a Voluntary was a technique that Stanley learnt from his teacher Maurice Greene; in fact the style of each composer has many points in common. Sometimes the connecting link is obvious, as in Op. 7, No. 1 (the notes E—F—G—A of the first bar); sometimes the point in common may be one of general outline, as in Op. 7, No. 8.

Example 44

a) Voluntary in A minor, Op. 7. No. 8   ·Stanley
(Opening of first movement)
Andante staccato

b) (Fugue subject)

[The minor third *motif* (a) gives rise to two subsidiary motifs in the fugue; a^2 is a retrograde, a^3 is a retrograde inversion.]

Or again, the harmony of one movement may be a distillation of the melody of the other:

Example 45

Sometimes the harmonic progressions implied in the first movement are pursued in the second.

Example 46

A certain subtlety connects the movements of Op. 6, No. 9, in which the subject is inverted and augmented in the second half.

Example 47

Like the Voluntaries of his teacher Greene, Stanley's work is polished, refined, complete; and deservedly popular.

COMPOSERS AND EXTANT REPERTOIRE UP TO 1759

Composer	Work	MS Source	Printed Editions
ANONYMOUS	(late seventeenth century)		
	Untitled pieces (Voluntaries?)		
	1 Voluntary in D minor	b^2, z^1	
	2 Voluntary in D minor	b^2, z^1	
	3 Voluntary in G	b^2, z^1	
	4 Voluntary in G	b^2, z^1	
	5 Voluntary in D minor	ee	
	6 Voluntary in G minor	y	
	7 Voluntary in D minor	z^1	
	8 Voluntary in D	b^2, z^1	
	9 Voluntary in D	b^2, z^1	
	10 Voluntary in C	b^2, z^1	
	11 Voluntary in D minor	b^2	
	12 Voluntary in G	b^2, z^1	
	13 Voluntary in D minor	b^2, w^1	
	14 Voluntary in A minor	b^2	
	15 Voluntary in A minor	b^2	
	16 Voluntary in C	z^1	
	17 (Prelude?) in C	z^1	
	18 Double Voluntary in D minor	z^1	86
	19 Double Voluntary in A minor	w^1	
	20 Double Voluntary in C		
	('Diaps. & Flutes')	w^1	
	21 Voluntary in A minor	a	
	22 Trumpet Voluntary in G	a	
	Untitled pieces (Verses?)		
	1 Verse in A minor	a	
	2 Verse in G	a	
	3 Verse in G	a	
	4 Verse in C	a	
	5 Verse in D minor	a	
	('A verse to play after prayer')		
	6 Verse in G minor	a	
	7 Verse in A minor	a	
	8 Verse in G	a	
	9 Verse in D minor	ee, t^3	
	10 Untitled piece in D minor	dd	
	11 Double Verse in A	y, ee	
	12 Verse in C	ee	
	(early-mid eighteenth century)		
	'A collection of Voluntaries . . .		
	by Dr Green, Mr Travers and		
	several other eminent masters'.		105
	(The pieces are not severally		
	attributed)		
	1 Voluntary in C (prob. Greene)		

Composer	Work	MS Source	Printed Editions
ANONYMOUS			
—*contd.*	II Voluntary in C		105
	III Voluntary in D		
	IV Voluntary in C		
	V Voluntary in C (incomplete)		
	VI Voluntary in C		
	VII Voluntary in C		
	VIII Voluntary in D minor		
	IX Voluntary in C		
	X Voluntary in A minor (prob. Greene)		
	'Ten select Voluntaries . . . by Orlando Gibbons, Blow, Purcell, Doctor Green, Doctor Boyce, Mr James Martin Smith & J. Stafford Smith'.		108
	(The pieces are not all attributed)		
	I Voluntary for double organ (prob. Gibbons)		
	III Voluntary in F		
	IV Voluntary in G (prob. Greene)		
	VI Voluntary in G		
	VII Voluntary in A minor (prob. Boyce)		
	IX Voluntary in D		
	'Ten select voluntaries . . . by Mr Handel, Dr Green etc.'		109
	(The pieces are not severally attributed)		
	I Voluntary in D (prob. Handel)		
	II Voluntary in C		
	III Voluntary in G minor		
	IV Voluntary in C		
	V Voluntary in F		
	VI Voluntary in G minor (perhaps Handel)		
	VII Voluntary in A		
	VIII Voluntary in A minor		
	IX Voluntary in G minor		
	X Voluntary in E minor		
	Voluntary in G	f[3]	
	Voluntary in C	l[2]	
BARRETT,	Voluntary in C*	w[1], f[3]	57, 51
John	Voluntary in D minor	x[1], l[2], f[3]	

* Ascribed to Purcell (in Ed. 51) See editorial note in Ed. 52.

Composer	Work		MS Source	Printed Editions
BLOW, John	*For numbers see Edition 90*			
	1 Verse	G	a^2, z^1, b^2 a, v	90, 91★
	2 Verse	C	a^2, z^1, b^2	90
	3 Verse	G	a^2, z^1, b^2, c^2	90, 91
	4 Verse	G	a^2, z^1, v	90
	5 Verse	(one flat) F	a^2, z^1, v, c^2	90, 91
	6 Verse	(one flat) D minor	a^2, v	90, 91
	7 Verse	G	a^2	90, 91
	8 Verse	(two flats) G minor	a^2, c^2	90, 91
	9 Verse	(one flat) D minor	c^2	90
	10 Verse	(one sharp) G	c^2	90
	11 Verse	A minor	$a^2, b^2, a,$ w^1, c^2, v	90
	12 Verse	D minor	c^2, v	90
	13 Verse	A minor	c^2	90
	14 Verse (for single organ) (three sharps) A		a^2, z^1	90, 91
	15 Untitled piece	G	z^1, c^2	90, 91
	16 Voluntary for the two diapasons & flute	C	a^2, z^1, b^2 w^1, c^2	90, 91
	17 A Voluntary for the single organ (two sharps) D		a^2	90, 91
	18 Voluntary for single organ (one flat) D minor		a^2, b^2	90
	19 Fugue	G	b^2	90, 91
	20 Prelude in A re	A minor	b^2	90, 91
	21 Untitled piece	C	b^2	90, 91
	22 Untitled piece (two flats) G minor		ff	90
	23 Untitled piece	G	y, a	90
	24 Voluntary	G	y, ee	90
	25 A Voluntary for the Double Organ	D minor	z^1	90
	26 Another double Voluntary	C	$x^1, b^2, a^2, z^1,$ h^2, l^2, f^3	90, 91
	27 A Verse for the Double Organ	D minor	a^2, a	90, 91
	28 A Voluntary for the Cornett stop	A minor	a^2, c^2	90, 91
	(Verse for the Cornett and single Organ)			
	29 A Double Verse	G	b^2	90, 91
	30 The 100th Psalm tune: set as a lesson†		b^2	90
	31 Voluntary‡	A		87
	32 Echo Voluntary‡	G		87
	33 Voluntary	C	x^1, f^3	57

★ Edition 91 has been edited ,with occasional additions, on three staves, to include pedals, and is to this extent unreliable.

† Also attributed to Purcell; see editorial note in Ed. 90 (c.f. Ed. 52).

‡ From the Nanki Manuscript, Tokyo; see editorial note in Ed. 87.

Composer	Work	MS Source	Printed Editions
CLARKE, Jeremiah	Trumpet tune ('Prince of Denmark's March')	y^1	
CROFT, William	1 Voluntary in D minor	g^2	
	2 Voluntary in D	g^2	
	3 Voluntary in D	g^2	
	4 Voluntary in G minor	g^2	
	5 Voluntary in C	g^2	
	6 Voluntary in G	g^2	
	7 Voluntary in D minor	g^2	
	8 Voluntary in C	g^2	
	9 Voluntary in A minor	g^2	
	10 Voluntary in D	g^2	
	11 Voluntary in D minor for double organ	g^2	
	12 Voluntary in D	g^2	
	Voluntary in D minor	h^2	
	Voluntary in D minor	x^1, l^2, f^3	
	Voluntary in A minor	x^1, l^2, f^3	
	Voluntary in D	f^3	
FROUD ?	Siciliano in G	l^2	
GIBBONS, Christopher	Voluntary for the Double Organ in A minor	ee, z^1 a^2, b^2, y	53
	(Voluntary) in C	y, ee, t^3	53
	Voluntary for the Double Organ in D minor	$a^2, b^2, y,$ ee, z^1	53
	(Verse) in D minor	b^2, y, ee, t^3	53
	(Verse) in A minor	d^2	53
	Voluntary (for Double Organ) in C	y, ee, t^3	53
	Verse for Single Organ in D minor	u^3	
	Verse for Single Organ in F	dd	
GREENE, Maurice	Voluntary in G		47, 104$^{(1)}$
	Voluntary in D minor		47, 104$^{(10)}$
	Voluntary in D minor	l^2, f^3	
	Voluntary in F	l^2, f^3	
	Voluntary in F	l^2, f^3	
	Voluntary in C minor/major	l^2	
	Voluntary in G	f^3	
	Voluntary in E minor	f^3	
	Voluntary in A minor/C	f^3	
	'Twelve Voluntaries for the Organ or Harpsichord'		112
	I Voluntary in A		112
	II Voluntary in F minor		46, 112
	III Voluntary in A minor		112, 113
	IV Voluntary in G minor		112
	V Voluntary in G		112
	VI Voluntary in B flat		46, 112

Composer	Work	MS Source	Printed Editions
GREENE,	VII Voluntary in E flat		47, 112
Maurice	VIII Voluntary in C minor		47, 112
—contd.	IX Voluntary in E minor		112
	X Voluntary in D minor		112
	XI Voluntary in B minor		46, 112
	XII Voluntary in E		112
	Probable attribution		
	Voluntary in C		105[1]
	Voluntary in A minor		105[10]
	Voluntary in G		108[4]
HANDEL,	'Twelve Voluntaries and Fugues for		
G. F.	the Organ or Harpsichord'		
	I Voluntary in C		55, 95, 101
	II Voluntary in C		55, 95
	III Voluntary in A minor		95
	IV Voluntary in G minor		55, 95
	V Voluntary in D		95
	VI Voluntary in C		95
	VII Voluntary in C		95
	VIII Voluntary in C		55, 95
	IX Voluntary in C minor		95
	X Voluntary in D		95, 101
	XI Voluntary in D		95
	XII Voluntary in F		95
	Numbers refer to Ed. 96		
	I Double Fugue in G minor		54, 96
	II Fugue in G	f^3	54, 96
	III Double fugue in B flat	f^3	54, 96
	IV Fugue in B minor		54, 96
	V Fugue in A minor		54, 96
	VI Fugue in C minor		54, 96
	Fugue in B minor		103
	Fugue in C minor		103
	Voluntary in D minor		
	(probably attributable, in style)		109[1]
	Fugue in E minor	f^3	
HART,	Fugues for the Organ or Harpsichord		
Philip	in A, in C minor, in F		66
HINE,	Voluntary in F	h^2	102
William			
HINGSTON,	Voluntary in A	ee, y	
John	(for Double Organ)		
JAMES,	Voluntary in A minor	l^2, o^2, f^3	104[4]
John	Voluntary in D	h^2	110*
	Voluntary in G	l^2	
KUKNAN,	Voluntary in F		104[9]

* Ed. 110 is not reliable.

Composer	Work		MS Source	Printed Editions
LOCKE, Matthew	Voluntary in E			94, 49[*]
	Voluntary in D			94, 49
	Voluntary in G			94, 49
	Voluntary in A			94, 49
	Voluntary in A		y[1]	94, 49
	Voluntary for a double organ			94, 49
	Voluntary in F			94, 49
PURCELL, Henry	Verse in E	E	d[2]	52
	Verse	(one flat) F	y[1]	52
	Voluntary in C	C	d[2]	52
	Voluntary	(one flat) D minor	z[1]	52
	Voluntary for Double organ			
		(one flat) D minor	a[2]	51, 52
	Voluntary	(one sharp) G	b[2]	52
	Doubtful work			
	Voluntary on the old 100th[†]	A	b[2]	51, 52
READING, John	Voluntary in G[‡]		l[2], x[1], f[3]	57, 104[(7)]
	Cornet Voluntary in D minor		x[1], l[2], f[3]	104[(5)]
	Voluntary in C		l[2]	
	Voluntary in D minor		l[2]	
	Air in D		l[2]	
	Air in G		l[2]	
	Trumpet Air in D (i)		l[2]	
	Trumpet Air in D (ii)		l[2]	
ROBINSON, John	Voluntary in A minor			72
ROGERS, Benjamin	Voluntary		e[2], f[2]	87
ROSEINGRAVE, Thomas	I Fugue in F minor			93
	II Voluntary in F minor (leading into)			93, 20
	III Fugue in F minor			93, 20
	IV Voluntary in G minor			93, 35
	V Fugue in D minor			93, 20
	VI Fugue in F			93
	VII Voluntary in G minor			93, 20
	VIII Voluntary in G minor			93, 2r
	IX Voluntary in G			93
	X Fugue in G			93, 20, 35
	XI Voluntary in G			93
	XII Voluntary in G minor			93
	XIII Fugue in E minor			93
	XIV Voluntary in G			93, 20
	XV Voluntary in C minor			93, 20

[*] Edition 49 is somewhat unreliable in the treatment of ornaments, and lacks a textual commentary.

[†] Also attributed to Blow. See editorial note in Ed. 52 (c.f. Ed. 90).

[‡] MS l[2] and Ed. 104 show alternative introductory movements.

Composer	Work	MS Source	Printed Editions
ROSEINGRAVE,	I Double Fugue in B flat major		92, 20
Thomas—*contd.*	II Double Fugue in G minor		92
	III Double Fugue in F major		92, 20
	IV Double Fugue in E minor		92, 20
	V Double Fugue in D minor		92, 35
	VI Double Fugue in D minor		92
SEDO, ?	Voluntary in D flat minor/major	l^2	
SELBY, ?	Voluntary in A		104$^{(8)}$
SKINNER, ?	Voluntary in E minor		104$^{(2)}$
SMITH,	Voluntary in D		108$^{(2)}$
J. Stafford	Voluntary in G		108$^{(8)}$
	Voluntary in A minor		108$^{(10)}$
SMITH, Martin	Voluntary in G		108$^{(5)}$
STANLEY, Charles John	*Ten Voluntaries*, Op. 5		
	1 Voluntary in C	i^2	61, 62, 63, 113, 133/4
	2 Voluntary in D minor	i^2	61, 62, 63, 133/4
	3 Voluntary in G	i^2	61, 62, 63, 133/4
	4 Voluntary in E minor	i^2	61, 62, 63, 133/4
	5 Voluntary in D	i^2	61, 62, 63, 133/4
	6 Voluntary in D minor		61, 62, 63, 133/4
	7 Voluntary in G minor	i^2	61, 62, 63, 133/4
	8 Voluntary in D minor	i^2	45, 61, 62, 63, 133/4
	9 Voluntary in G minor	i^2	61, 62, 63, 133/4
	10 Voluntary in A minor	i^2, l^2	61, 62, 63, 133/4
	Ten Voluntaries, Op. 6		
	1 Voluntary in D minor	i^2, l^2	61, 62, 63, 133/4
	2 Voluntary in A minor	i^2, l^2, x^1	61, 62, 63, 133/4
	3 Voluntary in G minor	i^2	61, 62, 63, 133/4
	4 Voluntary in F	i^2	61, 62, 63, 133/4
	5 Voluntary in D minor/major	l^2, x^1, f^3	61, 62, 63, 133/4
	6 Voluntary in D	l^2, x^1	61, 62, 63, 133/4
	7 Voluntary in G	i^2	61, 62, 63, 133/4
	8 Voluntary in A minor		61, 62, 63, 133/4
	9 Voluntary in E minor	x^1, h^2, i^2, l^2, f^3	61, 62, 63, 133/4
	10 Voluntary in G minor	i^2, l^2	61, 62, 63, 133/4
	Ten Voluntaries, Op. 7		
	1 Voluntary in A	i^2, qq	61, 62, 63, 133/4
	2 Voluntary in C	i^2	61, 62, 63, 133/4
	3 Voluntary in D minor		61, 62, 63, 133/4
	4 Voluntary in D minor		61, 62, 63, 133/4
	5 Voluntary in D	i^2	61, 62, 63, 133/4
	6 Voluntary in F	i^2	61, 62, 63, 133/4
	7 Voluntary in E minor	i^2	61, 62, 63, 133/4

Composer	Work	MS Source	Printed Editions
STANLEY, Charles John —contd.	8 Voluntary in A minor	i^2, l^2, o^2	61, 62, 63, 133/4
	9 Voluntary in G	i^2	61, 62, 63, 133/4
	10 Voluntary in F	i^2	61, 62, 63, 133/4
	Fugue in G	f^3	
	Fugue in E minor	f^3	
	Fugue in D minor	f^3	
	Voluntary in A minor★	x^1, l^2	
STUBLEY ?	Voluntary in C		$104^{(3)}$
	Voluntary in F		$104^{(3)}$
THORLEY, Thomas	*Ten Voluntaries*		167
	I Voluntary in C		
	II (Trumpet) Voluntary in D minor/major		
	III Voluntary in C		
	IV Voluntary in G minor		
	V Voluntary in C		
	VI Voluntary in D minor		
	VII Voluntary in C		
	VIII Voluntary in D minor		
	IX Voluntary in C		
	X Voluntary in F		
TRAVERS, John	'Twelve Voluntaries for the Organ or Harpsichord composed by the late ingenious Joannis Travers.'		106
	I Voluntary in D (minor/major)		106
	II Voluntary in F		106
	III Voluntary in D (minor/major)		106
	IV Voluntary in C		106
	V Voluntary in D		106
	VI Voluntary in A (minor/major)		106
	VII Voluntary in C (minor/major)		106
	VIII Voluntary in C/G		106
	IX Voluntary in C/G minor		106
	X Voluntary in D		106
	XI Voluntary in D minor		106
	XII Voluntary in F minor		58, 106
	Also unascribed Voluntaries in Ed. 105 (see *Anon.*)		

★ Attributed 'anon.' in MS l^2.

BIOGRAPHICAL NOTES ON THE COMPOSERS

BARRETT, John.

1674?–1735? Pupil of John Blow. *c.* 1707 Music master at Christ's Hospital. *c.* 1710 Organist at Christ Church, Newgate Street and St Mary-at-Hill. Compositions chiefly vocal, for the stage.

BLOW, John.

1649–1708. Born Newark. 1660 Chorister under Henry Cooke in the Chapel Royal at the Restoration. Later a pupil of Christopher Gibbons. 1668 Organist of Westminster Abbey. 1669 Musician for the Virginals to Charles II (after Giles Tomkins). 1673 (16th March) Gentleman of the Chapel Royal. 1674 Master of the children—Later (1676?) Organist (after C. Gibbons?). 1679 Succeeded at Westminster Abbey by his pupil Henry Purcell. 1682 Purcell & Blow both organists of the Chapel Royal. 1687 Almoner at St Paul's Cathedral (succeeded by Jeremiah Clarke 1703). 1689 Composer in the Private Musick. 1695 Resumed as organist at Westminster Abbey after Purcell's death. 'Tuner of the regalls, organs, virginalls' etc, with 'Father' Smith. 1697 Wren's new St Paul's opened. 1699 Composer for the Chapel Royal; first holder of new office. Compositions include Church Music, Choral Odes, Stage Songs, and a Masque 'Venus and Adonis'. Pupils included: Croft, Clarke, Daniel Purcell, Gates, Roseingrave, Barrett and Reading.

CLARKE, Jeremiah.

1673?–1707. Chorister in the Chapel Royal under Blow. 1692 Organist at Winchester College. 1695 Organist at St Paul's Cathedral. 1699 Vicar Choral. 1703 Almoner at St Paul's Cathedral. 1707 (July 7th) Gentleman of the Chapel Royal and joint organist with Croft (1704). 1707 Committed suicide, perhaps after an unhappy love-affair. Compositions include Church music, vocal music and keyboard works.

CROFT, William.

1678–1727. Chorister at Chapel Royal under Blow. 1700 (July 7th) Gentleman of the Chapel Royal; organist of St Anne's Soho. 1704 (May 25th) Joint organist of the Chapel Royal with Clarke. 1708 Succeeded Blow as organist of Westminster Abbey and as Master of the Children & Composer of the Chapel Royal. Compositions include Anthems, Odes, instrumental Chamber music and harpsichord pieces.

GIBBONS, Christopher.

1615–1676. Second son of Orlando Gibbons (q.v.). Chorister of Chapel Royal while his father was organist. After his father's death, chorister at Exeter under his uncle Edward Gibbons (q.v.). Knew Matthew Locke (q.v.) when latter was at Exeter, and later collaborated with him in Shirley's *Masque of Cupid and Death*. 1638–44 Organist Winchester Cathedral. During Commonwealth he was heard by John Evelyn (in July, 1654) playing the organ in Magdalen College, Oxford. 1660 (17th Nov.) Musician upon the Virginals to Charles II. Organist of Chapel Royal, Westminster Abbey. Compositions include Church music, Fantasias for strings.

GREENE, Maurice.

1695–1755. Chorister at St Paul's Cathedral. 1716 Organist at St Dunstan's in the West. 1717 Organist at St Andrew's, Holborn. 1718 Organist at St Paul's Cathedral. 1727 Joint organist, with John Weldon, and composer of the Chapel Royal. 1730 Succeeded Thomas Tudway as professor of Music at Cambridge. 1735 Master of the King's Band. Compositions include Oratorios, Anthems, Operas, Songs and keyboard pieces.

HANDEL, George Frideric.

1685–1759. Born in Halle. 1693 studied under Zachau, organist of the Liebfrauenkirche. 1702 Organist of Domkirche, Halle. 1703 played violin and harpsichord at Hamburg Opera House. 1706 Left Hamburg for Italy; Florence 1706, Rome and Venice 1707, Naples 1708. 1710 Kapellmeister to Elector Georg of Hanover—first visit to London. 1712 Returned to London, where he remained when Elector of Hanover became George I (1714).

HART, Philip.

1676–1749. 1724 First organist of St Dionis Backchurch. Also organist of St Andrew Undershaft (1696–1749) and St Michael, Cornhill (1704–1723). Composer of minor vocal pieces.

HINE, William.

1687–1730. Pupil of Jeremiah Clarke. Chorister at Magdalen College, Oxford (1695). 1705 Clerk. 1710 Organist of Gloucester Cathedral. *Harmonia Sacra Glocestriensis*, including one organ Voluntary, published posthumously by his widow Alicia.

HINGSTON, John.

?–1683. Musician to Charles I. Organist to Cromwell at Hampton Court, music teacher to Cromwell's daughters. After Restoration 'Keeper of the organs' to Charles II (succeeded by Purcell).

JAMES, John.

?–1745. Organist at St Olave's, Southwark. Later (1738) St George in the East.

LOCKE, Matthew.

1630–1677. 1638–41 Chorister at Exeter Cathedral under Edward Gibbons. 1648 Visited the Netherlands. 1660 'Composer in the private musick', in place of Coperario. Organist of the Queen's Catholic Chapel in Somerset House.

PURCELL, Henry.

1659–1695. Chorister of the Chapel Royal under Henry Cooke, after 1672 under Pelham Humfrey. Later pupil of Blow. 1679 Succeeded Blow as organist of Westminster Abbey. 1682 Joint Organist with Blow and Child of the Chapel Royal, in succession to Edward Lowe. Gentleman of the Chapel Royal. Composer in ordinary to Charles II, and 'keeper of the organs'.

READING, John.

1677–1764. Born at Winchester, son of John Reading, organist of Winchester Cathedral (1675–1681). Chorister of the Chapel Royal under Blow. 1700 (22nd April) Organist at Dulwich College. 1702 Junior Vicar and poor clerk of Lincoln Cathedral, as his father had once been. 1704 'Instructor of the choristers in vocal music' at Lincoln. 1708 Organist St John's, Hackney. Organist of various churches, including St Mary Woolnoth (1727?) and St Dunstan in the West, where he remained until his death. His pupils included John Stanley. Most famous composition the hymn tune *Adeste fideles*.

ROBINSON, John.

1682–1762. Chorister of Chapel Royal under Blow. 1710 Organist St Lawrence Jewry. 1713 Organist St Magnus the Martyr, London Bridge. Assistant to Croft at Westminster Abbey. 1727 Organist Westminster Abbey (after Croft).

ROGERS, Benjamin.

1614–1698. Son of lay-clerk of St George's Chapel, Windsor, where he himself was chorister under Giles. 1639–41 Organist of Christ Church Cathedral, Dublin. Returned to Windsor with rebellion, taught, composed. 1660 (5th July) 'Hymnus Eucharisticus' for Guildhall Banquet for Charles II. 1661–64 Organist of Eton College. 1662 Lay-clerk at St George's Windsor. 1664–85 Organist and *Informator* of Magdalen College Oxford. Compositions mainly vocal after 1660 —instrumental before then.

ROSEINGRAVE, Thomas.

1690–1766. His father Daniel (1650–1727) was under Blow & Purcell, and was organist of Gloucester, Winchester and Salisbury Cathedrals, before moving to Dublin in 1698. Thomas was born at Winchester before moving to Salisbury (1692), then Dublin. 1707 Entered Trinity College. 1710 Travelled to Italy and knew Scarlatti, whose sonatas he edited. Studied counterpoint and admired Palestrina's style. 1720 Composer at King's Theatre, London. 1725–37 First organist of St George's Hanover Square. Retired, owing to mental instability, to Ireland where he died at Dunleary. Compositions for organ and harpsichord, also cantatas, songs etc.

STANLEY, Charles John.

1713–1786. Blind from the age of two. Pupil of John Reading (1720) and Maurice Greene. 1724 Organist All Hallows, Bread Street. 1726 Organist St Andrews, Holborn (after Daniel Purcell). 1734 Organist Temple Church. 1779 Master of the King's Band of Musicians (after Boyce, q.v.). Played violin in the Swan Tavern, Cornhill. Directed Oratorios at Drury Lane. Compositions include Stage works, songs, instrumental works. Pupils include John Alcock (q.v.).

TRAVERS, John.

1703(?)–1758. Chorister at St George's Chapel, Windsor, pupil of Maurice Greene at St Paul's, and Pepusch. 1725 Organist at St Paul's Covent Garden, also of Fulham Church. 1737 Organist Chapel Royal.

The following composers seem to be otherwise unknown: FROUD, KUKNAN, SEDO, SELBY, SKINNER, SMITH J. S., SMITH M., STUBLEY, THORLEY.

THE ORGAN OF THE PERIOD (1656–1759)

By a curious irony, the restrictive policies of the Common-wealth period finally resulted in a great renewal of activity in organ building, and acted as a most effective spur to progressive design. The final years of the seventeenth century saw some of the most marked advances that there have ever been in England.

Two main reasons may be advanced for this apparent paradox. First, there was hardly a Cathedral, College or Church in the country after 1660 that was not anxious and enthusiastic to restore its organs, that had been silenced or removed for some fifteen years. In many cases former organs were re-built or re-erected; Magdalen College, Oxford, and Salisbury Cathedral were two prominent examples. But in many other cases new instruments were asked for; The King's Chapel in Whitehall, and Exeter and Winchester Cathedrals for instance. Organ builders were hence-forward increasingly in demand.

The second reason is that during their period of enforced idle-ness, organ-builders travelled and worked on the continent; for instance, Robert Dallam, and Thomas Harris carried on work in France (where Renatus was born); while Bernard Smith himself lived on the continent. Thus continental styles and techniques were later to reach this country.*

Allied with both these fortunate circumstances is the fact that, from now on, records become gradually more numerous, with the result that our knowledge of this period is much less fragmentary than of the earlier ones.

It is generally accepted that at this time two organ-builders out-strip all others in importance; Bernard ('Father') Smith, and Renatus Harris. The new tonal structure that between them they had established by 1700 was to remain the standard pattern for the rest of the eighteenth century; much as Dallam's style had been the pattern for the earlier period up to the Commonwealth.

---

* A similar process took place during the second world war, 1939–45, when English musicians, while serving with the armed forces, gained experience of European styles of organ design, which gradually affected taste after 1945.

The chief features of the new style were the addition of reeds and mixtures, as well as a third manual—the Echo, later to become the Swell. Another equally important improvement was the avoidance of duplication of stops. Whereas Dallam's Great Organs were built round double choruses, with two stops at each pitch, this practice was abandoned after 1660 in favour of the much more effective technique of building up the tonal chorus with different, single ranks.

The three chief reeds introduced were the Trumpet, Cremona (or Crumhorn) and Vox Humana; variants included also at 8ˡ pitch the Bassoon, French Horn, and Hautboy, and as the eighteenth century progressed the Clarion at 4ˡ pitch.★

The commonest Mixtures were the Sesquialtera, usually three ranks, which completed the Diapason Chorus, and the five-rank solo Cornet, usually mounted separately, whose first appearance in England was in Exeter Cathedral (John Loosemore, 1665).†

But the change to the new style was gradual. Many of the instruments that were replaced immediately after the Restoration were still of the early seventeenth-century design; such a one was (the elder) Thomas Harris's organ for Magdalen College, Oxford, which was originally built in 1637.

The introduction of the new design was noticeable in the work of several other builders than Smith or Harris. Pride of place, if only because it was the first, must be given to the Exeter Cathedral organ built by John Loosemore in 1665/6. Loosemore, whose family came from Devonshire, was Clerk of the Works at Exeter, and his duties covered many other more humdrum tasks than organ-building; plumbing and road-works, for instance. He also made Virginals.‡ But the Dean and Chapter of Exeter Cathedral, where there had for long been a particularly strong musical tradition, looked for excellence; they required Loosemore to select the finest material, such as tin from the Cornish mines, and to consult as many colleagues and musicians as possible. Accordingly he in-

★ For instance Salisbury Cathedral (1710), St George's Hanover Square (1725).
† For an account of a Mixture at Staunton Harold, Leicestershire, in an organ built by Christian Smith, see Noel Mander in *Musical Times*, May 1956.
‡ One may be seen at the Victoria & Albert Museum.

spected (the younger) Thomas Harris's organ at Salisbury;* and it
is reasonable to suppose (his specification strongly suggests it) that
among others he also heard the opinion of a former Exeter chorister, now organist at Westminster Abbey, as well as private
organist to Charles II—Christopher Gibbons. Indeed the compositions of Gibbons represent the transition to the new style of organ
music in much the same way as Loosemore's organ heralds what is
to come as far as tonal design is concerned. The two correspond.
The Exeter specification was as follows:

Exeter Cathedral
(John Loosemore, 1665/6)

Great		Chair	
Double Diapason	16	Stopped Diapason	8
(Bass only, 14 pipes)		Principal	4
Open Diapason I	8	Flute	4
Open Diapason II	8	Fifteenth	2
Stopped Diapason	8	Bassoon	8
Principal	4		
Twelfth	$2\frac{2}{3}$		
Fifteenth	2		
Sesquialtera	V		
Cornet	V		
Trumpet	8		

Such an instrument was remarkable not merely for first introducing the Double Diapason, an imaginative attempt to meet the
English lack of pedals, but more especially for the remarkable step
forward it represented tonally. Here for the first time in England
appear reeds and mixtures—several years before Smith's best
known work.

The Exeter organ was destined to have a long life of notoriety.
Loosemore's workmanship must have been of a remarkably high
standard. It was repaired fifty years later, by Christopher Schrider†
in 1713; while in 1740 the Dean and Chapter once again took outside advice, from the Westminster Abbey organist John Robinson,

* See p. 191.
† See p. 199.

which resulted in Abraham Jordan* (the younger) repairing and altering the instrument. He carried the famous Double Diapason through the whole range of the 55 notes, and also added a small Swell Organ—which his father had pioneered since 1712; the rest of the organ remained tonally as Loosemore built it. The next alterations were not made until the nineteenth century.

A number of accounts of distinguished visitors mentioned the organ. Macaulay describes the visit to the Cathedral by the Prince of Orange in 1688:†

> As he passed under the gorgeous screen, that renowned organ, scarcely surpassed by any of those which are the boast of his native Holland, gave out a peal of triumph.

Much later, another well-known visitor to Exeter, John Wesley, was to record in his diary:‡

> *29th August, 1762*
> Such an organ I never saw or heard before, so large, so beautiful, and so finely toned; and the music of 'Glory to God in the highest', I think, exceeded the *Messiah* itself.

Another important builder whose work developed with the times was Thomas Thamer ('of Cambridge'). His new organ for Winchester Cathedral, which he built in 1665, was practically identical to Thomas Dallam's Double Organ at Worcester, of fifty years previously, except that Thamer added a mixture to the Great ('one furniture of Tynn'). However, nine years later, the organ he made for Pembroke College, Cambridge, was much more adventurous, and included on the Great, apart from the traditional Diapason stops, a Twelfth, Sesquialtera, Cornet and Trumpet.§ Clearly he had become aware of new developments during the intervening years. But Thamer's organ at Winchester did not last long; in 1693 the Dean and Chapter invited Renatus Harris to replace it.

* See p. 199.
† See Betty Matthews *The Organs & Organists of Exeter Cathedral* p. 7.
‡ See Erik Routley *The Musical Wesleys*, p. 10.
§ This organ, still with some original material, now stands in Framlingham Church, Suffolk.

Renatus Harris (165?–1724)

Renatus Harris, grandson of Thomas Dallam, was one of a continuous line of organ builders spanning at least six generations:

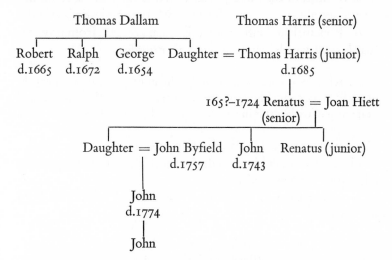

The organ which Thomas Harris (junior) re-built in Salisbury Cathedral at the Restoration was a traditional and unexceptional double organ; it can hardly have been from this source that Loosemore derived his exciting ideas for his Exeter specification. Nevertheless this 1661 organ was for the Harris family the beginning of a long and highly fruitful association with Salisbury.

Although Renatus Harris's first cathedral organ was built in 1677 at Chichester, his most characteristic work was done after 1690 at such London churches as St Bride's, Fleet Street (1696), St Andrew's, Undershaft (1696) and St Andrew's, Holborn (1699). Following Winchester (1693), his finest cathedral organ was without doubt that at Salisbury, in 1710.

Already in 1688, after his father's death, he had repaired and altered the old Salisbury instrument. The modifications that he carried out included altering one of the Great Organ Fifteenths into a Choir Organ Larigot. He did similar work at Norwich Cathedral in 1690, where he added a Furniture and Mixture to

Robert Dallam's organ (built in 1663); also at Magdalen College, Oxford, in 1690. These modifications reflect his French influence,* and also one of his chief contributions to the development of tonal design at this period, namely the avoidance of the traditional duplication of stops of the same pitch. Whereas the early seventeenth century specifications normally included two ranks each of Diapasons, Principals and Fifteenths, this practice ceased from now on. Harris's own words† sum up the new attitude:

> . . . when two unisons are together in an organ as two principals, two fifteenths, etc, (that) they never agree well together in tune, and one stop of each sort is in a manner as loud as two of the same name.

Renatus Harris avoided duplication of stops of the same quality and pitch; as a result his tonal designs consisted of the progressive build-up of separate ranks.

The culmination of this process was reached in the Salisbury specification (1710):

Salisbury Cathedral
(Renatus Harris, 1710)

Great		Choir		Echo	
(playable on 2 manuals)					
Open Diapason I	8	Open Diapason	8	Open Diapason	8
Open Diapason II	8	Stopped Diapason	8	Stopped Diapason	8
Stopped Diapason	8	Principal	4	Principal	4
Principal	4	Flute	4	Flute	4
Flute	4	Twelfth	$2\frac{2}{3}$	Twelfth	$2\frac{2}{3}$
Twelfth	$2\frac{2}{3}$	Fifteenth	2	Fifteenth	2
Fifteenth	2	Bassoon	8	Tierce	$1\frac{3}{5}$
Tierce	$1\frac{3}{5}$			Larigot	$1\frac{1}{3}$
Larigot	$1\frac{2}{3}$			Trumpet	8
Sesquialtera	IV			Cromhorn	8

* Harris used several French stop-names, such as Tierce, Larigot, Furniture and Cart (or quart).

† From 'The proposal of Renatus Harris to the Reverend the President and Fellows of Magdalen College in Oxford, for the repairing and making several alterations in their organ, 17 July 1686'. c.f. Rimbault *The Early English Organ Builders* pp. 89–92.

Great (contd)		Choir (contd)	Echo (contd)	
Cornet	V		Vox Humana	8
Trumpet	8			
Clarion	4			
Cromhorn	8			
Vox Humana	8			

The Great Organ stops were available, except for one of the Open Diapasons, on another manual. Salisbury thus possessed the first four-manual instrument in England. It is extremely unfortunate that the marvellous potential of this organ does not seem to have been fully realised and sustained by eighteenth-century Salisbury musicians. Evidently the musical tradition of the Cathedral, at one time the strongest of any in England,[*] had fallen into desuetude and laxity; whereas earlier organists had included such front-ranking musicians as Giles Tomkins[†] and Daniel Roseingrave (Thomas's father), the eighteenth century shows no such comparable figures. At all events, for whatever reason, mediocrity and reaction finally triumphed in 1789–1792, when Harris's fine organ was replaced with a nondescript one by George III's favourite organ builder Samuel Green—a dismal foretaste of what the nineteenth century held in store.

Renatus Harris's style is equally well shown in the instrument he built for St Andrew's Church, Holborn in 1699. Indeed this specification may almost be said to be the standard one round which the eighteenth century organ composers worked. Moreover, for the first time, a 4ˡ reed appears:

St Andrew's, Holborn
(Renatus Harris, 1699)

Great				Choir	
Open Diapason	8	} from	⌠	Open Diapason	8
Stopped Diapason	8	} Great	⟨	Stopped Diapason	8
Principal	4	}		Principal	4
Twelfth	2⅔		⌡	Principal	4

[*] C.f. p. 8.

[†] Thomas's half brother, who succeeded his brother John at King's College, Cambridge. His appointment to Salisbury caused a dispute between the Bishop & the Dean. (Stevens *Thomas Tomkins* pp. 16–19.)

Great (contd)		*Choir* (contd)	
Fifteenth	2	Flute	8
Tierce	$1\frac{3}{5}$	Open Flute	4
Larigot	$1\frac{1}{3}$	Twelfth	$2\frac{2}{3}$
Sesquialtera	III	Fifteenth	2
Mixture	II	Tierce	$1\frac{3}{5}$
Cornet	V	Bassoon	8
Trumpet	8	Vox Humana	8
Clarion	4		

Harris's last instrument, that of St Dionis Backchurch (1724) was very similar to St Andrew's, Holborn, including the Great 4¹ Clarion; it also added a third manual, a Swell organ of seven stops.*

Renatus Harris visualised the possibility of pedals, though he never included them in any of his organs. They were mentioned as part of a visionary scheme,† which needless to say never materialised, for a six-manual organ to end all organs, in the West end of St Paul's Cathedral. No doubt his rivalry with 'Father' Smith had something to do with it; more importantly, there may well have been in his mind, since his childhood, memories of French instruments—a *Grande Orgue*, separate and independent from the choir, against a wall which would reflect the sound; grand, majestic, remote.

But meanwhile he had to deal with the facts of the situation; and in England, where churches and cathedrals were generally smaller than in France, the organ could not be so remote. Moreover it continued to be thought of partly as an accompaniment to voices, and not so much for solo playing, as was the case on the continent. As far as introducing pedals was concerned, the chief hindrance by far was the tradition and style of playing and composition that had developed in England since the very beginning of keyboard music. Organists, whether composers or executants, did not conceive of music which used pedals, whether indepen-

* It was largely constructed by his son. (See correspondence in the Guildhall Library.)
† Quoted in Clutton and Niland *The British Organ*, pp. 80–81.

dently or not. Their introduction therefore would need to be very gradual; and it is highly significant that an ambivalent attitude was to persist right through the nineteenth century, since neither builders nor organists were fully aware of the need for, and purpose of, a pedal organ. The mistaken idea that pedals are a downward extension of the manuals was to persist for many years; indeed its origin may be seen in Loosemore's Double Diapason at Exeter. Loosemore had made his Double Diapason available just for the lowest 14 notes of the Great manual; and it was merely the logical continuation of this principle to allot these notes to the pedals. This was done, and the pedal board thereby made an early appearance, at St Mary Redcliffe, Bristol, in the organ built by Renatus Harris's son John in 1726, working with his brother-in-law, John Byfield. The instrument otherwise carries on the established tradition of Renatus Harris. So pedal keys appeared—but not yet a 'pedal organ'.

Father Smith

Bernard Smith came from Halle soon after the Restoration. It is quite likely that he was of English extraction. An organ built in Diss Manor House, Norfolk, in 1643, is signed clearly Christian Smith, probably Bernard's uncle. It is reasonable to suppose that the family moved to the Continent during the Commonwealth. After 1660 Bernard became established and well-known in England slightly earlier than Renatus Harris; moreover he had the benefit of Royal patronage, starting with the King's commission to build the new organ for the Chapel at Whitehall in 1662. This advantage stayed with him throughout his life. Not only did he build the organs in Westminster Abbey and St Paul's Cathedral, but during that extraordinary episode, the six-year 'battle of the organs' (1682–1688),[*] he was able to call on the King's musicians, Blow and Purcell, to demonstrate his instrument, while his less fortunate

---

[*] Between the Benchers of the Middle Temple, who favoured Smith, and the Benchers of the Inner Temple, who favoured Harris, as the builders of their new instrument for the Temple Church.

rival Renatus Harris had to be content with an Italian player, Giovanni Battista Draghi. It is therefore not altogether surprising that Smith's instrument was finally chosen.

Temple Church
(Father Smith, 1684/8)

Great		*Chair*		*Echo* (short compass)	
Prestand	8	Gedackt	8	Gedacht	8
(open Diapason)		(Stop Diapason)		(Stop Diapason)	
Holflute	8	Hohlflute	4	Flute	4
(Stop Diapason)		(Nason)		(Principal)	
Gedackt	4	'A Sadt'	4	Gedackt	4
(Nason)		(Principal)		(Nason)	
Principal	4	Spitts Flute	2	Super Octavo	2
		(Fifteenth)		(Fifteenth)	
Quinta	$2\frac{2}{3}$	'A violl & violin'	8	Cornet	III
(Twelfth)		(Cromhorn)			
Super Octavo	2	Voice Humane	8	Sesquialtera	IV
(Fifteenth)		(Vox Humana)			
Cornet	IV			Trumpet	8
Sesquialtera	III				
Mixture	IV				
Trumpet	8				

Names in brackets are the equivalents later used by Smith's foreman and son-in-law, Christopher Schrider. Not the least of the novel features of this instrument, by which no doubt Smith sought to outbid his rival, were the introduction of the Echo manual—its first appearance in England—and also the use of double keys for G♯–A♭ and D♯–E♭.* The continental names of some of the stops show the Dutch and North German influence on him.

During his first years in England, after the Whitehall Chapel organ (1662), Smith built small organs, such as Dulwich College Chapel (1670), and the Sheldonian Theatre, Oxford (1671). The first of these was remarkable in that its Great, although only of

---

* Organs were tuned to mean-tone temperament; equal temperament was not used until the nineteenth century. However, such quarter-notes were not generally used, as they presented great problems to the player.

seven stops, included a Sesquialtera, Cornet and Trumpet; while
the second probably resulted in his being asked back to Oxford a
few years later to build a new organ in Christ Church (1680), in
which he consolidated his ideas of tonal design, as they then stood:

Christ Church, Oxford
(Father Smith, 1680)

Great		Chair	
Open Diapason	8	Stopped Diapason	8
Stopped Diapason	8	Principal	4
Principal	4	Flute	4
Twelfth	$2\frac{2}{3}$	Fifteenth	2
Fifteenth	2		
Tierce	$1\frac{3}{5}$		
Sesquialtera	III		
Cornet	V		
Trumpet	8		

An almost identical instrument, but with the addition of a Vox
Humana, and 'Trimeloe' was built for St Mary-at-Hill in 1692/3
and he further pursued the possibilities of the short-compass third
manual, which he had introduced in the Temple organ, in the
organs for St Paul's Cathedral (1695/7), and the Whitehall Banqueting House, (1699). The St Paul's Cathedral organ was without
doubt one of his most important, if only because so many composers (notably Greene and Handel), used it as their model. It was
officially opened on 2nd December, 1697 at a service of thanks-
giving for the Treaty of Ryswick.*

St Paul's Cathedral
(Father Smith, 1695/7)

Great		Chair		Echo (short compass)	
Open Diapason I	8	Stopped Diapason	8	(Stopped?) Diapason	8
Open Diapason II	8	Quintadena	8	Principal	4
Stopped Diapason	8	Principal	4	Nason (Flute)	4
Principal	4	Holfleut	4	Fifteenth	2
Holfleut	4	Great Twelfth	$2\frac{2}{3}$	Cornet	II[?]

* The Cathedral itself was not fully completed until 1715.

Great (contd)		*Chair* (contd)		*Echo* (contd)	
Great Twelfth	2⅔	Fifteenth	2	Trumpet	8
Fifteenth	2	Cimball	III[?]		
Small Twelfth	1⅓	Voice Humaine	8		
Sesquialtera	III[?]	Crumhorne	8		
Mixture	III[?]				
Cornet	V				
Trumpet	8				

The Banqueting House organ was very similar to this, but with fewer stops (nineteen, as compared with twenty seven). Although the Westminster Abbey specification has not survived, it is no very difficult task to deduce what it must have been, in the light of Smith's established style by this time. His organ in St Paul's stood on the choir screen, and remained unaltered for over a century. It was not removed until the screen itself was, in 1860.

Apart from such major contracts, which represent the summit of his achievement, Smith did highly characteristic work in building smaller organs, and especially chamber organs. Several are even still preserved to-day in private collections.* The most outstanding by far, because Noel Mander has restored it to playing condition, is the organ at Adlington Hall, near Macclesfield in Cheshire,† which Smith built in *c.* 1670, at about the same time as the Dulwich College instrument. It stands in a gallery between two oak trees at the end of the Great Hall. The specification is as follows:

(The original spelling is reproduced)

Adlington Hall
(Father Smith, *c.*1670)

Great		*Choir*	
Opn Diopason	8	St Diopason	8
St Diopason	8	St Flute	4

---

* Such as that of the Marquis of Northampton at Compton Wynates. Noel Mander possesses one, which was built for New College, Oxford, and is still in its original state, except for the later addition of a Mixture by Bishop in 1845.

† The home of the Legh family since the fourteenth century.

Great (contd)		Chair (contd)	
Principall	4	Vox Humana	8
Twelfth	$2\frac{2}{3}$		
Bl Flute Bas	2		
Bl Flute Trib	2		
Fifteenth	2		
Ters	$1\frac{3}{8}$		
Sm Twelfth	$1\frac{1}{3}$		
2 and Twenty	1		
Bassoon	8		
Trumpet	8		

After Smith's death in 1708, his business was carried on by Christopher Schrider, his son-in-law; meanwhile his nephews Gerard and Christian Smith had begun to build organs independently. Gerard Smith built an organ in a newly-built church in Hanover Square, which was to be of great importance, as it was the instrument that Thomas Roseingrave played, and later John Keeble:

St George's, Hanover Square
(Gerard Smith, 1725)

Great		Choir		Echo (short compass)	
Open Diapason	8	Stopped Diapason	8	Open Diapason	8
Stopped Diapason	8	Principal	4	Stopped Diapason	8
Principal	4	Flute	4	Cornet	III
Twelfth	$2\frac{2}{3}$	Fifteenth	2	Hautboy	8
Fifteenth	2	Vox Humana	8	Trumpet	8
Sesquialtera	IV			Cremorne	8
Cornet	V				
Trumpet	8				
Clarion	4				

This specification only departs from Father Smith's style in the 4¹ reed. This was an addition of the eighteenth century, introduced by Renatus Harris, not by Smith, whose reeds were invariably of just 8¹ pitch. The other main addition at this time was the Swell box, with adjustable shutters, which Abraham Jordan introduced at St Magnus the Martyr, London Bridge in 1712. Henceforward therefore the *Echo* manual becomes the *Swell*; also the *Chair* becomes the *Choir*.

But the invention of the Swell box, which simulates a crescendo or diminuendo, was a purely mechanical innovation, whose origin was in the mind of an organ builder, and was of little or no concern to the composers of organ music. Its effect was of limited musical interest, and it therefore found very little place in eighteenth-century organ music, because it was out of keeping with the organ style of the Voluntary or Fugue, that had by this time become securely established.

5

1759–1837

THE EIGHTEENTH CENTURY VOLUNTARY (II)

The background

By the death of Handel, the Voluntary had come into its own. This was a period which saw a great spread in the performance of music of all kinds, and the organ was in demand in many other places than just cathedrals and churches; it was now used in theatres, in taverns, in coffee-houses, in the newly fashionable concert-rooms, in pleasure-gardens, and in private houses. The eighteenth century was one of popularisation of music; the diatonic idiom was universally accepted; music spread to include the newly-emerging middle class, the prosperous merchants, the *bourgeoisie*. The well-to-do, the aristocratic, patronised the Italian opera, or the concerts at one of the fashionable *salons*, such as the Argyll Rooms, or Hanover Square; those of a humbler calling patronised, in their teeming hundreds, the pleasure-gardens of Marylebone, Vauxhall or Ranelagh.

No doubt this great increase in the popular demand for music was related to the declining influence of the Chapel Royal. The days when the greatest composers were as a matter of course in the service of the monarch were now gone; by the later eighteenth century not one organ composer of significance was organist of Westminster Abbey or St Paul's Cathedral; the last representative of the former tradition was William Boyce. Instead the more active organists and composers were appointed to London churches, of which there were a large number. Thus would they have time to spare for the increasingly numerous opportunities which eighteenth-century London had to offer. The greatest composer of this period, Samuel Wesley, was entirely independent of any church appointment, or indeed an appointment of any kind, royal or otherwise, until he was nearly sixty years old. The outward form of the Chapel Royal remained, but the inner substance was lacking.

Certain London churches developed strong musical reputations, and were much sought after as a result. The Temple church, St Dionis Backchurch, St George's Hanover Square, St Martin's-in-the-Fields, the Foundling Hospital were among the best known, and attracted the finest musicians of the day.

The duties of the organist in these churches were not onerous. Frequently he would be required to improvise—which no doubt partly explains why the *extempore* style became so ingrained into eighteenth-century organ music, whether written or performed. The ability to improvise, made possible by the universal acceptance of a common diatonic idiom, was an essential part of an organist's technique.

The liturgical organ repertoire had long since disappeared. There were no hymns in the Anglican liturgy, and the people only sang psalms. Between the verses of the psalms, and again before the first Lesson, the organist would play interludes on the psalm-tune. Several organ composers published their versions of psalm-tunes with interludes; Reading, Hook, Kirkman, Keeble, Blewitt and Goodwin. Musically this procedure is of very slight value; but the introduction of the congregational hymn was of greater importance, and this was due to the Methodists. Both John and Charles Wesley saw the importance of filling this need; later, in the 1820s, Samuel Wesley wrote over a hundred harmonised tunes, modelled on Bach chorales; but these have remained out of use. Meanwhile the chief developments of organ music of this time, in the form of the Voluntary and Organ Concerto, were non-liturgical, or secular.

The Music

Just because the Voluntary had become securely established by the middle of the eighteenth century, it is only natural to expect that the work of many composers of the rank and file should be somewhat stereotyped and formal. One such is Burney, whose Voluntaries continue fairly and squarely in the mainstream of his predecessors. His style is straightforward, and the Handel influence is particularly marked; the right hand part is chiefly melodic, while the secondary left hand part provides the harmonic background.

Another minor composer, more strongly influenced by Stanley, who was his senior by twelve years, was the Oxford organist William Walond. His music, however, lacks the subtlety of Stanley; the sequences are more direct, and occasionally mechanical (such as those of the Fugue in Op. 1 No. 6), or disjointed (such as those of Op. 2 No. 3). A comparison of a Siciliano by each composer illustrates the difference of phrase construction between them:

Example 48

a) Voluntary in D minor, Op. 6 No. 1   Stanley

b) Voluntary in D minor, Op. 1 No. 3   Walond

Walond makes no thematic or motivic link between the movements of a voluntary; several are in one single movement—Op. 2, Nos. 3, 6, 7, 8. He was however one of the first to allow for a Swell box crescendo.

Far the most remarkable work of the immediate post-Handel period* was that of an otherwise unknown and obscure organist, John Bennett. He must have enjoyed an enviable reputation, since the list of those who subscribed to the publication of his Voluntaries, which were published when he was only twenty-three, reads like a roll-call of the most notable musicians of the day; apart from Handel, Travers and Burney, it included Savage, organist of St Paul's, Langdon, organist of Exeter Cathedral, and Imings, a lutenist of the Chapel Royal.

What makes Bennett's Voluntaries particularly interesting is his avoidance of stereotyped, ordinary figures associated at this time with such solo stops as the Trumpet, French Horn, or Cornet; instead the composer makes great expressive use of the full range of the keyboard. He is also a master of chromaticism, and the harmonic interest goes a long way towards sustaining the tension of the music. He combines homophony with polyphony; he has a genuine contrapuntal ability, as well as a sense of organ sonority.

The Voluntaries, of which the last four are fugal, are written in three parts. The slow opening movements are substantial, and often finish with flourishes or quick scales. The exception to this general rule is the Voluntary for full organ No. 9, in which after an Adagio of only four bars, finishing on a half-close, the composer suddenly breaks into an Allegro, with semiquaver runs. This is marked 'Full organ without the trumpet'—meaning, presumably, that the opening Adagio was 'Full organ with the Trumpet'. Is Bennett deliberately surprising the audience, who would naturally expect the slow section to continue? But once he is embarked on the Allegro, nothing can stop it. There follows another Adagio section; then a final fugue, which is confined to quaver movement, until the end, when it recalls the semiquaver runs. This work is therefore, in effect, a four-movement Voluntary.

---

* His Voluntaries were published in 1758.

After Bennett, it was over twenty years before the Voluntary
was injected with fresh vitality, and given a fresh sense of direction,
in the hands of the highly inventive and original composer and
organist of St George's Hanover Square, John Keeble. In the mean-
time several sets were published whose merits were very real, but
which did not effectively extend the territory already opened up.

Samuel Long's output though small was of a high standard;
it was published posthumously by his widow in 1770. His four
harpsichord 'lessons' are charming pieces in the *galant* style usually
associated with J. C. Bach; his two organ Voluntaries, both fugal,
are somewhat more severe, though their substantial subjects are
well maintained. The slow sections give the composer an opportunity for the use of characteristic rhythmic patterns; that of the first
Voluntary is in triplets, that of the second in dotted notes.

The interest in Nares's Voluntaries centres chiefly on those that
have Introductions—Nos. 1, 3, 5. He calls his works 'Six fugues
with introductory Voluntaries'—a confusion of terms if ever there
was one. If his fugue subjects are somewhat ordinary and lack
spontaneity, it is in the three introductions that Nares shows a
possible way towards an individual expansion of the Voluntary—
such an expansion as was indeed to come later. The three introductions all differ, finishing on a half-close, and show the composer
at his most natural, in the style that he put to further use in his
'lessons' for harpsichord. The introduction to the first fugue is a
long, rhapsodic, unfolding melody; that to the third is full, homophonic; that to the fifth develops freely, like a fantasia, full of
colour.

The danger that the Voluntary, as a form, was becoming ossified
by about 1770 is further suggested by the work of three other
composers; John Alcock (senior), Starling Goodwin, and George
Green. Alcock's pieces, published after he left Lichfield Cathedral
and was at Sutton Coldfield, show him as somewhat conventional
in his figurations, ordinary in his invention of themes, and rudimentary in his structures. Moreover, except in one case, the fifth
Voluntary, he is ill at ease in modulatory or chromatic passages.
For instance the Trumpet tune in the sixth Voluntary only makes
one brief modulation outside the key of D throughout the entire

course of its 101 bars. Harmonic progression is not the strongest aspect of Alcock's technique, and occasionally, as in the seventh Voluntary, becomes laboured. Indeed the chromatic fourth with which this piece interestingly opens, is unfortunately not maintained.

And so it is the exceptional points of style that stand out in such surroundings, like trees in a desert. For instance, he is one of the first composers to use the Cremona as a solo stop; again, the ninth Voluntary begins with a *moto perpetuo* in quavers, which is carried over with a dotted rhythm into the trumpet tune, with simple but telling effect. The dot is reversed in the descending phrase:

Example 49

Voluntary No. 9 in D minor/major
(Opening of first and second movements)   Alcock

Far the most original of the set is the fifth Voluntary, in which a texture of two equal and characteristic parts is maintained with great effect. Against held chords for the Choir flutes in the right hand the left hand has a moving part in crotchets, with Diapason, Principal and Sesquialtera; a bold and unusual organ colour. Only one of the Voluntaries, the tenth, ends with a fugue; Alcock was not a great contrapuntist.

Starling Goodwin and George Green might serve as the typical eighteenth century composers. Thoroughly competent, speaking the standard language, following the established patterns. The melodic shapes, the cadences, the sequential harmonies, in short the musical style as a whole, represents a reaping of that harvest already sown by Handel, Greene and Stanley. Rules and conventions are important for a musical or artistic tradition, even if they are bad rules; they provide the point of departure for future development. The Voluntaries of these two composers represent the standard, conventional pattern that had evolved by 1770. Only very occasionally can they be brought up on technical grounds—such as Goodwin's use of chords for the Cornet stop; but then they rarely, if at all, venture outside or beyond what had already been tried and proven by others.

John Keeble 1711–1786

After such comparatively minor figures, a very different picture, and a foretaste of what was to come, is presented by the work of John Keeble. The first three of his four books of Organ works, which he called 'Pieces' not 'Voluntaries', were published by himself; the fourth by Longman and Broderip.

His musical thought was intricate, contrapuntal, his structures large-scale; his double fugues make him the successor to Roseingrave—who had also been his predecessor at St George's, Hanover Square. His fugues are substantial, and thus allow time for the working out of the possibilities inherent in their subject-material. The construction of themes or subjects out of many contrasted particles is not confined to fugues; for instance the Trumpet Voluntary (No. 8) is another example of this process, which gives a breadth to the music.

Keeble was fond of the spread chord, *arpeggiando*;* also of the half-close in an arioso movement—the essence of the *galant* style, which thus gained a momentary but quite real foothold in organ music at about this time. He gives only the most general indication of registration, as if he were thinking more of pure counterpoint, and less of specific organ colours.

His use of harmony is often most unusual, and voice-entries erratic. If there was to be a choice between theory and practice, Keeble invariably opted for practice. The opening of the fugue in the ninth Voluntary is a case in point; the third beat of the third bar is a $^6_4$ chord. Another example of his highly personal and expressive chromaticism (of the sort that Nares objected to) occurs in the Largo of No. 16:

---

* For example in No. 1, second movement, and No. 8, first movement.

Example 50

Voluntary No. 16 in D minor   Keeble
(bars 10-12)
Largo

etc.

The first three volumes of his pieces all contain the same preface, which clearly reflects the considered views of an active professional organist in the mid-eighteenth century:

> The obligato style of writing, which consists of fugues, inversions, canons, double descants, and the like, is interwoven in many parts of these compositions; and figures are placed over each of these parts, as they occur, more readily to compare one with the others.
>
> This style of writing, so proper for the church, has of late been too much neglected by the young professors, from an opinion of its dryness, want of wit, and destroying the true and original spirit of genius. How far I have succeeded in removing this objection, by the freedom of modulation, is now submitted to the public. . . .
>
> The subject proper for a Fugue may be considered as a kind of Canto Fermo, on which a great variety of Descant is discovered. It should be such as may engage the attention and, like a Theme, or simple Proposition, be capable of divisions and sub-divisions; by which means we have not only a greater variety of modulation, but very often other subjects of a secondary nature are discovered, which in their turn relieve the attention from a too frequent repetition of the first, or principal one, and at the same time prevent that sameness, so often objected to in this species of writing, which rather fatigues than pleases.
>
> For this reason, the most artful parts of composition should be employed, especially when it is considered that we have no articulation, as in choral music, to mark and give strength to the subjects; nor the assistance of different species of voices, to distinguish them in their places of Acute and Grave; and above all that we are destitute of Poetical sentiment, which stamps a character so truly animating on the subjects of the chorus.
>
> The Fugue, on the organ, being destitute of these advantages must

seek to supply the defect, as much as possible, by art; and thus imitations, points, inversions, double descant, canons and the like, or some of them, may be called in to our aid; which, as they contribute so much to relieve and enliven the principal subject, lead us with greater pleasure towards a conclusion; whose every power of harmony must be exerted, and, if possible, the several scattered parts should be collected, like the rays of light, into one point of view, that the whole may receive an additional strength, from the union of the several parts.

The placing of numbers over the subject-entries was a most useful idea,* and served to pinpoint the nature of the composer's thought. This had two chief sides to it, the lyrical and the architectural; the lyrical side, the *cantabile* element of Keeble's style, led him to a certain expansiveness, often with two parts over a bass, like chamber music; the architectural side led him to build large structures, often fugues, and to explore the full range of the keyboard. This was the way forward for the Voluntary; Keeble thus prepared the way for Samuel Wesley.

Keeble used the major and minor key of each note.† His twenty-four pieces fall into the following scheme:

Key	Major	Minor
C	4, 8, 12	14, 22
D	2, 20, 6	10, 16
E	18	(3rd movement of 12)
F	11, 13, 23	3, 7
G	1, 15	5, 9
A	17	21
B flat	24	—
(G) Chromatic—19		

No. 19 is experimental, without a key; beginning and ending on a D major chord, the middle movement is in E flat. If this is an

---

* A similar procedure was followed much later in the published scores of Schönberg, Berg & Webern and others of the second Viennese School—whose textures were also contrapuntal.

† Organs were still tuned in mean-tone temperament. Keeble was also a theorist; his *The Theory of Harmonics* was entered at Stationers' Hall on 10th December, 1784.

exceptional case, Keeble's harmony is always complex; the transition section of No. 3 illustrates this point.

Every one of his pieces is differently constructed. His mastery of counterpoint is formidable; for instance the fugue in No. 10 is a striking example of canon at the twelfth. Another interesting case is No. 12, which is a solitary and exceptional example at this time of variations on a rising and falling 4-note figure—like the old hexachord variations, which fell into disuse after the Restoration.

William Boyce 1710–1779

If Keeble's work was disturbing, as it no doubt was, to his more orthodox contemporaries, the mainstream of the Voluntary continued to flow serenely, yet effectively, in the ten Voluntaries of William Boyce,* which were published five years later, in 1785.

They are all in two movements, of which the second, quick, movement presents a different thematic treatment of the material inherent in the first. This procedure, inherited from Greene, suggests an analogy with the Prelude and Fugue of the German School.

Example 51

Voluntary No. 8 in C   Boyce
(Opening of first and second movements)   [Vivace]
    [Largo]
Full organ   etc.

As in the case of Travers, the last four Voluntaries of Boyce's set are fugal. His fugues are short, polished, and registered for Full Organ. No. 10 ends with a double fugue. As in the solo movements, the composer introduces modulations in the middle sections; the recapitulations in Nos. 7, 8 and 9 occur in the bass part, which would be effectively played on a double stop, if available.

* Whose work was also published by Thompson.

Those quick second movements that are not fugal are also fairly short; the music is not involved.

Voluntary No. 2 uses the Vox humana as a solo stop, while numerous felicities of technique may be noticed in the other pieces; the recapitulation in No. 1 takes up the trumpet theme half way; in No. 4 it occurs an octave higher; while the middle section of No. 5 is an ingenious diminution of the subject.

These two aspects of the Voluntary, the orthodox (Boyce) and the experimental (Keeble), represent the farthest points reached in the later eighteenth century, whose closing years produced nothing further of any original worth. Kirkman, who was Keeble's successor at St George's, Hanover Square, was not an original composer, and his style varies according to his source. Worgan also was more of an executive than a creative musician, and his extremely simple pieces—perhaps improvisations recollected—show little more than rudimentary powers of invention. Blewitt was a teacher, who also wrote simple ballads with which he regaled his audience at the Spa Gardens, Bermondsey. It would be vain to pretend that his organ pieces were intended as anything more than illustrations for his treatise *On the Organ*; this is however quite a useful summary of the late eighteenth-century instrument.

In spite of his large output, Dupuis broke no fresh ground either. Indeed the majority of his pieces were technically easy, and directed at the young or inexperienced player. Dupuis fell in with this well-known commercial habit of publishers to produce volumes of short and simple pieces that require no practice, and are thus more likely to find acceptance among the less assiduous organists—who form a disarmingly large proportion; but in so doing he fettered his creative freedom.

His real work was concentrated into nine of his Voluntaries which were published posthumously in 1800. Although his modifications to the Voluntary, as far as organ style is concerned, are minimal, he does introduce some colourful and skilful writing. He was a painstaking composer, whose every effort was carefully calculated; yet there is no figuration or harmonic progression that would have caused a moment's heart-searching to his teacher Travers.

Nor for that matter did George Guest write anything in his Voluntaries Op. 3, published in 1808,* that Greene could not have written seventy-five years earlier. Guest was cast in a conservative mould, like Nares; there is only one fugue, in the last Voluntary, which closes the set, perhaps appropriately, with a Handelian flourish.

James Hook's talent lay in light music; those simple, tuneful ballads, so much in demand at this time, with which he caught the ear of the less discriminating pleasure-seekers in Vauxhall Gardens, and of which his best-known example was *The Lass of Richmond Hill*. His organ Voluntaries form a very unimportant part of his work, and while containing clean-cut, serviceable music, make no pretensions whatever to any lasting merit.

Two other minor figures hardly contributed materially. After his brilliant early years as an infant prodigy, who had played to the King at the age of three, and also to the aged Stanley, Crotch's work deteriorated and became merely academic. And Wesley's friend Thomas Adams was clearly more of a virtuoso performer than a composer. Though he explored certain avenues which Wesley was to follow up, his pieces otherwise suggest those less desirable aspects of nineteenth-century organ writing that were later to supplant the traditional style; orchestral writing for instance, with a greater importance laid on harmony at the expense of counterpoint.

Pre-Wesley composers

In spite of some overlapping of dates, two composers' work may be seen chiefly as preparing the ground for Wesley, in so far as their Voluntaries foreshadowed change; these were Battishill and Cooke. A third composer, born eleven years after Wesley, worked very much under his shadow, and thus clearly belongs in the same line of musical descent—William Russell.

* The date is known from a mention of Beckwith at Norwich (1808).

Jonathan Battishill, whose work was published posthumously by John Page, a Vicar Choral of St Paul's, composed on a miniature scale; nevertheless his pieces, however small, indicate a fresh approach to the Voluntary. His are exquisite miniatures in the *galant* style—which Wesley was to adopt and incorporate into the Voluntary itself. The second of Battishill's Voluntaries is the longest, in the form of a Rondo in A major.

Benjamin Cooke's pieces, too, are slender and, like Battishill's, were published after his death. Yet his organ textures are new, as the seventh piece shows. His structures are not stereotyped, and he frequently writes in more than three parts. But Cooke was not a fluent contrapuntist, and his parts soon ossify into chords; he even uses thick chords against fugue subjects; yet sometimes, as in the sixth fugue, he betrays the ingenuity of a good Pepusch* pupil, with inversion, stretto and so on. And occasionally some bold, dramatic strokes, such as occur in the fifth piece, betray the stirrings of that romantic temperament, beneath which the Voluntary was shortly to evolve. Like Keeble, Cooke avoided the word 'Voluntary'; indeed he sometimes wrote with little relationship to the traditional Voluntary. For instance the Cornet tune in the second piece is most untypical of an eighteenth-century Cornet Voluntary. Cooke wrote arpeggios, not scale runs; and his tempo is measured, not fast.

William Russell 1777–1813

But apart from Wesley himself, the composer who contributed most to the growth of the Voluntary at this time was, without doubt, William Russell. It is not impossible that he may even have been Wesley's pupil; certainly they were closely acquainted. The elder man must have been delighted when he (Russell) became organist at the Foundling Hospital in 1805, where only seven years earlier he had himself been rejected, in favour of a nonentity.

Russell's two books of Voluntaries were published in 1804 and

---

* J. C. Pepusch (1667–1752) was a German, resident in London, who taught counterpoint and composition. He directed concerts of the Academy of Ancient Music, and arranged various pastiche-operas, including *The Beggar's Opera* (1728).

1812 respectively, and dedicated 'to the Governors and Guardians of the Foundling Hospital'. Apart from their originality of effect and freedom of invention, their greatest characteristic is a more precise, systematic approach to registration. Russell carefully calculated the degree of contrast between different organ sonorities.

Thus in a Cornet Voluntary, with the left hand playing on the Choir, the echo to the Great Cornet is another Cornet on the Swell. The Trumpet however, on the Great, is always set against a contrasting tone on the Swell, while the left hand is allotted Choir Stopped Diapason 8 and Flute 4.

Again, with the left hand accompanying on the Great, a Swell oboe is set against a Choir Cremona; or a Choir Cremona is set against a French Horn, 'or diapasons'.

A movement with reed-tone will be followed by one for Full Organ, or other foundation stops; similarly a movement with flute-tone will be followed by one for reeds; or reeds may be set against diapasons or flutes within the same movement.

Full organ movements are either marches or fugues; the last five Voluntaries of the second book are Preludes and Fugues for Full organ. Russell's idiom allowed for powerful moments; these might come about through the registration, as when he brings both hands onto the Great in a Trumpet movement; or through the structures themselves, which are big and massive. His fugue subjects are impressive; climbing, or arpeggio-centred. The Voluntaries are in three or four movements, whose structure enlarged the scope of the Voluntary as a form, as much as their style extended the expressive range of the eighteenth-century organ—which was the instrument available to all composers up to Wesley.

His structures are never inconsistent. The link between movements is usually one of mood, key or metre rather than theme, though there are exceptions to this. In the seventh Voluntary of the first book, the link is one of a dotted rhythm, while in the eighth Voluntary of the same book the fugue subject is a 3-note *motif* in augmentation. Often a fugue in $\frac{4}{4}$ or duple metre is preceded by a prelude in triple metre; or vice versa. The exception, in this as in other respects, is the last piece in the second book.

Like Wesley, Russell's style shows the composer's assimilation of many facets of the early organ tradition—new as well as old. He not only adapted the *galant* style, he also harked back to that old form, beloved by organ composers of an earlier age, the hexachord variations. The fugue in the twelfth Voluntary of the first book is a nineteenth century, chromatic version of this timehonoured organ style.

Russell's harmony is rich and adventurous. Again like Wesley, he strongly favoured the minor ninth and the augmented sixth. If the influence of Haydn is clear, the use of violent dynamic changes suggests Beethoven—whose work was not widely known in England until after Russell's death in 1813. He seems to have been the first composer to write a trumpet tune in the minor key; and like Keeble he wrote his Voluntaries in all the keys of the mean-tempered scale. One of his fugue subjects, the tenth of the first book, is very similar to one of Wesley's.

In this way the ground was prepared for Wesley, in whose hands the Voluntary reached far beyond anything hitherto attained. The years which he dominated extended from about 1790 onwards, and represent the consummation of the early English tradition; they also represent its conclusion.

Samuel Wesley 1766-1837

The final phase of the early English organ tradition was, as it happened, a glorious one, and was focused on the work of one composer. Many factors combined to make the organ compositions of Samuel Wesley the consummation that they undoubtedly were. He was not only the most outstanding composer that this country had produced for a long time—or indeed was to produce for many a year to come; it also happened to be for the organ that he wrote many of his most characteristic and mature works.

Next, he was a musician with an acute sense of historical perspective; much more so than his contemporaries. He was both knowledgeable about the past and curious about the present. His output exceeded, in size and scope, that of his more fashionable, and infinitely more provincial, colleagues.

His outlook on the musical art, and his creative achievements,

were, within the limits of his environment, a reflection of those of
J. S. Bach, of whose work he was both disciple and champion. The
limitations, both social and cultural, of the England of 1800 were
obvious and very immediate; yet Wesley's aesthetic intentions
were similar in many essential respects to those of his great German
predecessor. His innate and enthusiastic response to Bach's music,*
which he himself pioneered in England, was creative, not parasitic.
Both composers summarised, and consummated, the traditions
of their respective countries; each, in so doing, discovered fresh
techniques and styles of organ composition proper to them.

This fact is all the more remarkable when one considers the
dates between which Wesley worked. His most active years were
1790–1830; that is to say before the birth of Mendelssohn,† when
the torch of Bach's music was kept alight only through the devoted
vision of small, esoteric groups.

There were several ways in which Wesley could have heard
some of Bach's works in London. It could have been through
J. C. Bach, who died when Samuel was 16, or C. F. Abel, who
died in 1787 and had been a former pupil of Bach in Leipzig, and
whose father had played under Bach himself at Cothen; both these
musicians however lacked any depth of understanding of Bach's
greatness. It could more likely have been through the German
violinist and impresario Salomon, or one of the many musicians
(such as Pinto) and composers (such as Haydn) who visited London
through his agency.

Two German musicians, settled in London, in particular deserve
mention in this respect. K. F. Horn, was music teacher to the
Queen and Princesses, and eventually (1823) organist of St George's
Chapel, Windsor; he collaborated with Wesley in 1810–13 in
bringing out an edition of the '48'‡ and the Trio Sonatas, arranged
for three hands on the pianoforte; and A. F. C. Kollmann, originally

---

* So vividly shown in the letters to his friend, the organist Benjamin Jacobs.

† Mendelssohn's discovery of Bach, under his teacher Zelter, and his famous
  'first performance' of the *St Matthew Passion* in Berlin in 1829, are landmarks of
  the nineteenth century.

‡ Though this was not the first edition in England. Lavenu and Broderip each
  printed an edition in 1800 (see Redlich *The Bach revival in England*).

from Hanover, was primarily a teacher, writer and editor, as well as organist of the German Chapel, St James's. Both actively propagated Bach's music.

Clearly Wesley's contemporaries had the same opportunity as he; but only Samuel seems to have had ears to hear.

Strangely enough an external circumstance of Wesley's life bears a resemblance to that of Bach. Samuel's son, Samuel Sebastian, was also a minor composer, whose style was fashioned by a later age, and whose effect tended to obscure his father's full stature, which remained hidden for many years. In Wesley's case, he still awaits discovery; and the fact that his music was not lost was due to two musicians in particular—his friend Vincent Novello, who believed in his greatness, and was his assiduous copyist and propagandist; and his daughter Eliza, also an organist, at St Margaret Pattens, who not only published some of the piano works, but bequeathed many invaluable manuscripts to the British Museum.

His essential qualities have tended to elude biographers.* The trail is indeed set with so many conflicting scents. The nephew of the founder of Methodism, he himself became a Roman Catholic. Though he was acknowledged to be a fine organist and improviser, and many of his works were published in his lifetime (particularly the keyboard works; not so much the vocal works), he was not appointed to any official London church. His life coincided with a period both of decline in the vitality of the Church of England (that very decline which had made Methodism necessary), and of an acceptance of mediocrity which was shortly to lead to the total eclipse of the early musical tradition.

This was indeed a dismal phase of church music in England. Yet in his work, almost alone among British composers of his time, we are shaken out of the enclosed, constricted world of musical and spiritual provincialism, and brought into contact, however briefly, with wider movements; with those great forces that swept through, and transformed, European life and music in the tumultuous opening decades of the nineteenth century. The chief manifestations of this transformation were the discovery by countries of a fresh

---

* The extraordinarily inadequate notes in Ed. 50 are a case in point.

national identity, and by composers of a fresh, independent social status; also the spirit of Romanticism, of which the musical symbol, the embodiment, was the pianoforte; also the great re-birth of religious awareness, after the grim excesses of the Napoleonic wars. The countries of Europe wished to assert their national status and sovereignty, in music as much as in politics; they reacted violently against the hegemony of 'reason' and 'enlightenment'. The concept of European unity that was represented by the Holy Roman Empire had come to an end. Individualism was born.

All these factors, and more besides, underlie Samuel Wesley's music, which was so directly at variance with the eighteenth-century *Zeitgeist*.

The greatness of his achievement differed from that of earlier English composers, such as Byrd or Bull, chiefly because of this estrangement. It is only against the background of his tradition, cultural context and social ethos that a composer's work is best seen; and the England of 1800 was not nearly so susceptible of great music as the England of 1600.

He was born, the youngest of Charles Wesley's three children,* on 24th February, St Mathias's Day, 1766 at Bristol, which had been the place of his father's ministry since 1737. The family lived there until they moved to London in 1778.

Samuel was born into one of the most remarkable families in the land.† His father Charles, best known perhaps as a hymn-

---

* There were eight children altogether, five of whom died in infancy.

† The suggestion that the Wesley and Wellesley families were connected, and that Samuel Wesley was thus a blood-relation of the Duke of Wellington, is not proven. Nevertheless it is a belief which has gained an almost legendary status from frequent repetition, ever since Adam Clark's *Wesley Family* (1823), and many biographies since then of John and Charles Wesley. It has appeared in such eminently respectable works of reference as the *Oxford Companion to Music* and the D.N.B., and is even attributed to Samuel himself by the dilettante William Gardiner (*Music & Friends*, II, p. 654); but in every case the connection has been merely stated; in no case has it been genealogically demonstrated.

The existence of a kinship seems to have been assumed for three chief reasons:

(1) the similarity of name.

writer, and his uncle John, the founder of Methodism, have each been the subject of many biographies. His sister Sarah ('Sally') was born in 1759, and his elder brother Charles, nine years his senior, had displayed a precocious musical talent. From the age of two he played tunes, complete with a bass part, by ear. At the age of four it was suggested to his father that he might enter the Chapel Royal as a chorister. But Charles (senior) viewed his infant prodigy son with mixed feelings, and the thought that he might be launched on a musical career, with an evangelical aversion. In this he tellingly reflected the general opinion of a man of his attainments and social standing at this time.

'I had then no thoughts' he wrote in his journal, 'of bringing him up a musician'.

Nevertheless he was man-of-the-world enough to seek advice from the most eminent musicians, with the result that he had his eldest son professionally taught—by William Boyce. In the event Charles (junior) became a proficient organist, who enjoyed the King's favour—first as his private organist, then, no doubt at Lord Mornington's suggestion, at the Chapel of the Lock Hospital, Grosvenor Place. Afterwards he was at the Surrey Chapel, and then, until his death in 1734, he was at St Marylebone. He was also a minor composer, though after the early promise of the String Quartets (1778) and the Organ Concertos (1781) his creative

---

(2) The original connection of both families with the West country, and their sharing some mutual acquaintances, such as Mrs Mary Pendarves.

(3) The musical ability of the first Earl of Mornington, and his acquaintance with Charles Wesley and his family. Lord Mornington (1735–1781), father of Arthur Wellesley, Duke of Wellington, was a precociously musical child, who became Professor of Music at Dublin 1764–74, and was also a minor composer. When he moved with his family to London in 1776, he became well-known in musical circles, and conducted his own orchestra in charitable performances. He was also Chairman of the Governors of the Lock Hospital. Thus his attendance at the Wesley house-concerts need not occasion any surprise.

The lack of any direct evidence of kinship is summarised in Elizabethan Pakenham, *Wellington, the years of the sword* (1969) (footnote pp. 6–7), and discussed in Charles Evans, *The ancestry of the Wesleys* ('Notes and Queries', June 1948, pp. 255–9).

talent failed to develop. His few organ compositions are derivative of Handel and uninteresting.

According to the standards set by his brother, Samuel was a late starter; he was three before he started playing. Moreover he received none of the professional advice and encouragement that his father had procured for Charles. As a composer he was virtually self-taught. He said later, in his Reminiscences,[*] that when Charles was studying harmony under Boyce, he (Samuel) 'could have had all the same exercises to peruse and digest'.

But he acquired an early introduction to Church music at Bath Abbey, where the organist Trylee, 'used to suffer me to do the afternoon duty frequently on Sundays'. Also an organist in Bristol, David Williams, taught him the 8th Concerto of Corelli, and several of Handel's organ concertos.

When he was twelve his father moved to London, where the family lived at 1 Chesterfield Street, Marylebone. This house had been acquired as early as 1770, and Samuel had lived in London since 1776; but it was not until 1778 that their house in Bristol was finally given up. In London the two brothers, Samuel and Charles, were more directly exposed to the musical fashions and influences of the day. Samuel was chiefly impressed by Handel and Scarlatti; Roseingrave had helped to introduce the latter's work to England forty years earlier. It was perhaps with this model in mind from his childhood that Samuel himself was later to do the same propaganda-service for a much greater composer than Scarlatti.

Naturally the Wesley family became acquainted with the leading London musicians and organists.[†] Apart from Arnold, Stanley and Boyce, these included John Worgan at St John's Chapel, Bedford Row, who was best known as an *extempore* organist, and Joseph Kelway at St Martin's-in-the-fields, a most fashionable player and teacher, referred to by Burney as 'head of the Scarlatti sect'. For a while he taught Samuel's brother Charles. Samuel however, pre-

---

[*] MS r² f.131. These 'reminiscences' were written in 1836, the year before his death.

[†] Charles senior's account of Samuel's early life is quoted in full in Daines Barrington's *Miscellanies* (pp. 291–8).

ferred to learn the violin, and became an adequate, though not brilliant player.

The famous musical evenings at the Wesleys' house in Chesterfield Street began in 1779 and lasted until 1785. They were subscription concerts, attended by many of the nobility, such as the Earl of Mornington, and Daines Barrington. The list of subscribers* included, under the years 1780 and 1781, no less notabilities than Samuel Johnson, then aged 71, and the Lord Mayor of London.

Heading the list of those attending one of the concerts appears the somewhat alarming name of Oliver Cromwell, written in a large and childish hand. Clearly this was a joke on the part of young Samuel; or perhaps one that was shared by the Wesley family as a whole. At all events we are here afforded a tiny, but invaluable glimpse into some of the factors that contributed towards the composer's formative years. Indeed it is no exaggeration to see in these concerts the schooling of his technique; at a time when schools or colleges of music did not exist, and the Chapel Royal was gradually declining in importance, Samuel took the fullest advantage of what opportunities for music existed in London. By 1778 he had already written his first compositions, such as the eight 'Lessons' for harpsichord or pianoforte, which are far from being juvenilia.

The concerts reflected the tastes and abilities of the two brothers. Charles usually played the organ, in his own concertos or in duets with Samuel; the latter often played the violin. These early organ duets must have left a strong impression on the young 13-year old composer; thirty years later he was to write some substantial works for this combination.

The Wesley evenings were more than merely musical events; they were aristocratic 'at homes', which followed the example set by similar social gatherings in houses of the nobility, such as the Argyll Rooms and Carlisle House. Concerts began to be given in this way, under exclusive private patronage; and no doubt a certain element of rivalry was not unknown between competing

* MS x².

hostesses. The natural outcome of this process came with the formation of the Philharmonic Society, in 1813 (of which Vincent Novello was one of the founders) and the Royal Academy, in 1822.

Relations between Samuel and his father were, however, put to a severe strain when the former at the age of eighteen, and influenced by friends, became a Roman Catholic. This was not so much for doctrinal as for musical reasons; an interest in Gregorian Chant for instance, and particularly in Renaissance polyphony. Samuel was catholic in artistic outlook if not Catholic by religious faith. Indeed he later remarked, with a true Wesleyan mordacity, that if only the doctrines and dogmas of the Roman Church were as pure as its music, it could indeed call itself blessed.

The outward events of his later career present a somewhat disjointed, even menial appearance. The established Anglican church was inevitably closed to him. 'We want no Wesleys here' was the official response that greeted his brother Charles, on applying for St Paul's Cathedral in 1796. And Samuel himself, in spite of influential backing,★ was unable to secure the appointment to the Foundling Hospital (1798) and St George's Hanover Square (1824). The loss to the Anglican church, as a whole, was incalculable.

But his creativity developed in many directions. His life was constructed round several lasting and valuable friendships; with Vincent Novello, organist at the Portuguese Embassy since 1797, when he was sixteen; with the Jewish violinist and impresario Salomon; with Benjamin Jacobs,† organist at the Surrey Chapel, Blackfriars Road. He was a familiar figure on the London concert scene, both from his attendance at the Bach and Abel concerts in the New Rooms, Hanover Square, where he became acquainted with the music of Haydn and Mozart, Dussek and Cramer, and from his appearance as a brilliant keyboard performer and conductor.

He was 'conductor at the organ' for several seasons of theatre oratorios at Covent Garden; on one occasion, when his *Ode on*

★ Particularly from William Seward, friend and biographer of Samuel Johnson.
† Benjamin Jacobs (1778–1829) was organist of the Surrey Chapel 1794–1825. It was even suggested that Wesley might be his successor. He was also a minor composer, whose songs and hymns were entered at Stationers' Hall.

St Cecilia's Day was performed, he also provided the customary Handel organ concerto, and extemporised a fugue. When Haydn's oratorio *The Creation* was first presented by Salomon at the Opera House, Samuel played one of his own organ concertos between the first and second parts.

The other chief centres of music-making were the Argyll Rooms in Regent Street, where his *Confitebor* was performed; also the Pantheon in Oxford Street. The 'Concerts of Ancient Music' in Tottenham Street* were preferred by Charles who was not a modernist. For Samuel on the other hand music was a many-sided voyage of creative discovery; an evolving, living art. His horizons took in the major contemporary figures, Mozart and Haydn, as well as the host of lesser composers such as Clementi, Dussek, Cramer, Moscheles, and many others.

As far as church music was concerned, he was deeply aware of the immense heritage from the past of both the Roman and English churches. His Latin Motets and Antiphons, and Gregorian Mass, are his response to this awareness.

He was aware too, and intensely curious, about the latest technical discoveries of his day; equal temperament for instance, and the just-developing Piano Forte. The dominating influence of the last forty years of his life was the work of J. S. Bach, whose very name was quite unknown to many of his contemporaries. Wesley absorbed and propagated the work of Bach in every way open to him; by studying, by lecturing, by performing, by publishing.

He spent much of his time teaching, though he found it irksome. He was for twenty-five years (1784–1808) employed by the Misses Barnes to teach the Piano Forte at their 'establishment' at Oxford House, Marylebone. He also taught at four other schools, and later (1826–30) returned to Bristol to lecture on a variety of musical subjects at the Bristol Institution. He was well versed in Latin and Greek; he was a witty and well-spoken lecturer; also a considerable letter-writer. A number of his piano pieces, and keyboard duets, were written for teaching purposes, or for his daughter Eliza. Some of his pupils were more advanced, and when one of them

---

* Founded by Pepusch. The term 'ancient' meant at least twenty years old.

performed his Piano Concerto, Clementi's comment was 'Why, Wesley, you have brought us here a young man with two right hands!'

There are several references in his letters to suggest that he was subject to periodic bouts of depression; but to counterbalance this, from the direct evidence of his own writings, and of his portraits, two facets of his character stand out particularly sharply; his sense of humour and his generosity of spirit.

His sense of humour, so disapproved of by the Victorians, was a compound of ironical observation and keen wit. Two examples occur in the Reminiscences.*

(i) I was once addressed by an opulent individual in the following manner:
'Sir, if you will teach me how to play *extempore* like you, I will give you any sum you may think proper to demand!'
My reply to him was this:
'Sir, as soon as ever I myself know and can explain to you the nature of my extemporaneous faculty, I will teach you for nothing.'

(ii) When Dr J[ohnson] came to my father's house in Marylebone, he knowing the high character which my brother and myself had acquired for musical ability, asked us both to play, which when we began to do, he took up a stray book which he happened to find about, and continued reading therein, during the whole time that we were playing; after which he said 'Young gentlemen, I feel much obliged to you both for your civility.'

Several friends dedicated pieces to him in gratitude for his loyalty and generosity, chiefly Thomas Adams and Samuel Webbe. He was particularly closely attached to William Russell, who was eleven years his junior, but whose life was cut short at the early age of thirty-six. Russell, he says:†

Published a set of Voluntaries for the organ distinguished by richness, elegance and variety, among which are fugues which demonstrate his having studied that branch of the art very successfully.

* MS r².
† MS r² f. 95.

Vincent Novello compared* Wesley and Russell as organists. Russell was:

> not equal to the Great Samuel Wesley as an *extempore* fugist, yet as an accompanist he was superior to him; and as a general organist he was one of the finest players that ever lived.

In 1814, after Russell died, Wesley and Novello characteristically presented a memorial concert at the Foundling Hospital, for his widow and two children. Samuel made an adaptation of Russell's oratorio *Job*, and also wrote the organ duet in C minor, which he and Novello played as an introduction to Bach's 'St. Anne' Fugue.

Wesley's references to his contemporaries are invariably generous and full of praise. Battishill he calls 'a perfect master of the organ', while as for his friend Adams:

> Among our modern organists there seems to be none of more versatile ability than Mr Thomas Adams. His great skill and ability in the management of the pedals are deservedly admired.

Samuel Wesley continued his work up to his death. In 1836 he wrote his Reminiscences; several piano pieces also date from his last year. Then, as if in an unconscious act of homage to the ageing composer, Mendelssohn aged twenty-eight, visited London in September, 1837. Londoners heard the brilliant young German composer play some Bach works on the organ, first in St Paul's, then on 9th September at Christ Church, Newgate Street—where there was one of the very few organs in London to possess pedals.† Wesley, nearing the end of his life, met Mendelssohn, at the prime of his; and he played, or improvised, his fugue in B minor written for the occasion. As it stands, the manuscript was probably used as the basis for *extempore* playing, which was his particular strength.

That this was indeed the case, is confirmed by the words of someone who was present on that occasion‡:

* MS e³.
† The organ, originally built by Henry Lincoln, was rebuilt with pedals by H. J. Gauntlett.
‡ Quoted in *The Musical Times,* Dec. 1902 (my italics). See also Gardiner *op. cit.* (II, pp. 654/5).

Wesley *extemporised* with a purity and originality of thought for which he has rendered his name ever illustrious.

It was a moving as well as a significant occasion; the brilliant young German musician, and the greatest English composer of his time, were united as much by mutual respect as by admiration for Bach's music. Two days before the concert Mendelssohn had written a short counter-subject of his own on Wesley's fugue-subject, and presented Eliza with a signed copy.* The crowded church however, and the emotion of the occasion were too much for the eighteen-year-old girl, and when her father began to play she broke down and had to leave.

Perhaps she already knew that this was to be Samuel's last performance. At all events, he returned home that day for the last time. His final days were spent writing some hymn-tunes for a collection that Novello was publishing (Ed. 213). On 11th October he died, and was buried in Old Marylebone Church. With him died the tradition of early English organ music—which thus completed the course first indicated by John Redford some three hundred years before. It was perhaps fitting that the long story should thus end as it began—with the Hymns of the Church.

His epitaph was written by Vincent Novello in 1843 :† 'Samuel Wesley was one of the greatest musical geniuses that England has ever produced.'

The Music
(Numbers refer to the list of keyboard works p. 244)

Wesley's music is today virtually unknown; it is not yet published in a definitive modern edition; his only biography, that by Lightwood, is long since outdated; of those who have written about him only Hans Redlich penetrates deeply.

His compositions‡ covered a wide and diverse range. For instru-

---

* See Max Hinrichsen's preface to Ed. 56.

† In a foreword to MS d³, and elsewhere.

‡ The list in Grove is not reliable, and quotes heavily from Eliza Wesley's two lists in the *Bach Letters* (1895 edition).

ments, they included symphonic works, concertos, chamber music and keyboard pieces; for voices they included choral motets, anthems, antiphons, songs, hymns and glees—also some larger-scale pieces, such as the Gregorian Mass *Pro Angelis*, the *Ode to St Cecilia's day*, and the *Confitebor*. His earliest known composition was an oratorio *Ruth*, written between the ages of six and eight. According to Barrington it was composed at six, and written down when he was eight.

The keyboard works were written either for the pianoforte or organ; almost twice as many (about 110) for the organ as for the piano. Wesley did not write for the harpsichord, after the early set of eight sonatas (or lessons), written when he was eleven, and dedicated to Daines Barrington. In far the majority of cases there is a clear distinction in style between his piano and his organ compositions; in the latter he aimed to achieve a texture that was 'fine, smooth and close', while in the piano pieces he used broken chord figurations, double octaves, crossing of the hands and so on.

The expressive range in the keyboard works is a very wide one; from the light and easy piano pieces to the more extended sonata structures; from the intimate quality of a 'Desk Voluntary', or the concentrated expressiveness of a short piece, to the sustained grandeur of one of the organ duets or voluntaries. He revived the variations for keyboard on popular tunes. This particular form, so frequently used in Byrd's day, had fallen out of use with the growth of the eighteenth century Voluntary. Most of Wesley's variations are in the form of the Rondo, and are for the piano rather than the organ. But the influence of this style is also seen in the more *cantabile* movements of the organ works. In this way Wesley incorporated into his organ music the most common form of popular music of his day—the air, or ballad.

His fondness for duets, shared by many composers at this time, reflects the domestic nature of piano music of his day. Many duets such as Op. 5 were also written for pupils. In the case of organ music, the use of two players went some way towards meeting the lack of pedals. Duets occur throughout the early period of English organ music, but never before to the extent that Wesley used this device. It was also partly the result of his study of Bach. If a piece such as Bach's St Anne Fugue, or one of the Trio Sonatas, was to be played at all on an instrument without pedals, an arrangement of it for two players was one possible solution.

The Bach influence is most strong in the keyboard works, though it is apparent also in many other aspects of his style. Wesley not only introduced Bach to England; he assimilated many points of style and technique from him. His motet for double choir *In exitu Israel* was inspired by Bach's motet *Jesu meine Freude*; both these works were conducted by Wesley at concerts in the Hanover Square Rooms in 1809 and 1810. The sonata for three pianos is clearly a follow-up of Bach's three-harpsichord concerto; his four-part hymns are modelled on Bach's chorale-harmonisations; the setting of 'et expecto' in his Mass *Pro Angelis* is reminiscent of the equivalent point in Bach's *B minor Mass*. That Wesley knew this work is evident from the fact that he tried unsuccessfully to publish the 'Credo' section of it in 1815.

Another direct result of the Bach influence was Wesley's use of equal temperament. His preludes in each of the major and minor keys (1797) are highly characteristic pieces—the first of many sets by subsequent composers which owe their existence to Bach's '48'. Equal temperament was just beginning to be used by 1800 in England. Wesley ascribed it to sheer necessity; the symphonic works of Haydn and Mozart, which Salomon included in his Hanover Square concerts, could not be played except on instruments tuned in equal temperament; therefore, largely under the aegis of Salomon, this gradually became the practice. But organs naturally continued to be tuned in mean-tone temperament until well into the nineteenth century. Wesley's preludes are for the piano.

Other Bach influences may be detected in the construction and organisation of Wesley's fugue subjects; the juxtaposition of disparate elements, for instance, and the use of long phrases, building up into long sentences.

The two chief landmarks among his organ works are the Twelve Voluntaries, Op. 6, and the Thirteen Short Pieces. Both sets were published in his lifetime, the first in 1805 by Hodsoll, the second in 1812 by Clementi. Both works show signs of having been polished and carefully checked by the composer, which is by no means always the case, particularly with manuscript compositions. He was a great extemporaneous player, and some of the organ pieces appear to have been written down only in the form of the outline, to which the player, probably the composer himself, would be expected to fill in the details in performance. One such piece has already been referred to—the 'Mendelssohn' fugue in B minor, his last composition. Such a practice was entirely in conformity with the eighteenth-century conventions.

The Twelve Voluntaries and the Thirteen Short Pieces show Wesley's interpretation of the two possible directions in which the eighteenth century Voluntary might develop—first, into a substantial piece, of sonata-like dimensions; second, into short and concentrated preludes. It is probably not unreasonable to guess that Wesley modelled the general conception of the short pieces on the same sort of technical basis as Bach used for his *Orgelbüchlein*; that is to say each piece exploits a particular organ style, sonority or texture.

Since the Chorale Prelude was an impossibility within a tradition that lacked a popular repertoire of sacred songs, Wesley took instead the various tonal aspects of the eighteenth-century voluntary, and used them as the vehicles for highly concentrated studies; *Full with the trumpet, Full without the trumpet, Cornet, Flute,* etc.

His melodic and harmonic idiom is particularly characteristic in these brilliant little preludes. The structure of each is very taut, yet the *motifs* that make up each phrase are highly variable; the progressions are extremely chromatic, yet the harmony is never forced.

The material sometimes overlaps between pieces. For instance the gavotte of No. 8 is a diminished form of the material of No. 3; the subject of the final fugue, No. 12, is a continuation of the previous piece, in the form of a counter-subject to the bass line, but in duple metre.

The most striking characteristic is the integrated use of chromaticism, which is greater than in the more extended structures of the voluntaries. Wesley introduces chromaticism right from the very first piece, which opens like the slow diapason movement of a voluntary—but with a difference:

Example 52

Thirteen Short Pieces: No. 1 in G
(bars 11-12)
Diapasons
Wesley

Chromaticism is not confined to the harmonisations. The entire middle section of the Air of No. 8 is built round a chromatically ascending bass line; and the composer is particularly successful in his characteristic use of the dominant minor ninth:

Example 53

a) Thirteen Short Pieces: No. 8 in F
(bars 22-24)
Flute
Wesley
Diapasons
etc.

b) Thirteen Short Pieces: No. 9 in F
(bars 25-28)
Diapasons and Principal
Wesley
etc.

*Dominant minor ninth

Twelve Voluntaries, Op. 6

The twelve voluntaries, or sonatas, that make up Op. 6 are altogether bigger, not just in scale but in importance. They stand head and shoulders above other pieces of this time. They were written before the composer was forty, and thus may be taken to represent the prime of his organ work.

They exploit the expressive power of the eighteenth century

organ up to the very limit—if not beyond. The fact that Wesley had no official appointment to a church at the time he composed them makes his achievement all the more remarkable. But he found compensation in his close friendship with Benjamin Jacobs, who was organist to the Rev. Rowland Hill at Surrey Chapel, Blackfriars Road. This church, where his brother Charles was once organist, and where, says Wesley,* there was 'a capital organ by Elliot', was the scene of several important recitals, at which Wesley and Jacobs introduced the works of Bach. Samuel would play the violin, as he used to twenty years before at the musical evenings in Marylebone; or he would play some of the '48'. The absence of pedals naturally ruled out the larger organ works of Bach. About this time also Jacobs was the recipient of the famous 'Bach Letters', in which the two friends discussed the propagation of Bach's work.

We may safely assume that it was for this organ that the majority of the Op. 6 voluntaries were written, although one of them (No. 6) calls for a third manual, which the Surrey Chapel instrument did not have. Wesley however had access to a three-manual instrument at the Portuguese Embassy Chapel.† Hodsoll's editions (Ed. 175) contain Wesley's own registration, and are therefore of the first importance.

Wesley extends the customary two-movement structure of the voluntary into three or four movements. The pieces abound in characteristics of style; a fondness for the 'theme and variations' principle, the use of dotted rhythm, passages in thirds for the right hand, dramatic contrasts of tone quality and dynamics, and in particular a subtle harmonic chromaticism. He owes little or nothing to Handel, and the *style galant* that appeared for a while in the work of his brother Charles, and some other organ composers, was subjected to a highly personal treatment at his hands. The range between his bold, decisive themes, and his melodic *cantabile* movements, is a very wide one. Another characteristic feature is his fondness for a quiet ending, which may well be unexpected. Op. 6, No. 6 is an example.

* In MS r² f.107. The specification is given on p. 267.
† Mary Cowden Clarke *The life and labours of Vincent Novello*, p. 4.

I The first Voluntary, in three movements, straightaway shows great contrapuntal skill, at the same time being wholly underivative. The music gradually increases up to the full fugue, with a climax at the end, which is marked by the customary eighteenth-century improvisation-chords.

II Two movements played on the Great, at moderate speed, are varied in texture and rhythm, but connected by the material itself —a technique greatly favoured by Wesley. Each movement is introduced by a *Larghetto* in the metre appropriate to it; the first a *Siciliano*, the second in $\frac{2}{4}$.

III The two movements for Full Great that make up this Voluntary exploit the dramatic contrast of loud and soft, also a dotted rhythm. The second movement is a complex double fugue, whose ascending chromatic fifth makes it akin to the old hexachord variations-technique.*

IV The three movements of this Voluntary are all based on *Non nobis Domine*. The second is a canon 3 in 1, and the third a trumpet movement.

V Dynamic contrasts and chromaticism culminate in a theme-and-variations movement; the theme was a 'melody of the late Mr. Stephen Paxton'.† Thus Wesley combines sustained power with intimate organ colours.

VI The same principle is continued in the next Voluntary. After a flourish for Full organ, an Air is treated antiphonally with a fugal section for Full organ. Whether consciously or unconsciously, Wesley's style was partly based on that of the early English composers. His use of variation techniques singles him out from his contemporaries; while this use of alternating Air and Fugue,

* The same principle applied to the Twelfth Voluntary of Russell's First Book (1804).
† Stephen Paxton, 1735–1789, was a minor composer.

which Mendelssohn later followed in his first Organ Sonata in F minor, recalls the early sixteenth century style of alternating choral and organ polyphony.

VII The structure of the seventh Voluntary is a subtle one. The opening Diapason movement provides the harmonic basis for the concluding fugue, in which Wesley's characteristic chromatic harmony makes prominent use of the minor 9th.

But between the Prelude and its Fugue the composer inserts a third movement, *Andante quasi Allegretto*, for the Mixture, changing to Diapason half way. As the Prelude and Fugue are directly connected, the two movements might well have followed each other consecutively. Why the extra movement?

One possible solution to this structural riddle could be, yet again, Wesley's strong predisposition towards the theme and variations principle. The middle movement uses part of the fugue subject in its melodic form; thus the same material is variously treated in the three movements. So when the fugue at last enters, it is heard as the logical continuation of what has gone before.

A three-movement structure was used frequently by Wesley; the Prelude, Arietta and Fugue is an outstanding example.

A particularly brilliant example also occurs in the Voluntary for Thomas Attwood (No. 14), in which the three movements represent a gradual growth of dynamic strength, and a progressive increase of speed. The scheme is:

1 Diapasons; Moderately slow tempo.
2 Diapasons, Principal and Fifteenth, with alternating Swell Trumpet; Lively tempo.
3 Full Organ, with rich, chordal writing; Triple metre. Fast tempo.
  The sense of climax is further enhanced in this movement by greater use of chromaticism, and a strutting fugue-subject, in which the interval gradually widens—diminished fourth, fourth, diminished fifth.

VIII In the eighth Voluntary, Wesley exploits various organ textures; the repetition of chords or bass notes, for rhythmic definition; the alternation of chords, counterpoints and unison passages, at the Full Organ level; the use of the Trumpet unaccompanied; all these appear here for the first time.

IX After an opening superficially similar to Handel's No. 4, Wesley soon asserts himself. Like the seventh Voluntary, the three movements of this piece are also constructed on a variation basis. The fugal movement in the major key is simply the final version of the earlier theme; the fugue subject is a direct variant, with one note substituted, of the material of the opening movement:

Example 54

a) Voluntary in G minor/major, Op. 6 No. 9   Wesley
(Opening of first movement)

b) (Opening of third movement)

X The four movements alternate Diapason with Principal and Fifteenth (second movement), and Full Organ (fourth movement). Intricate harmony, small-note decoration, and complex counterpoint characterise the melodic writing. The fugue subject is more chromatic than usual, and the resulting harmonic opportunities are amply realised in the course of the movement.

XI This, like the third Voluntary, consists of two movements for Full Great. The first, which contains a quiet episode, also uses brilliant keyboard figuration, short-note runs and dotted rhythms.

The fugue subject, derived from the first two bars of the first movement, is very similar to one by Russell;* the melodic figure in each case derives from Handel.

XII The first and third movements are surprisingly subdued, like one of the short pieces. The subject of the Full Organ fugue that forms the second movement is a continuation of that of the eleventh Voluntary. Evidently Wesley has not said all he wishes to say on this theme.

The piece does not open with the subject, but with a dotted-rhythm, homophonic *ritornello*, which later recurs and acts as a framework for the contrapuntal section. This procedure is similar to that of the sixth Voluntary, and it may have been modelled on Bach's E♭ Prelude at the beginning of the Clavierübung (Part 3).

This great collection of Voluntaries ends, as it began, with a slow melody; this time a highly characteristic movement for the Cremona.

Several of Wesley's other Voluntaries compare equally with those of Op. 6. The massive *Prelude, Arietta and Fugue* (54) finishes with one of the most brilliant fugues he ever wrote. The published score describes it as an 'exercise for the improvement of the hands'. The Prelude and the Arietta are based on the same left hand pattern; the Prelude in that dotted rhythm that so appealed to Wesley, the Arietta with a varied melodic line, first in single notes, next in thirds. This left hand pattern then becomes the subject of the extended fugal finale. The subject contains great possibilities:

Example 55

Prelude, Arietta and Fugue   Wesley
(Opening of fugue)

* No. 10 of the first set.

Although this work was not published until 1840, it clearly belongs to the central period of Wesley's life, before 1820. A piece comparable to it is the *Full Voluntary* (13) which he placed at the end of the *Thirteen Short Pieces*—thus covering in one volume both main categories of his organ compositions.

Some of Wesley's organ works were published long after his death by Josiah Pittman, who was a pupil of Samuel's son Samuel Sebastian, and organist of Lincoln's Inn. He was a disciple of the Wesley-Jacobs-Mendelssohn school, and his editions therefore have an authenticity not found in others of the late nineteenth century. One of his editions (64) is the fine Voluntary in B flat. This is particularly noted for Wesley's use of unison, for full organ—one of his most personal features of style. The octave of the opening also appears at the beginning of the fugue subject; the slow middle movement in E flat, is a homophonic *cantabile*, with characteristic chromaticism.

In the extended voluntary, Wesley invariably differentiated between the characters of the different movements and sections. For the less bold moments, the 'second subject', he evolved a highly expressive *cantabile*, which, while owing something to the *galant* style, was compounded from many other sources as well, such as the introductory Diapason movement of the earlier eighteenth-century Voluntary, from the melodic patterns of Mozart and early Beethoven, and from the harmony of Haydn—particularly in the use of the augmented sixth.

This *cantabile* style appears frequently in the Voluntaries. Other fine examples are the Arietta (21), a sustained melody in ternary form, with a middle section in the minor key; the Larghetto (18), and the two sections of (63). The early Voluntary in D (16), after a brilliant, full opening, uses it to introduce a secondary idea, while still maintaining the dotted rhythm of the first theme.

The alternation of *Aria* with *Full Organ* sections has already been mentioned as one of Wesley's pronounced characteristics. In the B flat Voluntary (19) the second and third movements use this technique; the second movement is a homophonic one for Full Organ, with a middle section on the Choir organ; the third movement is a 'Soft Organ' *Aria*, interspersed with 'Full Organ' unisons.

Indeed the Voluntary opens with a bold unison, like an orchestral concerto, recalling Stanley's Op. 5, No. 8. The first movement also uses a particular effect (a held note over a moving part, both in the right hand) which occurs in earlier pieces, such as the Voluntary in D (17), written shortly before, and in some of the *Thirteen Short Pieces*.

We are often reminded, particularly in the closing bars of a movement, that improvisation on the part of the player was assumed by the composer. The technique of *extempore* playing, which flourished in the eighteenth century, and of which Wesley himself was such a master, passed out of use as the early organ tradition gradually receded into the past after his death. But a particularly fine opportunity for such improvisation is provided by the flattened sixth (G flat) of the penultimate bar of this first movement.

Wesley was as much a master of the short piece as he was of an extended one. Both are of equal importance in his output. No doubt the short organ piece partly at least owed its origin to those moments of necessity in divine service when the organist was required to fill with music an otherwise silent space; but partly also Wesley avoided too long a use of solo stops in his larger movements, and reserved this for the concentrated expressiveness of his miniatures.

Apart from the *Thirteen Short Pieces*, Wesley wrote many more in the last years of his life, such as the exquisite piece in C (25), and the *Desk Voluntaries*. These are short, single-movement works written for a desk or chamber organ. They require, however, two manuals and pedals. It is interesting to speculate whether Wesley possessed such an instrument in his house. Elliot, who built the Surrey Chapel organ, had been a pupil of Snetzler; did he perhaps also build a small organ for the composer's private use? Or perhaps Wesley acquired one from elsewhere. In his father's house in

Marylebone he and his brother Charles had two organs, which must have been the sort of instruments for which, fifty years later, the *Desk Voluntaries* (or *Introductory Movements*) were written.

Evidently the *Desk Voluntaries*★ were re-named for publication; but the three pieces so named are highly polished miniatures; all are slow, homophonic, alternating Diapasons (Great) with Swell, and written with that characteristic chromaticism of the earlier set.

The four short preludes (30), also written about the same time, are equally rich in expressiveness. They are only 14, 16, 15 and 11 bars respectively, yet each is different; the fourth piece even uses a miniature ternary form.

The years about 1830 were busy ones for Wesley; he also wrote twelve short and simple duets (81–88, and 102–105) for his daughter Eliza, who was born in 1819. She played them with her father 'when young'; they must have been written therefore about 1830. If the simplicity of these duets was for the benefit of a child, he also wrote about this time the six deceptively easy pieces of Op. 36. Characteristic chromatic progressions and melodic patterns, and tightly-knit *motifs,* show that Wesley was here addressing himself, in spite of the publisher's advertised intention, to a slightly older pupil. Some of the movements recall certain of the *Thirteen Short Pieces,* which perhaps is not surprising if the basis of both sets was to explore particular aspects of organ style. Wesley includes among the lessons to be learnt the art of *extempore* playing, and the first movement of the fifth piece in D (52) introduces chord progressions for improvisation.

Some of the manuscript pieces† written in the 1830s seem to be the basis for improvisation. The 'Mendelssohn' fugue (31) has already been mentioned; another is the fugue in D (28), which is written basically in just two parts, with an occasional holding note in the inner part. It is certain that this fugue follows directly after the movement in D (24), to form one Voluntary. A similar procedure occurs in the F major Voluntary (27), in which the first

---

★ MS t², f.51. The frayed edge of the manuscript page (No. 58) makes the date illegible. It could be 1830, or 1836.
† MS t².

cantabile movement leads straight into the ensuing fugue; no doubt the half-close, marking the link, was intended to form the basis of some improvisation. This fugue, for Full Organ, also ends, typically for Wesley, with unisons.

On her eighteenth birthday (6th May, 1837) Eliza was given a small collection of pieces and sketches★ by her father, then in the last months of his life. Two Voluntaries in G and D minor (32 and 33), and an effective fugue in G (35), form the substance of the collection; the opening movement of one of these (32) conceals considerable subtlety beneath a comparatively simple appearance, though the wedge-like subject of the fugue remains somewhat undeveloped. The short pieces which come at the end of the manuscript (176) were probably studies; the second in E flat bears a surprising resemblance to the quick section of Maurice Greene's seventh Voluntary, also in E flat (Ed. 112). It is effective if performed quickly and lightly; indeed Wesley often wrote some of his most effective movements *vivace*; the long *Presto* movement of the early Voluntary in D (16) is a case in point; also the finale ('lively') of another D major piece dating from 1830 (15).

The great C major Duet (79) was written specifically to be played by Vincent Novello and the composer at a concert in the Hanover Square rooms in 1812. It is a grand, majestic piece, highly characteristic of Wesley's maturity. The first movement, with its typical dotted rhythm, and *cantabile* secondary material, is much nearer to the sonata-form of an instrumental piece than the customary Diapason movement of a Voluntary. The second movement, in F, is a lyrical, chromatic, *affettuoso*, while the fugue subject is made up of contrasted and varied motifs, which make it well able to sustain the weight of the intricate musical argument that makes up the final movement. Wesley never surpassed this piece.

Indeed his duets are unique in English organ music. By this means he sought to overcome the deficiency of the eighteenth-century instrument that he knew, which lacked a pedal organ, even if it possessed, in a few cases, pedal keys.

★ MS s².

The other duet (80) is intended to lead directly into Bach's E flat triple fugue 'St Anne'; it is to that extent incomplete. It was written for the memorial concert for William Russell at the Foundling Hospital in 1814, and is therefore much shorter and more subdued a work than the earlier duet. It uses three tone-colours, and three manuals, simultaneously, like a Trio Sonata. It was no doubt suggested to Wesley after he and K. F. Horn had made an edition for three hands of Bach's Trio Sonatas. The three parts, Flute, Oboe, Diapasons, have independent material; two solo parts over an accompanimental bass.

Wesley's collection of over a hundred hymn-tunes (106), many of them to his father's words, broke new ground in several respects. It was not the first such collection in England; these can be found as early as the sixteenth century (Sternhold and Hopkins); and in 1623 appeared a collection of hymns with music by no less a composer than Orlando Gibbons. But it was the independent religious movements of the eighteenth century that provided the spur to congregational hymn-singing. Isaac Watts was one important writer; and John Wesley himself published not only psalms and hymns, but also collections of single-note tunes, which Samuel's brother Charles later edited. Two of them, from the *Foundery Collection* (1742), have even found their way into Anglican usage through the English Hymnal.* But Samuel's conception of a hymn was of something grander; modelled on the Bach chorale, in four parts, it was to be something altogether more musically important; sweeping yet simple. But the tradition of hymn-singing, innate in the German Lutheran church since the sixteenth century, in England moved very much according to popular taste, and Samuel's hymns lacked popular appeal both for the Methodists, and the Anglican church as a whole, which for long adhered obstinately to metrical psalms.

The greatness of Wesley's organ music consists in the main in his enlarging the expressive range, as well as the structure, of the eighteenth century Voluntary, and by his understanding, and suc-

---

* Herrnhut (135) and Milites (381).

cessfully combating, the inherent characteristics, and weaknesses, of the eighteenth century organ. The same spirit of enquiry and curiosity governs his other keyboard works, his very considerable compositions for piano. He assimilated what was new and valid from the many radical developments of his day.

Whereas his predecessor Keeble (and later Russell) wrote organ pieces in as many keys as possible, Wesley in 1797 wrote two preludes in each key, major and minor, for the piano. By this means he was able to include the keys E flat and A flat major, which on the organ would have sounded most discordant, due to lack of equal temperament.

Again, just as he embodied the *galant* into his *cantabile* style of organ composition, so he embodied popular Airs into his piano pieces. He would either use the Air as a basis for variations, in which he was particularly inventive, and which had once been the main boast of the English School, or else incorporate the tune into a Rondo. In this he was following the practice of his contemporaries Shield, Pleyel and Dussek.

If there are echoes of a former age in certain of Wesley's pieces, such as the 'hexachord variation' Voluntary, and his fondness for the variation principle, this is even more noticeable in the unashamed 'programme-music' of the 'Siege of Badajoz' Sonata. Its section-headings are vivid and specific:

'Fire opened by six batteries.'
'Groans of the dying.'
'Lord Wellingtons March.'

The popularity of 'programme-music' in the early nineteenth century was widespread. Louis Von Esch wrote many military pieces, while battle pieces included Koczwara's *Battle of Prague*, and Beethoven's *Battle of Vittoria*. Another composer was rash enough also to depict the Battle of Vittoria, Wesley's friend, to whom he dedicated a fine fugue, J. B. Logier. This genre later led to such a master-work as Schumann's *Carnaval*.

As with Wesley's organ pieces, so many of his piano pieces were simple, intended for pupils. The *Four Sonatas and Two Duets* is an example; clearly the recipients, the Miss Lambs, possessed no very advanced technique; yet that does not prevent Wesley writing characteristic music for them.

Samuel Wesley's was a most versatile genius. From an early age he showed extraordinary abilities, both as a performer and as a composer. This in itself need not be exaggerated; indeed his father seems to have been comparatively unexcited at the prospect of a second musical prodigy in the family. Yet whereas in the case of Charles (junior), and of another infant prodigy William Crotch, early promise led to nothing, Samuel's early musicianship was altogether different. It was noticed by Daines Barrington, a friend of the family, in his *Miscellanies* (1781), who understood that Samuel's genius was something quite unique, and described what he observed; how Wesley as a boy of ten would play *extempore* for long periods at a stretch; his remarkable powers of invention, particularly in the form of variations; his serenity of touch and technique, yet his bold and uncommon modulations. His early musicianship had that Mozartian spontaneity which impressed itself even on a hardened professional like William Boyce, who described him as 'dropped out of heaven'. The early harpsichord lessons dedicated to Barrington (125) are evidence of this early sparkle.

Wesley's abilities were many-sided. He sang counter-tenor, he was a competent violinist, a rewarding and brilliant conversationalist. He was also a Freemason. He appeared frequently in concerts, as organist and conductor, both in London and elsewhere; he conducted for instance at a Birmingham Festival in 1811. He was often asked to open new organs, and to give his opinion. Yet he held no official appointment of any kind.

The organ was his favourite instrument; and one of his favourite organs, apart from the Surrey Chapel, was one built by Snetzler in the German Savoy Chapel, where Kollmann was organist. Contact with German musicians in London brought him closer to Bach's music.

As for the reception of his work by his contemporaries and posterity, a most revealing sentence* in his Reminiscences (1836)

* MS r², f.40 v.

sums up, in its masterful understatement, the composer's awareness that the trends of organ design and organ playing in the nineteenth century were incompatible with the early English tradition,
which he represented:

> The powers of instrumental execution seem to have been much
> extended for the last forty or fifty years. The compass of the Piano-
> forte has been greatly augmented, and also organs, which latter have
> been carried up to a higher pitch than the genius of the instrument
> seems to require.

As far as his performance as an organist is concerned, the style
of *extempore* playing, now a thing of the past, was an integral part
of the eighteenth century, and found its chief exponent in Samuel
Wesley. Someone who witnessed his playing, though towards the
end of his life, was Edward Holmes, who has left a vivid and
unique account:*

> . . . I heard him, when invited to play at the close of many an
> excellent musical evening, put such a climax to it, that every thing
> which had before been heard was entirely swallowed up and lost in
> the last impression. He concentrated himself and warmed over his
> work with unequalled enthusiasm, and showed not only the con-
> structive head but the most impassioned feeling. . . . Mr V. Novello
> one evening, at his house in Percy Street, Bedford Square, selected
> for him, with admirable judgement and tact, the subject of the chorus
> in the *Messiah* 'He trusted in God'. The dramatic and impassioned
> style of that chorus exactly suited Wesley, who, I remember, used
> to revel with peculiar delight on a certain point of the fugue towards
> the end, where the trebles enter with the subject on the high G. On
> this occasion we were full of curiosity to know what Wesley would
> do, and how he would disunite from Handel. For a few bars he kept
> close to the original, but soon cleared himself of it, and sailed away
> into the heaven of his own invention. . . . By introducing new
> and florid counterpoints, he threw Handel's subject into an entirely
> new form—that of most elaborate, interesting, and artificially-
> constructed instrumental fugue.

Wesley took equal pleasure in extemporising variations of an
Air, as he did in contrapuntal ingenuity. His fancy was limitless.

* *Musical Times*, August, 1851.

THE EXTANT REPERTOIRE
Samuel Wesley—Keyboard Works (I)
Organ

MS Source Printed Editions

Thirteen Short Pieces with a Full Voluntary

(1)	i in G	n^3	50, 194
(2)	ii in G	n^3	50, 194
(3)	iii in G (Full)	n^3	50, 194
(4)	iv in A minor (Hautboy)	n^3	50, 194
(5)	v in A minor (Cornet)	n^3	50, 194
(6)	vi in A minor	n^3	50, 194
(7)	vii in A minor (Full without the Trumpet)	n^3	50, 194
(8)	viii & ix in F ('Air and Gavotte')	n^3	50, 194
(9)	x in F (Full without the Trumpet)	n^3	50, 194
(10)	xi in D (Flute)	n^3	50, 194
(11)	xii in D	n^3	50, 194
(12)	xiii in D (Full with the Trumpet)	n^3	50, 194
(13)	Full Voluntary in D minor	n^3	48, 194
(14)	Voluntary in B flat (27th February, 1829) (to Thomas Attwood)	p^3	204
(15)	Voluntary in D (6th September, 1830)	u^2	178,* 193
(16)	Voluntary in D (16th May, 1788)	b^3	
(17)	(Voluntary) in D (8th October, 1817)	y^2	
(18)	Larghetto and Coda in D (18th–20th October, 1817)	y^2	
(19)	Voluntary in B flat (5th–6th November, 1817)	y^2	
(20)	Voluntary in C	y^2	
(21)	Arietta in G (19th September, 1823)	t^2, r^3	
(22)	(Voluntary) in A	t^2	
(23)	Short piece in D ('Diapasons')	t^2	
(24)	Movement (of a Voluntary in D) +	t^2	
(25)	Short piece in C	t^2	
(26)	(Voluntary) in D	t^2	
(27)	(Voluntary) in F (18th October, 1836)	t^2	
(28)	Fugue (of a Voluntary) in D +	t^2	
(29)	Fugue in C	t^2	
(30)	Four short preludes (1834?) (i) in C, (ii) in G, (iii) in D, (iv) in A,	t^2	
(31)	Fugue in B minor (9th September, 1837) 'composed expressly for Dr Mendelssohn'	t^2	56
(32)	Introduction and Fugue (Voluntary) in G	s^2, z^2	
(33)	Introduction and Fugue (Voluntary) in D minor	s^2	
(34)	Air (anapaest)in D, from 'Salomon' Sonata for piano	s^2, r^3	180, 189
(35)	Fugue in G	s^2	

Twelve Voluntaries, Op. 6

(36)	i Voluntary in D minor/major	175, 177
(37)	ii Voluntary in C	175, 177
(38)	iii Voluntary in C minor	114, 175, 177
(39)	iv Voluntary in G minor/major (Trumpet duet)	175, 177

* Ed. 178 is unreliable.

Samuel Wesley—Keyboard Works (I)—*contd.*

		MS Source	Printed Editions
(40)	v Voluntary in D		175, 177
(41)	vi Voluntary in C		175, 177, 190[5]
(42)	vii Voluntary in E flat		175, 177
(43)	viii Voluntary in D		175, 177
(44)	ix Voluntary in G minor/major		175, 177
(45)	x Voluntary in F	u[2]	175, 177
(46)	xi Voluntary in A		175, 177
(47)	xii Voluntary in F		175, 177

Six Organ Voluntaries for young organists, Op. 36

(48)	i Voluntary in F	n[3]	176
(49)	ii Voluntary in A	n[3]	176
(50)	iii Voluntary in G	n[3]	176
(51)	iv Voluntary in B flat	n[3]	176
(52)	v Voluntary in D	n[3]	176
(53)	vi Voluntary in C	n[3]	176
(54)	Prelude, Arietta and Fugue in C minor		
	'to his friend Thomas Adams' (24th July, 1826)	m[3]	172
(55)	Grand Coronation March		190[6],★ 191

Six introductory movements to which is added a loud Voluntary

(56)	i in D ('Desk Voluntary' No. 5)	t[2]	193
(57)	ii in E		114, 193
(58)	iii in F ('Desk Voluntary' No. 3, 27th August,		
	1830[?])	t[2]	193
(59)	iv in A		193
(60)	v in C		193
(61)	vi in E minor ('Desk Voluntary' No. 4)	t[2]	193
(62)	A short and familiar Voluntary in A		205
(63)	Larghetto and Andante in E minor/major		185
(64)	Allegro, Andante and Fugue (Voluntary) in B flat		185
(65)	Introduction and Allegro (Voluntary) in D		185

Six Fugues with Introductions for young organists

(66)	i in D	n[3]	
(67)	ii in B flat	n[3]	
(68)	iii in F	n[3]	
(69)	iv in F	n[3]	
(70)	v in E flat	n[3]	
(71)	vi in C	n[3]	

Miscellaneous short pieces

(72)	'Scraps for the organ'	i[3], l[3]	190[5, 6]
	Andante in G		
	Air, Moderato in D minor		
	('for Miss Ogle of Bath')		
	Lento (Larghetto) in B flat		
	Allegretto Cantabile (Vivace) in E flat		
(73)	Untitled piece in C minor (24th June, 1829)	s[3]	
(74)	Hymnus Matutinus		190[1]

★ Ed. 190 is a doubtful one, consisting largely of arrangements. However for several short
pieces it is the sole source.

Samuel Wesley—Keyboard Works (I)—*contd.*

		MS Source	Printed Editions
(75)	Diapason melodies, in F & G		190^4
(76)	Pastoral melody in D (28th November, 1831)		190^4
(77)	Diapason pieces in C & A		190^4
(78)	Slow movement in F (9th September, 1800)		190^5

Organ Duets

(79)	Duet for the Organ in C (24th May, 1812)	d^3	184
(80)	Duet for the organ in C minor (1814) introduction to J. S. Bach's 'St Anne' Fugue in E flat	b^3, d^3, g^3, i^3, q^3	

(Short and easy Duets: one keyboard, four hands)

(81)	No. 1 in D	t^2	
(82)	No. 2 in G	t^2	
(83)	No. 3 in F	t^2	
(84)	No. 4 in A	t^2	
(85)	No. 5 in G	t^2	
(86)	No. 6 in B flat	t^2	
(87)	No. 7 in A	t^2	
(88)	No. 8 in G	t^2	

Airs, Variations and Arrangements

(89)	Eight variations in B flat on 'God save the King' (1st December, 1817)	y^2	
(90)	'Rule Britannia' (Arne)	t^2	
(91)	'Aileen Aroon'	t^2	
(92)	'Rousseau's Dream'	t^2	
(93)	'Coolun'	t^2	
(94)	Three Variations in D on 'God save the King'	m^3	179
(95)	Arrangement, with variation, of 'Rule Britannia' (Arne)	m^3	179
(96)	Arrangement of Dead March in 'Saul' (Handel)		179
(97)	Arrangement of Air in D (Handel)		179
(98)	An old English melody, harmonised with additions (June, 1806)	r^3	187, 190^1
(99)	Air in C minor	g^3, i^3	190^3
(100)	Air in G		190^6
(101)	Variations on 'Tantum ergo' (Stephen Paxton)		190^4
(102)	Duet No. 9 in D, Handel's Coronation Anthem	t^2	
(103)	Duet No. 10 in C, Mozart's 'O God when thou appearest'	t^2	
(104)	Duet No. 11 in F, Minuet by Mozart	t^2	
(105)	Duet No. 12 in G, Pergolesi's 'Gloria in excelsis'	t^2	

(106)   *Hymns*

'Original hymn tunes adapted to every metre in the collection by the Rev. John Wesley, A.M. Late Fellow of Lincoln College, Oxford, newly composed and arranged for four voices with a separate accompaniment for the organ or pianoforte'.

First Line	Metre		
i. Come ye that love the Lord	S.M.D.	o^3	196
ii Happy the souls to Jesus joined	C.M.	o^3	196

Samuel Wesley—Keyboard Works (I)—*contd.*

First Line	Metre	MS Source	Printed Editions
iii Happy the souls that first believed	L.M.	o³	196
iv Maker, Saviour of mankind	7.6.7.6.7. 7.7.6.	o³	196
v Ye simple souls that stray	6.6.6.6.8. 6.8.6.	j³	196
vi Behold the Saviour of mankind	C.M.	o³	196
vii Stand th' omnipotent decree	7.6.7.6.7. 8.7.6.	o³	196
viii Lo! He comes with clouds descending	8.7.8.7.4.7.	o³	196
ix A fountain of life	8 lines of 8	o³	196
x Come O thou traveller unknown	6 lines of 8	o³	196
xi O Jesus my hope	10.12.10.12	o³	196, 213
xii Jesus thy blood and righteousness	L.M.	o³	196
xiii Thee O my God and King	6.6.7.7.7.7.	o³	196
xiv O heavenly King	10.10.11.11	o³	196
xv My God, the spring of all my joys	C.M.		196
xvi Glorious Saviour of my soul	7.6.7.6.7. 7.7.6.	o³	196
xvii All thanks be to God	5.5.5.12. twice	o³	196
xviii Young men and maidens	6.6.6.6.8.8.	o³	196
xix Father of all	L.M.D.	o³	196
xx Hail! Father, Son and Holy Ghost	C.M.	o³	196
xxi O God! Thou bottomless abyss	L.M.	o³	196
xxii Father in whom we live	S.M.	o³	196
xxiii Glory be to God on high	4 lines of 7	o³	196
xxiv Worship and thanks and blessing	7.7.8.7. twice	o³	196
xxv God of all grace and majesty	C.M.D.		196
xxvi Come on my partners	8.8.6.8.8.6.	o³	196
xxvii Come Holy Ghost	8.8.8.8.8.8.	o³	196
xxviii Love divine, all loves excelling	8.7.8.7. twice	o³	196
xxix Jesu my Saviour	L.M.	o³	196
xxx Messiah, full of grace	S.M.	o³	196
xxxi Lamb of God	6 lines of 7	o³	196
xxxii Come let us anew	5.5.5.11	o³	196
xxxiii Come and let us sweetly join	8 lines of 7	o³	196
xxxiv Our friendship sanctify and guide	8 lines of 8	o³	196
xxxv Come thou all inspiring spirit	8.7.8.7. twice		196
xxxvi Come thou everlasting spirit	8.7.8.7. twice	o³	196
xxxvii Ye servants of God	4 lines of 10 and 11		196
xxxviii Come Lord from above	5.5.11 twice	o³	196

Samuel Wesley—Keyboard Works (I)—*contd.*

		MS Source	Printed Editions
First Line	*Metre*		
Let all that breathe		o³	
Meet and right it is to praise		o³	

'Three hymns, the words by the late
Rev. Charles Wesley, A.M., and set to music by
G. F. Handel, faithfully transcribed from his
autography in. . . . Fitzwilliam Museum,
Cambridge'

i Sinners obey the Gospel word	8.8.8.8.	203, 213
ii O love divine how sweet thou art	8.8.6. twice	203, 213
iii Rejoice! the Lord is king	6.6.6.6.8.8.	203, 213
We sing the wise, the gracious plan	8.8.8.8.8.8.	202

Hymn tunes included in *The Psalmist*
(Number in the collection shown in brackets)
† indicates an arrangement by Wesley of another composer's tune.

Name of tune	*Metre*	
Eversley (18)†, Northampton (41)†,	C.M.	213

Clifton (123), St Mary's (132)†,
Phillipi (133), Loughton (141),† Harlow (143),
Lystra (220)†, Kingsland (224), Canterbury (229)†
York (234)†, Bethany (236), Troas (239),
Westminster New (243)†, Arnsby (317),
Hertford (319), Colchester (321), Woodford (323),
Romsey (325), St David's (326)†, Walworth (329),
Watford (331), Snowdon (333), Daventry (335),
Tiverton (337), Bath (338), Chertsey (339).

Christchurch (101), Prague (110)†,   S.M.
Salamis (202), Shelford (210),
Lincoln College (213), Dunstable (302),
Reading (305), Amersham (308), Falmouth (309),
Norwich (312), Derby (313).

Arimathea (146), Leicester (160)†   L.M.
Bridgewater (165), Epworth (248),
Philadelphia (268), Hierapolis (347),
Thiatira (352), Ramah (356), Galatia (358)
Syria (359), Bristol (362), Thessalonica (365),
Lavendon (367), Lycaonia (369).

Joppa (294)	6.5.6.5. twice
Blandford (291)	6.6.4.6.6.4
Richmond (379)	6.6.4.6.6.6.4
Cesarea (292)	6.6.6.6.8.8.
Cyrene (315)†	(S.M.D.)
	6.6.8.6. twice
Llanberris (189)	7.6.7.6. twice
Weymouth (289)	7.6.7.6.7.8.7.6
Azotus (287)	7.7.7.5
Kettering (285)†	7.7.7.7.
Salisbury (290)	7.7.7.7.4.7.
Bedford (241)†	8.6.8.6.
Tarsus (275)	8.6.8.6.8.6.

Samuel Wesley—Keyboard Words (I)—*contd.*

		MS Source	Printed Editions
Name of tune	*Metre*		
Damascus (274)	8.6.8.6.8.8.		213
Portsea (283)†, Hebron (184)†	8.7.8.7.		
Bethlehem (296)	8.8.8.8.		
Chichester (186)	87.8.7. twice		
Dorking (188), Smyrna (397)	8.7.8.7.7.7.		
Gibeon (295)	10.10.10.10.		
Galilee (300)	13.11.13.11.		

Appendix, Juvenilia, Miscellaneous sketches

(107)	Alla breve in F	t^2	
(108)	Fugue in B flat (with imitation)	t^2	
(109)	Untitled pieces		
	(i) in F (18th November, 1822)	t^2	
	(ii) in D ('Denmark')	t^2	
	(iii) in C	n^3	
(110)	Sketch (harmonic outline) for slow movement in B flat	s^2	

Samuel Wesley—Keyboard Works (II)
Pianoforte

(111)	Preludes in the major and minor keys, two for each key (1797)	d^3, t^2	
	Major: C, D, E, F, G, A, B♭, B, E♭, A♭		
	Minor: A, B, C, D, E, F, G		
(112)	Untitled piece in D (6th September, 1797)	t^2	
(113)	Adagio in E minor	t^2	
(114)	Air in B flat, from a set of Sonatinas	t^2	
(115)	Sonatina in C	t^2	
(116)	(Sonatina) in D	t^2	
(117)	Prelude (Waltz) in D (18th October, 1836)	t^2	
(118)	Prelude (March) in E flat	s^2, t^2	
(119)	March in B flat (composed at 8, for military band)	s^2, t^2	180
(120)	Sonata in D minor/major, with fugue subject by Salomon	s^2, r^3	180, 189
(121)	(Minuet) in G	s^2	
(122)	Sonata in C, 'posthumous' (1813; 23rd March 1831)	u^2	180
(123)	Sonata in D, 'The Siege of Badajoz'		197
(124)	Three Sonatas Op. 3, to Miss Mary Grignon No. 1 in C, No. 2 in F, No. 3 in D		198
	Air from No. 2		190^2
(125)	Eight Sonatas (or lessons) for the harpsichord or pianoforte, to the Hon. Daines Barrington No. 1 in B flat, No. 2 in D, No. 3 in F, No. 4 in C, No. 5 in A, No. 6 in E, No. 7 in G, No. 8 in E flat		199
(126)	Fugue in D, to J. B. Logier		200
(127)	Grand Coronation March (also for organ)		191
(128)	Four Sonatas and Two Duets, Op. 5, to the Hon. Miss Lambs		186

Samuel Wesley—Keyboard Works (II)—*contd.*

		MS Source	Printed Editions
	Sonatas in A, B flat, D, E flat. Duets in F, D		186
	March from Duet in D		207
(129)	Sonata in E flat (8th November, 1788)	h³	
(130)	Sonata in B flat (28th January, 1793)	k³	
(131)	Sonata in A (5th October, 1794)	k³	
(132)	(Sonata) in G (23rd October, 1813)	n³	
(133)	Rondo in F (26th October, 1833)	n³	
(134)	Minuet in C	u²	
(135)	War Song in C (Amsterdam, 28th March, 1814)	u²	
(136)	Andante in A	u²	

Works for more than one player

		MS Source	Printed Editions
(137)	A trio for three grand pianofortes (20th April, 1811)	d³, t², u²	
(138)	Duet for the grand pianoforte (June, 1791)	d³	
(139)	Duet on 'God Save the King' in D (9th October, 1834)	t²	
(140)	Duet in G (19th January, 1832)	t²	
(141)	Duet (Gavotte) in D	t²	

Airs with Variations, or Rondos

		MS Source	Printed Editions
(142)	'The College Hornpipe' in B flat with variations	s²	
(143)	'A Frog he would a wooing-go', in D with variations	s²	
(144)	'Widow Waddle', Air in A	s²	
(145)	'Drops of brandy' (20th July, 1837)	s²	
(146)	'Weber's last Waltz', Air in A flat	s²	
(147)	Variations on an Italian Air in F, to Archdeacon Nares	t²	
(148)	'God rest you merry', Rondo on a Christmas Carol		180, 181, 190⁶
(149)	'Polacca', Rondo in G		180
(150)	'The Favourite Air of William Putty', Rondo	s², t²	188
(151)	'The Deserter's meditations', Rondo on an Irish Air (to the Misses Harrison)		171, 190⁶
(152)	Variations on a Polish Air		183
(153)	'Moll Pately', a celebrated dance arranged as a Rondo★		182
(154)	'Kitty alone and I', Rondo		201
(155)	'The Bay of Biscay', nine variations (to Clementi)		192
(156)	'Morgiana', Rondo	u²	
(157)	'Fairest Isle' (Purcell), Air and Variations (incomplete)	u²	
(158)	'Le Diable en Quatre', Air and Variations (28th October, 1801)	h³	
(159)	'Jessey of Dunblane', Air and Variations	n³	
(160)	'Jacky Horner', Rondo		168
(161)	'Off she goes', Rondo		195
(162)	'The Sky Rocket'		208
(163)	'Scots wha hae'		209
(164)	Cobourg Waltz		211

★ Referred to in *The Spectator*, Vol. 1, No. 67.

Samuel Wesley—Keyboard Works (II)—*contd.*

		MS Source	Other Editions
(165)	'Sweet enslaver', Air and variations		212
(166)	A favourite Air by Weber arranged as a Rondo		210
(167)	Introduction, Hornpipe and Variations (from an organ concerto)		206
(168)	'The Lass of Richmond Hill', Rondo	s^2, t^2	

Miscellaneous short pieces

(169)	Lento in F (1810)	l^3
(170)	Air in E flat	l^3
(171)	Waltz in D (21st November, 1818)	m^3
(172)	Gavotte in G minor	s^2, m^3, s^3
(173)	'Con discrezione' in D minor (10th July, 1829)	s^2, p^3
(174)	Introduction and Waltz in D	p^3
(175)	Short pieces in C, A	n^3
(176)	Short pieces in D (17th May, 1836), E flat	r^3, s^2, t^2

Other Composers

Composer	Work	MS Source	Printed Editions
ADAMS,	Fugue in D flat (Feb, 14th, 1810)	p^2	
Thomas	Fugue in F (Feb. 13th, 1810)	p^2	
	Voluntary in G (Jan. 31st, 1810)	p^2	
	Voluntary in E (Feb. 1st, 1810)	p^2	
	'Quant'è più bella', with variations		117
	Grand Organ piece		118
	Four books of Voluntaries		119
	Book I: 1 Voluntary in C		
	2 Voluntary in G		
	3 Voluntary in A		
	Book II: 4 Voluntary in B flat		
	5 Voluntary in D		
	6 Voluntary in E minor		
	Book III: 7 Voluntary in C		
	8 Voluntary in B flat		
	9 Voluntary in F		
	Book IV: 10 Voluntary in D		
	11 Voluntary in G		
	12 Voluntary in E		
	Three Organ pieces composed & dedicated to his friend Vincent Novello Esq.		121
	Voluntary in E		
	Voluntary in G		
	Voluntary in A minor		
	Six Voluntaries for the organ composed & dedicated to Mr Samuel Wesley		120
	1 Trumpet Voluntary in D		
	2 Voluntary in C		
	3 Voluntary in C minor/major		
	4 Voluntary in D		
	5 Voluntary in A minor		
	6 Voluntary in G minor		

Composer	Work	MS Source	Printed Editions
ADAMS, Thomas —contd.	*Six organ pieces composed & inscribed to* *T. Attwood Esq.* No. 1 in C minor No. 2 in B flat No. 3 in G minor No. 4 in C No. 5 in G minor No. 6 in D minor		122
	Six fugues for the organ or pianoforte *composed & dedicated to his friend* *Mr Henry May* 1 Fugue in B flat 2 Fugue in F minor 3 Fugue in C minor 4 Fugue in F minor 5 Fugue in E 6 Fugue in C		125
ALCOCK, John (Senior)	*Ten Voluntaries for the Organ or* *Harpsichord* 1 Trumpet Voluntary in C 2 Cremona Voluntary in G minor 3 Voluntary in E flat 4 Cornet Voluntary in C minor 5 Voluntary in D minor 6 Trumpet Voluntary in D 7 Voluntary in A minor 8 Voluntary in E minor 9 Trumpet Voluntary in D minor/ major 10 Voluntary in D		59, 128 59, 128 128 128 128 59, 128 128 128 128 59, 128
ALCOCK, John (Junior)	*Eight easy Voluntaries for the organ* 1 Trumpet Voluntary in D 2 Cornet Voluntary in G 3 Voluntary in F 4 Trumpet Voluntary in C 5 Voluntary in F 6 Trumpet Voluntary in D 7 Voluntary in G (fugue) 8 Voluntary in G minor (fugue, alla breve)		116
ANON.	*Six Voluntaries* 1 Voluntary in A minor 2 Cornet Voluntary in D minor 3 Cornet Voluntary in G 4 Cornet Voluntary in A minor 5 Voluntary in D 6 Voluntary in C		166
BATTISHILL, Jonathan	1 Voluntary in A 2 Voluntary in A		123 123, 124★

★ Ed. 124 is unreliable, and uses three staves.

Composer	Work	MS Source	Printed Editions
BATTISHILL	3 Voluntary in D		123
Johnathan	4 Voluntary in B flat		123
—*contd.*	5 Voluntary in A		123
	6 Voluntary in D minor		124*
BENNETT,	*Ten Voluntaries for the organ or*		
John	*Harpsichord*		129
	1 Trumpet Voluntary in D		
	2 Voluntary in B minor		
	3 Cornet Voluntary in G		
	4 Voluntary in C minor		
	5 Cornet Voluntary in A		
	6 Voluntary in F		
	7 Voluntary in D minor		
	8 Voluntary in G minor		
	9 Voluntary in F		
	10 Voluntary in D		
BERG,	*Ten Voluntaries for the organ or*		
George	*Harpsichord*, Op. 2		130
	1 Cornet Voluntary in D minor		
	2 Trumpet Voluntary in D		
	3 Cornet Voluntary in F		
	4 Trumpet Voluntary in C		
	5 Cornet Voluntary in G		
	6 Cornet Voluntary in G minor		
	7 Voluntary in D minor		
	8 Voluntary in D		
	9 Voluntary in G		
	10 Voluntary in G minor		
BLEWITT,	*A complete treatise* 'On the Organ'		
Jonas	*to which is added a set of* (twelve)		
	explanatory Voluntaries		143
	Ten Voluntaries or Pieces . . . for the		
	practice of juvenile performers		144
	Twelve easy & familiar movements . . .		
	for the use of juvenile performers		145
BOYCE,	*Ten Voluntaries for the organ or*		
William	*Harpsichord*		
	1 Trumpet Voluntary in D		60, 132
	2 Voluntary in G		132
	3 Trumpet Voluntary in C		132
	4 Cornet Voluntary in G minor		60, 132
	5 Trumpet Voluntary in D		131, 132
	6 Trumpet Voluntary in C		131, 132
	7 Voluntary in D minor		131, 132
	8 Voluntary in C		60, 131, 132
	9 Voluntary in A minor		60, 131, 132
	10 Voluntary in G		45, 131, 132
	Voluntary in A minor		108
	(see Anon., p. 176)		

* Ed. 124 is unreliable, and uses three staves.

Composer	Work	MS Source	Printed Editions
BURNEY, Charles	*Six Cornet Pieces with an introduction* *for the Diapason and a Fugue*		157
	1 Introduction and Cornet piece (Voluntary) in E minor		
	2 Cornet Piece in A		
	3 Cornet Piece in D		
	4 Cornet Piece in B minor		
	5 Cornet Piece in E flat		
	6 Cornet Piece in B flat		
	Fugue in F minor		
COOKE, Benjamin	*Fugues and other pieces (Book I)*		158
	1 Fugue in C minor		
	2 Cornet Piece (Voluntary) in C		
	3 (Voluntary) in G minor		
	4 (Voluntary) in B flat		
	Fugues and other pieces (Book II)		158
	5 (Voluntary) in C minor		
	6 (Voluntary) in C		
	7 Fugue in B flat		
	8 Fugue in A		
CROTCH, William	Fugue with 4 subjects (Oct. 7th, 1790)	n^2	
	Fugue with 2 subjects (Oct. 7th, 1790)	n^2	
	Twelve fugues based on Anglican chants		151
	Fugue on a subject of Muffat		174
DUPUIS, Thomas S.	Voluntary in D (Oct. 2nd, 1789)	m^2	
	Nine Voluntaries		44
	1 Voluntary in C		
	2 Voluntary in G minor		
	3 Voluntary in F		
	4 Voluntary in D minor/major		
	5 Voluntary in B flat		
	6 Voluntary in D minor		
	7 Voluntary in B flat		
	8 Voluntary in C		
	9 Voluntary in A		
	Nine Voluntaries for juvenile organists		141
	Pieces for the organ . . . for the use *of young organists,* Op. 8		150
	A second set of pieces . . . for the *use of young organists,* Op. 10		146
	Fugue in G minor, from above		58
GARTH, John	Voluntary in C (Op. 3, No. 2)	q^2	
	Voluntary in F (Op. 3, No. 3)	q^2	
GOODWIN, Starling	*Twelve Voluntaries (Book I)*		159
	1 Cornet Voluntary in A minor		
	2 Vox Humana Voluntary in G		
	3 Trumpet Voluntary in C		
	4 Cornet Voluntary in G		
	5 Voluntary in F		
	6 Trumpet Voluntary in C		

Composer	Work	MS Source	Printed Editions
GOODWIN,	7 Voluntary in D		159
Starling	8 Cornet Voluntary in D minor		
—*contd.*	9 Voluntary in B flat		
	10 Voluntary in D minor		
	11 Voluntary in A		
	12 Voluntary in D minor		
	Twelve Voluntaries (Book II)		160
	1 Voluntary in G		
	2 Voluntary in A minor		
	3 Trumpet Voluntary in C		
	4 Voluntary in A minor		
	5 Cornet Voluntary in A minor		
	6 Cornet Voluntary in G		
	7 Trumpet Voluntary in D		
	8 Voluntary in D		
	9 Voluntary in B minor		
	10 Cornet Voluntary in D minor		
	11 Trumpet Voluntary in D		
	12 Voluntary in G		
GREEN,	*Six Voluntaries*		165
George	1 Cornet Voluntary in E flat		
	2 Cornet Voluntary in A		
	3 Voluntary in E flat		
	4 Cornet Voluntary in E		
	5 Voluntary in E flat		
	6 Voluntary in B flat		
GUEST,	*Sixteen Pieces or Voluntaries,* Op. 3		147
George	1 Trumpet Voluntary in D		
	2 Voluntary in A		
	3 Voluntary in B flat		
	4 Voluntary in G		
	5 Voluntary in F		
	6 Trumpet Voluntary in C		
	7 Voluntary in F		
	8 Voluntary in G		
	9 Voluntary in D		
	10 Cornet Voluntary in F minor/major		
	11 Voluntary in E flat		
	12 Voluntary in G		
	13 Voluntary in F minor/major		
	14 Voluntary in F		
	15 Voluntary in C		
	16 Voluntary in D		
	Four fugues, Op. 13		126
	No. 1 in D, No. 2 in E flat, No. 3 in G,		
	No. 4 in B flat		
HAWDON,	*The Opening of an Organ*		
Matthias	Voluntary in C, and other pieces		148
	Six Sonatas or Voluntaries		167
	No. 1 in F, No. 2 in D minor, No. 3 in E flat		
	No. 4 in B flat, No. 5 in E flat, No. 6 in D		

Composer	Work	MS Source	Printed Editions
HERON, Henry	*Ten Voluntaries*		135
	1 Trumpet Voluntary in D ⎱ 2 Voluntary in B minor ⎰ (to be played cons.)		
	3 Cornet Voluntary in G		
	4 Cornet Voluntary in D minor		
	5 Trumpet Voluntary in C		
	6 Vox Humana Voluntary in A minor		
	7 Voluntary in D		
	8 Voluntary in G		
	9 Voluntary in G minor		
	10 Voluntary in A		
HOOK, James	*Ten Voluntaries*, Op. 146		142
KEEBLE, John	*Select pieces for the organ* (first set)		153, 156
	No. 1 in G		
	No. 2 in D		
	No. 3 in F minor/major		
	No. 4 in C		
	No. 5 in G minor		
	No. 6 in D (Cornet Voluntary)		
	Select pieces for the organ (second set)		154, 156
	No. 7 in F minor/major		
	No. 8 in C (Trumpet Voluntary)		
	No. 9 in G minor		
	No. 10 in D minor		
	No. 11 in F		
	No. 12 in C (Tetrachord variations)		
	Fugue only of No. 12		58
	Select pieces for the organ (third set)		155, 156
	No. 13 in F		
	No. 14 in C minor		
	No. 15 in G		
	No. 16 in D minor		
	No. 17 in A		
	No. 18 in E		
	Select pieces for the organ (fourth set)		156
	No. 19 in G (chromatic)		
	No. 20 in D		
	No. 21 in A minor		
	No. 22 in C minor/major		
	No. 23 in F		
	No. 24 in B flat		
	Diapason piece in F		190[5]
KIRKMAN, Jacob	*Six Voluntaries*, Op. 9		149
	1 Voluntary in D		
	2 Voluntary in B flat		
	3 Voluntary (Fugue) in E minor		
	4 Voluntary in E flat		
	5 Voluntary in A		
	6 Voluntary in B flat		

Composer	Work	MS Source	Printed Editions
LONG,	Voluntary in G minor		162
Samuel	Voluntary in D minor		162
MARSH,	Overture in D and six pieces		136
John	(No. 1 in A minor, No. 2 in D, No. 3		
	in C, No. 4 in D, No. 5 in G, No. 6 in C)		
	Two fugues (duet)		152
NARES,	*Six Fugues with Introductory Voluntaries*		137
James	1 Introduction & Fugue in F		
	2 Fugue in G minor		
	3 Introduction & Fugue in E flat		
	4 Fugue in G		
	5 Introduction & Fugue in A		
	minor/major		
	6 Fugue in F		
RUSSELL,	*Twelve Voluntaries* (set 1)		169
William	1 (Trumpet) Voluntary in C		
	2 Voluntary in F		
	3 Cornet Voluntary in G (a la Pollacca)		
	4 Voluntary in D		
	5 Cornet Voluntary in D minor		
	6 Voluntary in F		
	7 Voluntary in E flat (Pedals)		
	8 Voluntary in B flat		
	9 Voluntary in A minor		
	10 Voluntary in G minor		
	11 Voluntary in E minor/major		
	12 (Trumpet) Voluntary in C		
	minor/major (Pedals)		
	Twelve Voluntaries (set 2)		170
	1 (Trumpet) Voluntary in E		
	minor/major (Pedals)		
	2 (Cremona) Voluntary in C (Pedals)		
	3 Trumpet Voluntary in D		
	4 Cornet Voluntary in A minor		
	5 (Cremona) Voluntary in F		
	6 Voluntary in E flat (Pedals)		
	7 Voluntary in A		
	8 Voluntary in B minor		
	9 Voluntary in B flat		
	10 Voluntary in G (fugue on a subject		
	by Haydn) (Pedals)		
	11 Voluntary in D minor/major (Pedals)		
	12 Voluntary in C (Pedals)		
	Pastorale (from an Impromptu)		190²
	Introduction and Air in E minor/major		190⁴
	March in G		190⁴
	Two Airs in A		190⁴
	Air (Andantino) in E flat		190⁴
	March in C minor		190⁴
	Slow movements in A minor, C		190⁵

Composer	Work	MS Source	Printed Editions
RUSSELL,	Diapason piece in D		190[5]
William	Pastoral movement		190[5]
—contd.	Airs in E flat, E, F		190[5]
WALOND,	Trumpet Voluntary in D	o[2]	
William	*Six Voluntaries*, Op. 1		
	1 Cornet Voluntary in E minor		64, 138
	2 Voluntary in G		65, 138
	3 Cornet Voluntary in D minor		64, 138
	4 Cornet Voluntary in D minor/		
	major		65, 138
	5 Cornet Voluntary in G		64, 138
	6 Voluntary in D minor		65, 138
	Ten Voluntaries, Op. 2		
	1 Cornet Voluntary in E		45, 139
	2 Voluntary in B minor		139
	3 Voluntary in G		139
	4 Trumpet Voluntary in D		139
	5 Voluntary in C minor		139
	6 Voluntary in G		139
	7 Voluntary in B flat		139
	8 Voluntary in C		139
	9 Voluntary in E flat		139
	10 Voluntary in A minor		139
WEBBE,	Prelude and Fugue in A major		115
Egerton			
WEBBE,	*Three Voluntaries composed & dedicated*		
Samuel (Jun.)	*to his friend Samuel Wesley*		127
	1 Voluntary in D		
	2 Voluntary in A		
	3 Voluntary in C		
WESLEY,	*Six Voluntaries*		
Charles	1 Voluntary in D (based on Handel's		
	Julius Caesar)		173
	2 Voluntary in D minor/major		
	(based on 'Thou shalt bring them in'		
	Air from Handel's *Israel in Egypt*)		173
	3 Voluntary in G minor (based on		
	Handel's 'Then will I Jehovah Praise')		173
	Part only of No 3		114
	4 Voluntary in G		173
	5 Voluntary in A minor/major		
	(based on *Julius Caesar*)		173
	Part only of No 5		48
	6 Voluntary in C		173
WORGAN,	*Ten select organ pieces*		140
John	No. 1 in C minor/major		
	No. 2 in F, No. 3 in G		
	No. 4 in C, No. 5 in G		

Composer	Work	MS Source	Printed Editions
WORGAN John —*contd.*	No. 6 in C ('All the chords used in harmony in a sharp key')		140
	No. 7 in D minor ('All the chords used in harmony in a flat key')		
	No. 8 in G, No. 9 in C		
	No. 10 in A ('Swelling hautboy')		
	Organ pieces		111
	No. 1 in A, No. 2 in F, No. 3 in F		
	No. 4 in B flat, No. 5 in G minor		

BIOGRAPHICAL NOTES ON THE COMPOSERS

ADAMS, Thomas.

1785–1858. 1802–14 Organist at various London churches, incl. St George's, Camberwell, and St Paul's Deptford (1810) (Fugues played at the competition for St Paul's Deptford are in Ms p²). 1833 Organist St Dunstan in the West. Well-known performer and extemporiser. Friend of Samuel Wesley.

ALCOCK, John (i) 1715–1806 (ii) 1740–1791

(i) Chorister at St Paul's Cathedral. Pupil of John Stanley (1729). 1737 Organist St Andrew's, Plymouth. 1742 Organist St Lawrence's, Reading. 1749 Organist, Lay Vicar, Lichfield Cathedral. 1760 Organist Sutton Coldfield Parish Church. Songs, church music, keyboard music. (ii) Son of above, born Plymouth. 1758 Organist St Mary Magdalen, Newark-on-Trent. 1773 Organist Walsall Church, Staffordshire. Songs, church music.

ARNOLD, Samuel.

1740–1802. Chorister at Chapel Royal under Gates and Nares (q.v.). 1763 Engaged as composer at Covent Garden (oratorios, pastiches). 1783 Organist and composer to Chapel Royal (after Nares). 1786 Produced oratorios at Drury Lane (after Stanley). Edited Handel's works. 1790 Edited Cathedral music. 1793 Organist Westminster Abbey after Cooke (q.v.).

BATTISHILL, Jonathan.

1738–1801. Chorister at St Paul's Cathedral; pupil of William Savage. 1764 Organist St Clement, Eastcheap and St Martin, Ongar. 1767 Organist Christ Church, Newgate Street. Minor composer of theatre and church music (songs, ballads at Sadler's Wells); Sang in opera; deputy organist to Boyce (q.v.) at Chapel Royal.

BENNETT, John.

1735(?)–1784. 1752 Organist St Dionis, Backchurch, Fenchurch St, until his death. Great reputation as organist and composer. The subscribers to his Voluntaries (Ed. 129) included David Garrick, Handel, Travers, Worgan, Byfield, Dupuis, George England and many others as far afield as New England and Barbados.

BERG, George.

?(fl. mid-eighteenth century). German settled in London. 1771 Organist St Mary-at-Hill. Songs, glees.

BLEWITT, Jonas.

?–1805. 1795 (?) Organist St Margaret Pattens, Rood Lane with St Gabriel, Fenchurch and St Catherine Coleman, Fenchurch Street. Teacher, author of an organ treatise.

BOYCE, William.

1710–1779. Chorister at St Paul's Cathedral, later pupil of Maurice Greene. 1736 (21st June) Composer to the Chapel Royal. 1736–68 Organist St Michael's, Cornhill, where competitors included Froud, Kelway, Worgan. 1749–69 Organist All Hallows, Thames Street. 1757 Master of the King's Band of Musicians (on death of Greene). 1758 Organist of the Chapel Royal (on death of Travers). Resigned his appointment in 1769 owing to deafness. Compositions include Church music, Choral music, Stage works, Instrumental music.

BURNEY, Charles.

1726–1814. Attended schools in Shrewsbury and Chester. 1744 Associated, as harpsichordist, with Thomas Arne. 1748 Organist of St Dionis, Backchurch. Conductor of 'New Concerts' at the King's Arms, Cornhill. 1751 Moved to King's Lynn, Norfolk, where Snetzler built a famous organ (1754). 1770 Travelled extensively engaged in historical study. Writer, minor composer; *persona grata* to everyone of note in art, music, politics and religion of his day.

COOKE, Benjamin.

1734–1793. Pupil of Pepusch; apprentice (1743) to John Robinson at Westminster Abbey. 1752 succeeded Pepusch as conductor of the Academy of Ancient Music. 1757 Master of choristers at Westminster Abbey (after Gates). 1758 Lay Vicar at Westminster Abbey. 1762 Organist at Westminster Abbey (after Robinson). 1782 Organist St Martin's-in-the-Fields, where competitors included Burney. Compositions include Choral and Instrumental music. Son Robert Cooke —see under *Samuel Wesley*.

CROTCH, William.

1775–1847. Born Norwich, toured as infant prodigy (1778–9). 1786 Assisted Professor Randall at Cambridge, Organist at Trinity & King's Colleges. 1790 Organist Christ Church Oxford, succeeded Hayes as professor (1797).

DUPUIS, Thomas.

1733–1796. Huguenot family, Chorister of Chapel Royal under Gates. Pupil of John Travers. 1773 Organist of Charlotte Street Chapel. 1779 Organist of Chapel Royal (on death of Boyce).

GARTH, John.

1722–1810. Born Durham, now known only for Cello Concertos and Sonatas. Op. 3 consisted of six voluntaries.

GOODWIN, Starling.

? (fl. c. 1760–80). Organist St Mary's, Newington, St Mary Magdalen, Bermondsey. Nothing otherwise known. The Goodwins appear in the D.N.B. as a well-known ecclesiastical family.

GREEN (i) James (fl. c. 1743) (ii) George (fl. c. 1775–80).

(i) of Hull (?) Published psalm-tunes. (ii) nothing known.

GUEST, George.

1771–1831. Father was organist of St Mary's, Bury St Edmunds. Chorister of Chapel Royal under Nares. 1789–1831 Organist St Peter's, Wisbech. Probably taught at Lynn boarding school (see Ed. 147). Well-known all over East Anglia. Subscribers to Op. 3 include J. C. Beckwith (organist Norwich Cathedral 1808).

HAWDON, Mathias.

?–1787. Organist at Hull, Beverley Minster, Newcastle-upon-Tyne. Nothing otherwise known.

HERON, Henry.

18th cent. 1745 (?) Organist St Magnus the Martyr, London Bridge, Nothing otherwise known.

HOOK, James.

1746–1827. Born Norwich, crippled from birth, he had a permanent limp. Pupil of Thomas Garland, (organist Norwich Cathedral 1749–1808). Later of Burney. Precocious performer. 1764 Organist at a tea-house, White Conduit House, Clerkenwell. 1768–73 Organist at Marylebone Gardens. 1774–1820 Organist at Vauxhall Gardens. Composer of light music; concertos, overtures, 30 operas, 2000 songs, of which the most notorious was 'The lass of Richmond Hill'.

KEEBLE, John.

1711–1786. Chorister at Chichester Cathedral under Thomas Kelway. Later pupil of Pepusch. 1737 Organist St George's, Hanover Square (after Roseingrave). 1742 Organist at Ranelagh Gardens (from their opening).

KELWAY, (i) Joseph ?–1782, (ii) Thomas ?–1749.

(i). Pupil of Geminiani, Organist, Harpsichordist. 1730 Organist St Michael's, Cornhill. 1736 Organist St Martin's-in-the-Fields. Well known as a teacher; pupils included the young Charles Wesley. (ii) Brother of (i), Organist of Chichester Cathedral.

KIRKMAN, Jacob.

?–1812. Perhaps the nephew of well-known harpsichord maker. 1786 (?) Organist St George's, Hanover Square (after Keeble?). Published psalm-interludes with Keeble.

LONG, Samuel.

? (fl. *c.* 1760–70). Very small output; compositions include glees and catches.

MARSH, John.

1752–1828. Amateur musician, trained as a solicitor. Interests included astronomy and military affairs.

NARES, James.

1715–1783. Chorister in Chapel Royal under Gates and Croft. Deputy at St George's, Windsor. 1734 Organist of York Minster. 1756 Organist and Composer of Chapel Royal (after Greene). 1757–80 Master of the children (after Gates). Compositions include Church music, keyboard music. His brother became a judge.

RUSSELL, William.

1777–1813. Son of an organ-builder and organist, pupil of Arnold. 1789–93 Assistant to his father at St Mary, Aldermanbury. 1793–98 Organist Great Queen Street Chapel, until it became a Wesleyan meeting-house. 1798–1801 Organist St Ann's, Limehouse. 1800 Pianist and composer at Sadler's Wells. 1801–1813 Organist at Foundling Hospital, pianist at Covent Garden.

Compositions include 20 dramatic works, 2 oratorios.

WALOND, William.

1725–1770. 1757 *Organorum pulsator* 'at Oxford'. Three sons, William, Richard and George were all church musicians.

WEBBE, Egerton.

Son of (ii) below; nothing otherwise known.

WEBBE, Samuel (i) 1740–1816 (ii) 1770–1843.

(i) Organist, and composer of about 300 catches and glees. 1790(?) Organist of Sardinian Embassy Chapel. (ii) Son of above; Roman Catholic. Studied under his father and Clementi. 1798 Organist Unitarian Chapel, Paradise Street, Liverpool. 1817 Organist Spanish Embassy. ? Organist St Nicholas and St Patrick (R.C.) Chapels, Liverpool.

WESLEY, Charles.

1757–1834. Elder brother of Samuel. Organist of various London Churches, including Chelsea Hospital and St Marylebone; also (before 1794) Surrey Chapel, Blackfriars.

WORGAN, John.

1724–1790. Family of Welsh musicians, brother organist at Vauxhall Gardens. Studied under Roseingrave. 1749 (?) Organist St Andrew Undershaft, St Mary Axe 1753 Organist St Botolph, Aldgate. 1760 Organist St John's Chapel, Bedford Row. Played, composed and conducted at Vauxhall Gardens, with Hook (q.v.). Compositions included choral works and songs.

THE ORGAN OF THE PERIOD 1759–1837

The second half of the eighteenth century witnessed a consolidation of the style and tradition established by Smith and Harris. Among the most notable organ builders were Harris's son-in-law John Byfield, and his family; also John England, and his son George Pike England.

A remarkable example of an organ built by the second John Byfield in 1764 may still be seen at St Mary's, Rotherhithe. It has recently been restored by Noel Mander into playing condition.

St Mary's Rotherhithe
(John Byfield (II), 1764)

Great		Choir	
Open Diapason	8	Stop'd Diapason	8
Stop'd Diapason	8	Principal	4
Principal	4	Flute	4
Nason	4	Fifteenth	2
Fifteenth	2	Vox Humana	8
Sesquialtera	III		
Cornet	V		
Trumpet	8		
Clarion	4		

This design is entirely standard for the period, lacking only the third (Swell) manual. Further examples of this tradition, though extended to include a 4^1 Clarion on the Swell, were characteristic of John England's work, with such instruments as St Stephen's Walbrook, and St Mildred's, Poultry. His son George Pike England, who lived until 1816, carried this style over into the nineteenth century. His most typical organs were built at St Mary Magdalene, Holloway Road, and St James, Clerkenwell.

Another important organ-builder came from Germany in about 1740 and settled in this country. Johann Snetzler, who was born in Passau in 1710, came without any royal patronage, and moreover to an already-established tradition of organ design—within which he worked, and which he did as much as Byfield or England to consolidate.

The majority of his instruments were built outside London, particularly in the North of England. Beverley Minster was one of his chief ones. He was also well known for small chamber organs, some of which still survive today. One such instrument, a bureau organ dating from about 1725, is in the possession of Mr and Mrs George Warburg of London, and has been restored by Noel Mander.

Bureau Organ
(Johann Snetzler, 1759)

Diapason	8	
Flute	4	
Fifteenth	2	
Sesquialtera	II	(19th & 22nd up to middle C)
Cornet	II	(12th & 17th from middle C upwards)

Another chamber organ, highly characteristic of Snetzler's work, and restored to playing condition, is now in St Andrew-by-the-Wardrobe. It was formerly at Teddesley Hall, Stafford.

St Andrew-by-the-Wardrobe
(Johann Snetzler, 1769)

Stopt Diapason	8
Open Diapason	8
Dulciana	8
Flute	4
Principal	4
Fifteenth	2
Sesquialtera	III
Cornet	III

Three organs may be taken to be of central importance to the evolution of the eighteenth-century Voluntary—the instruments available to Boyce, Russell and Wesley; all clearly show the general style of organ design at this time.

Boyce's Organ at All Hallows, Thames Street
(Glyn and Parker, 1749)

Great		Choir★		Swell★	
Open Diapason	8	Open Diapason	8	Trumpet	8
Stopped Diapason	8	Stopped Diapason	8	Cornet	III

★ Played on the same manual.

Great		Choir		Swell	
Principal	4	Flute	4		
Twelfth	$2\frac{2}{3}$	Twelfth	$2\frac{2}{3}$		
Fifteenth	2	Vox Humana	8		
Sesquialtera	IV				
Cornet	V				
Trumpet	8				

Russell's Organ at St Ann's, Limehouse
(Richard Bridge, 1741; later modified)

Great		Choir		Swell	
Open Diapason I	8	Dulciana	8	Open Diapason	8
Open Diapason II	8	Stopped Diapason	8	Stopped Diapason	8
Stopped Diapason	8	Principal	4	Principal	4
Principal	4	Flute	4	German Flute	4
Twelfth	$2\frac{2}{3}$	Fifteenth	2	Cornet	III
Fifteenth	2	Mixture	II	Hautboy	8
Tierce	$1\frac{3}{5}$	Cremona	8	Trumpet	8
Sesquialtera	III			Clarion	4
Furniture	II–III				
Cornet	V				
Trumpet	8				

Pull-down pedals, one octave

Samuel Wesley's & Benjamin Jacobs's Organ
at Surrey Chapel, Blackfriars Road
(Elliot, ?)

Great		Swell (down to Tenor F)	
Open Diapason I	8	Open Diapason	8
Open Diapason II	8	Stopped Diapason	8
Stopped Diapason	8	Principal	4
Principal	4	Cornet	III
Flute	4	Trumpet	8
Twelfth	$2\frac{2}{3}$		
Cornet (Treble)	III		
Sesquialtera (bass)	II		
Mixture	II		
Trumpet I	8		
Trumpet II (Sw)	8		

Pull-down pedals, $1\frac{1}{2}$ octaves

But already by the late eighteenth century, symptoms of the changes that were to come in the nineteenth century began to be apparent; that gradual erosion of an active tradition of organ music, coupled with a growth of the monumental, display instrument; the 'romantic' organ.

The displacement of the Harris–Byfield tradition was gradual. The case of Salisbury Cathedral has already been mentioned.* At Norwich Cathedral the same process can be more clearly seen by comparing the Byfield instrument of 1760 with that of J. C. Bishop, built in 1834.

Norwich Cathedral
(John Byfield (II), 1760)

Great		Choir		Echo	
Open Diapason I	8	Stopped Diapason	8	Open Diapason	8
Open Diapason II	8	Principal	8	Stopped Diapason	8
Stopped Diapason	8	Flute	4	Principal	4
Principal	4	Stopped Flute	4	Cornet	III
Twelfth	$2\frac{2}{3}$	Fifteenth	2	Trumpet	8
Fifteenth	2				
Tierce	$1\frac{3}{5}$				
Sesquialtera	IV				
Cornet	V				
Trumpet	8				

(J. C. Bishop, 1834)

Great		Choir		Swell	
Open Diapason I	8	Dulciana	8	Open Diapason	8
Open Diapason II	8	Stopped Diapason	8	Stopped Diapason	8
Stopped Diapason	8	Principal	4	Principal	4
Clarabella	8	Stopped Flute	4	Hautboy	8
(In place of Cornet V)		Fifteenth	2	Trumpet	8
Principal	4	Cremona	8		
Twelfth	$2\frac{2}{3}$				
Fifteenth	2	*Pedal*			
Tierce	$1\frac{3}{5}$	Open Diapason 16			
Sesquialtera	IV	(lowest $1\frac{1}{2}$ octaves)			
Trumpet	8				

* See p. 193.

The modifications are highly significant, and reflect the function expected of the organ in the early nineteenth century, that of an accompanimental instrument to the singers—which had been the starting point more than three centuries earlier. The general tendency was to reduce the upper-work, and to revert to the former duplication of stops of the same pitch. The Great mounted Cornet, one of the most colourful and characteristic stops of the early organ tradition, was removed in favour of this particular builder's patent 8' Clarabella (or large-scale, unison flute); the Echo Mixture III was replaced by an 8' Oboe. The mechanical improvements, such as the enclosed Swell, and composition pedals, were of slight and highly questionable musical use. In short, in several important respects, this reactionary instrument may be taken as symptomatic of the approaching decadence.

As the nineteenth century progressed, the British genius for mechanics was applied to organs, often with dire results. While on the Continent the instruments remained largely untouched, in England the design of organs assumed a quite different character as a result of the pneumatic lever, electric action, and other inventions.

The two chief features of the British organs built at the beginning of the nineteenth century, which marked them out from those built on the Continent were, first, the continuing lack of a pedal organ and, second, the lack of a clearly defined character for the divisions other than the Great. These were problems which, in a vital and growing tradition, would have required urgent solution. In the event however neither problem was solved before the death of Samuel Wesley in 1837; and thereafter the stagnation of the nineteenth century overtook the British musical scene. By then, therefore, in spite of several promising innovations by some builders, such as William Hill, and the corresponding challenge of an exceptional composition like Egerton Webbe's *Prelude and Fugue*, it was too late to matter.

The problems were related; indeed in a sense they were the two sides of the same problem. The absence of a pedal division, and the absence of a musically-based and distinctive purpose for the Choir and Swell organs, were symptoms of the same disease; which was a general decline in solo organ music itself, and a consequent inevitable divorce between the composer and the organ-builder. Later, as the nineteenth century progressed, this divorce was to become indecently clear; organs reflected not the needs of composers, nor the traditions of an accepted musical style, but the public taste of the day, and the wishes of 'recital' organists, who fed on it. Standards became gross, vulgar and overwhelmingly reactionary. The ultimate stage in this line of development was reached in the instruments of Henry Willis,* which however 'unrivalled' they might be, were monuments to a vacuum. Their musical justification was more than questionable; their original repertoire negligible. Transcriptions were substituted for organ music; the town-hall organist became a 'one-man band', whose principal *raison d'être* was that he cost less to employ than a 50-man orchestra. Indeed this retrograde and reactionary trend was pursued even by Vincent Novello, whose 'Cathedral Voluntaries' were merely transcriptions of anthems.

If we need a particular point in time which can be shown to mark this process, such a moment was the year of the Great Exhibition, 1851. By then, if not before, the pattern and direction of organ building of the nineteenth century, to say nothing of its taste, were clearly fixed; by then the centuries-old tradition of early English organ music had become irretrievably a thing of the past.

* St George's Hall, Liverpool, (1855) and the Royal Albert Hall, London (1871) were the best known.

Select Bibliographies

Bibliography I: Books
Bibliography II: Articles in Magazines and periodicals.
Bibliography III: Catalogues, Dictionaries, Encyclopaedias, Works of reference.

BIBLIOGRAPHY I
Books
(Published in London unless otherwise stated)

AMBROSE, Holmes. *The Anglican Anthems and Roman Catholic Motets of Samuel Wesley*. Unpublished Ph.D. Dissertation, Boston University U.S.A. 1969.

APEL, Willi. *Geschichte der Orgel—und Klaviermusik, bis 1700*. Bärenreiter (Kassel). 1967.

— *Gregorian Chant*. Burns & Oates. 1958.

— *Solo instrumental Music* (in New Oxford History of Music, Vol. IV—1540–1630). Oxford University Press. 1968.

— *The Notation of Polyphonic Music* 900–1600. The Mediaeval Academy of America (2nd edition). 1944 (reviewed—see Bukofzer in Bibl. II).

ATKINS, Ivor. *The Early Occupants of the Office of Organist . . . of the Cathedral Church . . . Worcester*. Worcestershire Historical Society. 1918.

AYLWARD, Theodore. *The Sarum Hymnal*. Salisbury. 1869.

BARBOUR, J. Murray. *Tuning and temperament. A historical survey*. Michigan State College Press, U.S.A. 1951.

BARRINGTON, Daines. *Miscellanies* (includes Charles Wesley's account of Samuel Wesley's early life). J. Nichols. 1781.

BEDBROOK, G. S. *Keyboard Music from the Middle Ages to the beginning of the Baroque*. Macmillan. 1949.

BEDOS de CELLES, Dom François. *L'Art du facteur d'orgues*. Paris. 1761.

BENSON, Louis F. *The English Hymn*. Hodder & Stoughton. 1915.

BLOM, Eric. *Music in England*. Pelican Books. 1942 (revised 1947).

BLUME, Friedrich. *Two centuries of Bach*. Oxford University Press. 1950.

BORREN, Charles Van den. *The Sources of keyboard Music in England* (translated from the French, *Les origines de la musique de clavier en Angleterre*, by James E. Matthew). Novello. 1914.

BOSTON, Noel. *The musical history of Norwich Cathedral*. Norwich. 1963.

BRAGARD, Roger and De HEN, Ferdinand J. *Musical instruments in art and history*. Barrie and Rockliff. 1967.

BRITTAIN, F. see under GRAY, A.

BUHLE, Eduard. *Die Musikalischen Instrumente in den Miniaturen des frühen Mittelalters* (I—Die Blasinstrumente). 1903.

BUKOFZER, M. *Music in the Baroque Era*. Dent. 1947.

BUMPUS, John S. *A history of English Cathedral Music*. T. Werner Laurie. 1908.

— *The Organists and Composers of St Paul's Cathedral*. Bowden, Hudson & Co. 1891.

BUTLER, Charles. *The principles of musik*. London. 1636.

CALDWELL, John. *English keyboard music before the nineteenth century*. Blackwell, Oxford, 1973.

CLARKE, Mary Cowden. *The life and labours of Vincent Novello*. Novello, 1864.

CLUTTON, Cecil & NILAND, Austin. *The British Organ*. Batsford. 1963.

COBB, G. F. *A brief history of the organs . . . Trinity College, Cambridge*. Cambridge, 1913.

CURTIS, Alan. *Sweelinck's keyboard Music*. Leiden University Press (London: Oxford University Press). 1969.

DART, Thurston. *The interpretation of Music*. Hutchinson. 1954 (4th edition 1967). See also under MORLEY, T. and PARTHENIA IN-VIOLATA.

DAVEY, Henry. *History of English Music*. Curwen (2nd edition). 1921 (1st edition 1895).

DEARNLEY, Christopher. *English Church Music 1650–1750*. Barrie and Jenkins. 1970.

DEGERING, Hermann. *Die Orgel*. Münster. 1905.

De HEN, Ferdinand J. See under BRAGARD, R.

DENT, Edward J. *Foundations of English Opera*. Cambridge University Press. 1928.

DEUTSCH, Otto Erich. *Handel, A documentary Biography*. A. & C. Black. 1955.

DONINGTON, Robert. *The interpretation of early music*. Faber. 1963.

DOUGLAS, Winfred. *Church Music in history and practice*. Faber. 1963 (revised by Leonard Ellinwood).

DOWNES, R. *Purcell: An organist's view of the organ works*. Oxford University Press. 1959 (in *Henry Purcell, 1659–1695*, ed. I. Holst).

ELLINWOOD, Leonard. See under DOUGLAS, W.

FARMER, Henry George. *The Organ of the Ancients, from Eastern sources*. Reeves. 1931.

FELLOWES, Edmund H. *English Cathedral Music from Edward VI to Edward VII*. Methuen. 1941.

— *Organists . . . of St George's Chapel in Windsor Castle*. S.P.C.K. 1939.

FELLOWES, Edmund H. *Orlando Gibbons and his family.* Oxford University Press. 1925.

— *William Byrd.* Oxford University Press. 1936 (2nd ed. 1948).

FLOOD, W. H. Grattan. *A history of Irish Music.* Browne and Nolan, Dublin. 1905.

— *Early Tudor composers.* Oxford University Press. 1925.

FREEMAN, Andrew. *English Organ-cases.* Mate. 1921.

— *Father Smith.* London. 1926.

GALPIN, Francis W. *Old English instruments of Music.* Methuen. 1965 (4th edition).

— *The water-organ of the ancients and the organ of today.* Walter Scott Pub. Co. 1906.

GARDINER, William, *Music and Friends.* (3 vols.) Longman, Orme. 1838–53.

GILLMAN, Frederick J. *The evolution of the English Hymn.* Allen & Unwin. 1927.

GLYN, Margaret H. *About Elizabethan Virginal Music and its Composers.* Reeves. 1934.

GRAY, Arthur and BRITTAIN, Frederick. *A history of Jesus College, Cambridge.* Heinemann. 1960.

HARMAN, R. Alec. See under MORLEY, T.

HARRISON, Frank Ll. *Music in mediaeval Britain.* Routledge and Kegan Paul. 1958.

HINRICHSEN, Max. *A Purcell compilation (Tallis to Wesley,* Vol. 10). Hinrichsen. 1961.

— *Wesley and Mendelssohn in England (Tallis to Wesley* Vol. 14) Hinrichsen. 1962.

HOPKINS, E. J. *The English mediaeval Church Organ.* Pollard, Exeter. 1888.

HOPKINS, E. J. and RIMBAULT, E. F. *The Organ, its history and construction.* Robert Cocks, 1855 (3rd Ed. 1872).

HUGHES, Dom Anselm (ed.). *Ars Nova and the Renaissance* 1300–1540. Oxford University Press. 1960 *(New Oxford History of Music* Vol. III).

LANDOWSKA, Wanda. *Landowska on music* edited by Denise Restout. Secker and Warburg. 1965.

LEFFLER, Henry. *Notes on English Organs.* London. 1912 (see PEARCE, Charles W.).

LEFKOWITZ, Murray. *William Lawes.* Routledge and Kegan Paul. 1960.

Le HURAY, Peter. *Music and the Reformation in England*—1549–1660. Jenkins. 1967.

LIGHTWOOD, James T. *Samuel Wesley, musician.* The Epworth Press. 1937.

LONGFORD, E. See under PAKENHAM, E.

MARSH, John. *The Latin Church Music of Samuel Wesley.* Unpublished D. Phil. Thesis, York University. 1972.

MATTHEW, James E. See under BORREN, Charles van den.

MATTHEWS, Betty. *The organs and organists of Exeter Cathedral.* Exeter. 1965.

— *The organs and organists of Salisbury Cathedral.* Salisbury. 1966.

— *The organs and organists of Winchester Cathedral.* Winchester. 1967.

MAYES, Stanley. *An organ for the Sultan.* (An account of Thomas Dallam's journey to Constantinople in 1599 and 1600). Putnam, 1956.

MEYER, Ernst H. *English Chamber Music from the Middle Ages to Purcell.* Lawrence and Wishart. 1946.

MIDDLETON, R. D. *Dr. Routh.* Oxford University Press. 1933.

MORLEY, Thomas. *A plaine and Easie Introduction to Practicall Musicke* (1597) edited by R. Alec Harman. Dent. 1952 (3rd, revised, ed. 1962, with foreword by Thurston Dart).

NAYLOR, E. W. *An Elizabethan Virginal Book: A Critical Essay on the Contents of the Fitzwilliam Virginal Book.* Dent. 1905.

NEWMAN, Ernest. See under SCHWEITZER, Albert.

NILAND, Austin. See under CLUTTON, Cecil.

OHL, John F. See under PARRISH, Carl.

PAKENHAM, Elizabeth, Countess of Longford. *Wellington—The years of the sword.* Weidenfeld and Nicolson. 1969.

PARRISH, Carl and OHL, John F. *A treasury of early music.* Faber. 1959.

— *Masterpieces of Music before 1750.* Faber. 1942.

PARTHENIA IN-VIOLATA. Edited with Historical introduction by Thurston Dart and bibliographical note by Richard J. Wolfe. New York Public Library. 1961.

PEARCE, Charles W. *Notes on English Organs of the period 1800–1810, taken chiefly from the MS of Henry Leffler.* London. 1912.

— *Notes on Old London City Churches, etc.* London. 1909.

PFATTEICHER, Carl Friedrich. *John Redford, Organist and Almoner of St Paul's Cathedral in the reign of Henry VIII.* Bärenreiter. 1934.

PRAETORIUS, Michael. *Syntagma musicum.* Wolffenbüttel. 1619.

PULVER, Jeffrey. *Music in England during the Commonwealth.* London. 1934 (extracted from 'Acta Musicologica').

REDLICH, Hans. *The Bach Revival in England.* Hinrichsen. 1952 (in Hinrichsen Music Book, Vol. VII).

— *Virginal Music.* Macmillan. 1954 (in Grove's Dictionary, 5th edition, Vol. IX).

REESE, Gustav. *Music in the Middle Ages.* Dent. 1940.

— *Music in the Renaissance.* Dent. 1954 (revised ed.).

RIMBAULT, E. F. *The Early English Organ builders and their work.* Reeves. 1925 (1st ed. 1865). See under HOPKINS, E. J.

ROKSETH, Yvonne. *La musique d'orgue du XVe siècle et au début du XVIe.* E. Droz, Paris. 1930.

— *The instrumental music of the middle ages and early sixteenth century.* (New Oxford History of Music, Vol. III) Oxford University Press. 1960.

ROUTH, Francis. *Samuel Wesley Keyboard works—Thematic index.* Unpublished. 1972.

ROUTLEY, Erik. *The Musical Wesleys*. Jenkins. 1968.

SACHS, Curt. *The history of musical instruments*. W. W. Norton, New York. 1940.

— *The rise of music in the ancient world*. Dent. 1944.

SCHWEITZER, Albert. *J. S. Bach*. Translated by Ernest Newman. A. & C. Black. 1923 (first issued Breitkopf & Härtel, London 1911).

STEELE, H. J. Unpublished Ph.D. Dissertation Vol. 1 *English Organs and Organ Music from 1500 to 1650*. Vol. 2 *An Anthology of early English Organ Music* (manuscript transcriptions of 110 pieces). Cambridge University. 1958.

STERNFELD, F. W. *Music in Shakespearean tragedy*. Routledge & Kegan Paul and Dover Pub. New York. 1963.

STEVENS, D. *The Mulliner Book: a commentary*. Stainer & Bell. 1952.

— *Thomas Tomkins*. Dover Publications, New York. 1967 (1st ed. Macmillan 1957).

— *Tudor Church Music*. Faber. 1961.

SUMNER, W. L. *The Organ: Its evolution, principles of construction and use*. Macdonald. 1962 (3rd edition).

— *The organs of St Paul's Cathedral*. Musical Opinion. 1931.

SUTTON, Frederick H. *A short account of organs built in England from the reign of Charles II to the present time*. Masters, Aldersgate St. 1847.

TREVELYAN, G. M. *English social history*. Longmans, Green & Co. 1946 (2nd edition).

VENTE, Maarten A. *Die Brabanter Orgel*. Amsterdam. 1963.

VIDERØ, Finn. *European Organ Music of the 16th and 17th centuries*. Hansen, Copenhagen. 1969.

VULLIAMY, C. E. *John Wesley*. Geoffrey Bles. 1931.

WARLOCK, Peter. *English Ayres, Elizabethan and Jacobean, a discourse*. Oxford University Press. 1932.

— *The English Ayre*. Oxford University Press. 1926.

WERNER, Eric. *Mendelssohn*. Collier-Macmillan. 1963.

WESLEY, Charles. See under BARRINGTON, Daines.

WESLEY, Eliza (ed.). *Letters of Samuel Wesley to Mr Jacobs*. S. W. Partridge. 1875.

WILLIAMS, C. F. Abdy. *The story of organ music*. Walter Scott Pub. Co. 1905.

WILLIAMS, Peter. *The European Organ 1450–1850*. Batsford. 1967.

WILSON, Michael I. *The English Chamber Organ: history and development 1650–1850*. Cassirer, Oxford. 1968.

WOLFE, Richard J. See under PARTHENIA IN-VIOLATA.

WOOLDRIDGE, H. E. *Early English Harmony from the 10th to the 15th century*. Vol. 1 Facsimiles. Vol. 2 Transcriptions and notes. The Plainsong & Mediaeval Music Society (Bernard Quaritch). 1897–1913.

BIBLIOGRAPHY II
Articles in magazines and periodicals
(Published in London unless otherwise stated)

List of abbreviations used:

Af Mw	Archiv für Musikwissenschaft (Bückeburg)
BRLM	Bulletin of the John Rylands Library, Manchester
CM	Church Music
JAMS	Journal of the American Musicological Society (Princeton)
JHI	Journal of the History of Ideas (Lancaster, Pa.)
Kgr-Ber	Kongress-Bericht (Hamburg)
MD	Musica Disciplina, (published by the American Institute of Musicology, Rome)
ML	Music and Letters
MMR	Monthly Musical Record
MQ	Musical Quarterly
MR	Music Review
MS	Music Survey
MT	Musical Times
NQ	Notes and Queries
Org.	The Organ
PRMA	Proceedings of the Royal Musical Association
RS	Recorded Sound
Sc	The Score
Sp	Speculum, a journal of mediaeval studies (Cambridge, Mass.)
TVNM	Tijdschrift der Vereeniging voor Nederlansche Muziekgeschiedenis (Amsterdam)
ZIMG	Zeitschrift der Internationalen Musikgesellschaft (Leipzig)
Zf Mw	Zeitschrift für Musikwissenschaft

ANONYMOUS. *Organ—Playing in England*. ZIMG. 11, 1909.
— *Progress of Bach's music in England*. MT. June, 1851.
APEL, Willi. *Early history of the Organ*. Sp. 23. April, 1948.
— *The early development of the Organ ricercar*. MD. 3, 1949.
BAILLIE, Hugh. *A London church in early Tudor Times*. ML. 36, 1955.
— *Nicholas Ludford*. MQ, 44. April, 1958.
BEECHEY, Gwilym. *A new source of seventeenth century keyboard music*. ML, 50, 1969.
BEER, R. *Ornaments in old Keyboard Music*. MR, 13. 1952.
BERGSAGEL, J. D. *An introduction to Ludford*. MD, 14. 1960.
— *On the performance of Ludford's alternatim Masses*. MD, 16. 1962.
BOSTON, J. L. *Priscilla Bunbury's Virginal Book*. ML, 36. 1955.
BROWN, Alan. '*My Lady Nevell's Book' as a source of Byrd's keyboard music*. PRMA, 95. 1969.

BUKOFZER, Manfred F. *The notation of polyphonic music.* MQ, 30. Jan. 1944 (review of book by Apel, see Bibl. I).
BUTCHER, Vernon. *Thomas Roseingrave.* ML, 19. 1938.
CALDWELL, John. *Duddyngton's organ: another opinion.* MT. March 1967 (correspondence MT April, 1967).
— *The organ in the mediaeval Latin liturgy, 800–1500.* PRMA, 93. 1966.
— *The pitch of early Tudor organ Music.* ML, 51. 1970.
COLE, Elizabeth. *Seven problems of the Fitzwilliam Virginal Book.* PRMA, 79. 1953.
COLLINS, H. B. *John Taverner.* ML, 6. 1925.
CUDWORTH, C. L. *An essay by John Marsh.* ML, 36. 1955.
— *The English Organ Concerto.* Sc. Sept. 1953.
DART, Thurston. *A new source of early English organ music.* ML, 35. 1954.
— *English organ music for the Roman Rite.* ML. 52, 1971.
— *John Bull's 'Chapel'.* ML, 40. 1959.
— *Sweelinck's Fantazia on a theme used by John Bull.* TVNM, 18. 1959.
— *Two new documents relating to the Royal Music, 1584–1605.* ML. 45, 1964.
DAWES, Frank. *Nicholas Carlton and the earliest keyboard duet.* MT. Dec. 1961.
— *The music of Philip Hart.* PRMA, 94. 1968.
DEARMER, Geoffrey. *The fall and rise of the hymn tune.* ML, 6. 1925.
DICKINSON, A. E. F. *A forgotten collection: A survey of the Weckmann Books.* MR, 17. 1956.
— *John Bull's fugal style.* MMR, 84. 1954.
EDWARDS, F. G. *Bach and Wesley.* MT. Feb. 1896.
— *Bach's music in England.* MT. Sept., Oct., Nov., Dec. 1896.
— *Samuel Wesley.* MT. Aug., Dec. 1902.
EVANS, Charles. *The ancestry of the Wesleys.* NQ. June 1948.
FELLOWES, E. H. *My Ladye Nevell's Booke.* ML, 30. 1949.
FULLER-MAITLAND, J. A. *The notation of the Fitzwilliam Virginal Book.* PRMA, 21. 1895.
GLYN, Margaret H. *The national school of Virginal Music in Elizabethan Times.* PRMA, 43. 1917.
GUPPY, Henry. *Miles Coverdale and the English Bible 1488–1568.* BRLM, 19. July 1935.
HARRISON, Frank Ll. *Faburden in practice.* MD, 16. 1962.
HENDERSON, A.M. *Old English keyboard Music.* PRMA, 44. 1938.
HENDRIE, Gerald. *Keyboard music of Gibbons.* PRMA, 89. 1962.
HOLMES, Edward. *Cathedral music and composers: Nos. 13 and 14, Samuel Wesley.* MT. July, Aug. 1851 (correspondence MT. Aug. 1851).
HOPPE, Harry R. *John Bull in the Archduke Albert's service.* ML, 35. 1954.
HUGHES, Dom A. *Old English Harmony.* ML, 6 .1925.
INGRAM, R. W. *Operatic tendencies in Stuart drama.* MQ, 44. Oct. 1958.
IZON, John. *Italian musicians at the Tudor Court.* MQ, 44. July, 1958.
JEANS, Susi. *Geschichte und Entwicklung des Voluntary für Double Organ in der engl. Orgelmusik des 17 Jh.* Kgr-Ber. 1956.

— *17th and 18th Century Organ Music in England*. RS, 12. Oct. 1963.

KINSKY, G. *Kurze Oktaven auf besaiteten Tasteninstrumenten*. Zf Mw II, 2. Nov. 1919.

LAMBERT, Constant. *Thomas Roseingrave*. PRMA, 58. 1932.

LEFKOWITZ, Murray. *New facts concerning William Lawes and the Caroline Masque*. ML, 40. 1959.

LEICHTENTRITT, Hugo. *The Reform of Trent and its effect on music*. MQ, 30. July 1944.

LEVY, Kenneth Jay. *New material on the Early Motet in England* (a report on Princeton MS Garrett 119). JAMS 4. 1951.

LOWINSKY, Edward E. *English Organ Music of the Renaissance*. MQ, 39. July 1953.

— *Music in the Culture of the Renaissance*. JHI, 15. 1954.

MANSFIELD, Orlando A. *J. S. Bach's first English Apostles*. MQ, 21. April 1935.

MARK, Jeffrey. *The Jonsonian Masque*. ML, 3. 1922.

MASLEN, Benjamin J. *The earliest English organ pedals*. MT. Sept. 1960 (correspondence MT. Nov. 1960).

MELLERS, Wilfrid. *John Bull and English keyboard music*. MQ, 40. July, Oct. 1954.

MEYER, Ernst Hermann. *Form in the . . . 17th century*. PRMA, 65. 1938.

— *The 'In Nomine' and the birth of polyphonic instrumental style in England*. ML, 17. 1936.

MILLER, Hugh H. *Fulgens praeclara*. JAMS, 2. 1949.

— *John Bull's Organ works*. ML, 28. 1947.

— *Sixteenth century English faburden compositions for keyboard*. MQ, 26. Jan. 1940.

— *The earliest keyboard duets*. MQ, 29. Oct. 1943.

NEIGHBOUR, Oliver. *New keyboard music by Byrd*. MT. July 1971.

OLSON, Clair C. *Chaucer and the music of the fourteenth century*. Sp, 16. Jan. 1941.

REANEY, Gilbert. *John Dunstable and late Mediaeval music in England*. Sc. Sept. 1953.

REESE, Gustav. *Origin of the 'In Nomine'*. JAMS, 2. 1949.

ROSE, B. W. G. *Thomas Tomkins*. PRMA, 82. 1956.

SACHS, Curt. *Some remarks about old notation*. MQ, 34. July 1948.

SCHRADE, L. *Die Messe in der Orgelmusik des 15 Jh*. Af Mw 1. 1918.

SHARP, Geoffrey. *English composers abroad*. CM, 2. April 1965.

STEVENS, Denis. *A unique Tudor Organ Mass*. (Philip ap Rhys.) MD, 6. 1952.

— *Pre-Reformation organ music in England*. PRMA, 78. 1951.

— *The background of the 'In Nomine'*. MMR, 84. 1954.

— *The keyboard music of Thomas Tallis*. MT, 93. 1952.

— *Thomas Preston's Organ Mass*. ML, 39. 1958.

STEVENSON, Robert. *Thomas Morley's 'Plaine and Easie' Introduction to the Modes*. MD, 6. 1952.

VAN der MEER, J. H. *The keyboard works in the Vienna Bull MS*. TVNM, 18. 1957.

WHITTAKER, W. G. *Byrd's and Bull's 'Walsingham' Variations.* MR, 3. 1942.

WILLIAMS, Peter F. *Some interesting organ terms (Diapason, Principal, Bourdon, Dulciana, Cremona).* MT. June, July, Aug., Oct., Dec. 1965.

— *J. S. Bach and English organ music.* ML. 44, 1963.

WILSON, John. *John Stanley. Some opus numbers and editions.* ML, 39. 1958.

BIBLIOGRAPHY III
Catalogues, Dictionaries, Encyclopaedias, Works of reference

APEL, Willi. *The Harvard Dictionary of Music.* Heinemann. 1944 (2nd edition, 1969).

ARKWRIGHT, G. E. P. *Catalogue of music in the library of Christ Church, Oxford* (Part I). Oxford University Press. 1915.

BLOM, Eric. See under *Grove's Dictionary.*

BLUME, Friedrich (ed.). *Die Musik in Geschichte und Gegenwart* (Vol. 1–14). Bärenreiter. 1949–68.

BROWN, James D. and STRATTON, Stephen S. *British Musical Biography.* Birmingham. 1897.

BURN, John Henry. *Bibliography of the organ* (in *Dictionary of Organs and Organists*). Mate & Son. 1921 (2nd edition).

De GRAAF. *Literature on the organ principally in Dutch libraries.* Amsterdam. 1957.

De LAFONTAINE, Henry Carl. *The King's Musick 1460–1700.* London. 1909.

DICTIONARY of National Biography (D.N.B.).

DICTIONARY of Organs and Organists. Mate & Son. 1921 (see under BURN, John Henry and FREEMAN, Andrew).

FÉTIS, F. J. *Biographie universelle des musicians* (Vols. 1–8). Leroux, Brussels. 1835.

FREEMAN, Andrew. *Records of British Organ-Builders 940–1660* (in *Dictionary of Organs and Organists*). Mate & Son. 1921 (2nd edition).

FROTSCHER, Gotthold. *Geschichte des Orgelspiels und der Orgelkomposition* (Vol. 1–2). Max Hesses, Berlin. 1935.

GROVE'S Dictionary of Music and Musicians. Macmillan. 1954 (5th edition, ed. by Eric Blom).

HUGHES-HUGHES, Augustus. *Catalogue of Manuscript Music in the British Museum.* (Vol. III—Instrumental). British Museum. 1909.

LAVIGNAC, Albert. *Encyclopédie de la musique.* Delagrave, Paris. 1926 (Part 2, Vol. 2 André Pirro *L'art des organistes*).

MADAN, Falconer. *A summary catalogue of Western manuscripts in the Bodleian Library at Oxford* (Vol. 4, 5). Oxford, Clarendon Press. 1897/1905.

— Index to the above, by P. D. Record (Vol. 7). Oxford. 1953.

MARCUSE, Sibyl. *Musical Instruments. A comprehensive dictionary.* Doubleday, New York. 1964.

NEW OXFORD HISTORY of music. Oxford University Press. 1954–.

Oxford Companion to music. See under SCHOLES, Percy A.

PIRRO, André. See under LAVIGNAC.

PULVER, Jeffrey. *A biographical dictionary of Old English music.* Kegan Paul, Trench Trubner & Co. 1927.

RECORD, P. D. See under MADAN, F.

RIEMANN, Hugo. *Musik-Lexicon.* Schott, Mainz. 1967.

RIMBAULT, E. F. *The Old Cheque-Book. Book of remembrance of the Chapel Royal 1561–1744.* Da Capo Press, New York. 1966 (1st ed. 1872).

SCHOLES, Percy A. *The Oxford Companion to Music* (10th edition, ed. by John Owen Ward). Oxford University Press. 1970.

SEIFFERT, M. *Geschichte der Klaviermusik.* Breitkopf & Härtel, Leipzig. 1899.

STATIONERS. Entries of copies in the Register Book of the Company of Stationers. 1746–:

STRATTON, Stephen S. See under BROWN, James D.

WARD, John Owen. See under SCHOLES, Percy, A.

ZIMMERMAN, Franklin B. *Henry Purcell 1659–1695 An analytical catalogue of his music.* Macmillan. 1963.

Key to Manuscripts and Printed Editions

I—Manuscripts

Code Letter	Whereabouts	No. of Manuscript	Title or Description
a	British Museum	Add.31403	
b	British Museum	Add.23623	
c	British Museum	Add.36661	
d	British Museum	Add.30485	
e	British Museum	R.M.23.1.4	Cosyn's Virginal Book
f	Paris Conservatoire	rés. 1186 (18546)	
g	Paris Conservatoire	rés. 1122 (18547)	
h	Paris Conservatoire	rés. 1185 (18548)	
i	Paris Conservatoire	rés. 1186/bis II (18570)	
j	New York Public Lib.	Drexel 5612	
k	Christ Church, Oxford	Mus.MS 1113	
l	Christ Church, Oxford	Mus.MS 431	
m	Christ Church, Oxford	Mus.MS 1003	
n	British Museum	R.M.24.d.3	Will Forster's Virginal Book
o	Vienna, Nat. Lib.	MS 17771	
p	Fitzwilliam Museum, Cambridge	Mus.Ms 32.g.29	Fitzwilliam Virginal Book
q	Christ Church, Oxford	Mus.MS 1207	
r	Nat. Lib., Edinburgh	Panmure MS 9	Clement Matchett's Virginal Book
s	British Museum	Add.10337	Elizabeth Rogers' Virginal Book (Feb. 27th 1656)
t	British Museum	Add.29996	
u	Christ Church, Oxford	Mus. MS 371	
v	Bodleian Lib., Oxford	C.93	

Code Letter	Whereabouts	No. of Manuscript	Title or Description
w	New York Public Lib.	Drexel 5611	
x	Bodleian Lib., Oxford	F.575	
y	Christ Church, Oxford	Mus.MS 47	
z	Christ Church, Oxford	Mus.MS 89	
aa	Christ Church, Oxford	Mus.MS 92	
bb	Christ Church, Oxford	Mus.MS 378	
cc	Christ Church, Oxford	Mus.MS 437	
dd	Christ Church, Oxford	Mus.MS 1142a	
ee	Christ Church, Oxford	Mus.MS 1176	
ff	Christ Church, Oxford	Mus.MS 1177	
gg	Christ Church, Oxford	Mus.MS 1236	
hh	New York Public Lib.	Drexel 5609	
ii	Fitzwilliam Museum Cambridge	Mus.MS 52.B.7	
jj	Nat. Lib. Edinburgh	Panmure MS 8	Lady Jean Campbell's Virginal Book
kk	British Museum	Add.22099	
ll	British Museum	Add.31723	
mm	Royal College of Music	MS 2093	
nn	Berlin State Lib.	Ly. A1 and A2	Count zu Lynar's MS.
oo	Private		Priscilla Bunbury's Virginal Book (1645)
pp	Christ Church, Oxford	Music MS 1175	
qq	British Museum	Add.35039	
rr	Nat. Lib. Edinburgh,		Duncan Burnett's Music Book
ss	British Museum	Add.31392	
tt	Private		My Ladye Nevell's Booke
uu	Fitzwilliam Museum, Cambridge	Marlay Additions, No.15	Tisdale's Virginal Book
vv	British Museum	Add.30486	
ww	Nat. Lib., Edinburgh	Panmure MS 10	Kinloch MS.
xx	British Museum	Add.15233	
yy	Christ Church, Oxford	Mus.MS 1034a	
zz	British Museum	Add.30513	Mulliner Book
a^1	British Museum	Roy.App.56	
b^1	British Museum	Add.5465	Fairfax Manuscript
c^1	British Museum	Add.29246	
d^1	British Museum	Roy.App.74	
e^1	British Museum	Add.4900	
f^1	Bodleian Lib., Oxford	D.212–6	

Code Letter	Whereabouts	No. of Manuscript	Title or Description
g¹	British Museum	Add.31390	
h¹	British Museum	Add.29372	
i¹	British Museum	Add.30087	
j¹	British Museum	Add.30478	
k¹	British Museum	Add.31443	
l¹	British Museum	Add.22597	
m¹	Bodleian Lib., Oxford	E.423	
n¹	British Museum	Add.30480	
o¹	Christ Church, Oxford	Mus.MS 67	
p¹	Christ Church, Oxford	Mus.MS 1004	
q¹	Christ Church, Oxford	Mus.MS 49	
r¹	British Museum	Roy.App.58	
s¹	British Museum	Eg.2485	
t¹	British Museum	Harl.7340	
u¹	Fitzwilliam Museum, Cambridge	52.d.25	John Bull Virginal Book
v¹	British Museum	RM 24.k.3	
w¹	British Museum	Add.17852	
x¹	Dulwich College	MS (second series) 92b	F. B. Bickley cat.
y¹	British Museum	Add.31465	
z¹	British Museum	Add.31446	
a²	British Museum	Add.31468	
b²	British Museum	Add.34695	
c²	British Museum	Eg.2959	
d²	Christ Church, Oxford	Mus.MS 1179	
e²	British Museum	R.M.21.d.8	
f²	Royal College of Music	MS 820	
g²	British Museum	Add.5336	
h²	British Museum	Add.31814	
i²	British Museum	Add.14335	
j²	British Museum	Add.29485	Suzanne van Soldt's keyboard book
k²	British Museum	Add.28550	Robertsbridge Codex
l²	Dulwich College	MS (second series) 92a	F. B. Bickley cat.
m²	British Museum	Add.27753	
n²	British Museum	Add.30392	
o²	British Museum	Add.35040	
p²	British Museum	Add.34693	
q²	British Museum	Add.16155	
r²	British Museum	Add.27593	
s²	British Museum	Add.35006	Eliza Wesley's Organ Book

Code Letter	Whereabouts	No. of Manuscript	Title or Description
t²	British Museum	Add.35007	
u²	British Museum	Add.35008	
v²	British Museum	Add.35014	
w²	British Museum	Add.35015	
x²	British Museum	Add.35017	
y²	British Museum	Add.34089	
z²	British Museum	Add.31239	
a³	British Museum	Add.31764	
b³	British Museum	Add.14340	
c³	British Museum	Add.14343	
d³	British Museum	Add.14344	
e³	British Museum	Add.31120	
f³	Dulwich College	MS (second series) 92d	F. B. Bickley cat.
g³	Royal College of Music	MS 640	
h³	Royal College of Music	MS 1039	
i³	Royal College of Music	MS 1151	
j³	Royal College of Music	MS 2227	
k³	Royal College of Music	MS 4018	
l³	Royal College of Music	MS 4021	
m³	Royal College of Music	MS 4022	
n³	Royal College of Music	MS 4025	
o³	Royal College of Music	MS 4027	
p³	Royal College of Music	MS 4028	
q³	Royal College of Music	MS 4029	
r³	Royal College of Music	MS 4038	
s³	Royal College of Music	MS 2141b	
t³	Christ Church, Oxford	Mus. MS 15	
u³	Wimborne Minster	Mus. MS P. 10	

II—Printed Editions

(Published in London unless otherwise stated)
+ Collections and Anthologies of works by more than one composer

Code No.	Title	Editor	Publisher	Date
1+	The Fitzwilliam Virginal Book★	J. A. Fuller Maitland & W. Barclay Squire	Breitkopf & Härtel, Leipzig	1899
			(ii) reissued	1906
			(iii) reissued: Dover Publications, N.Y.	1963
2+	Parthenia	Thurston Dart	Stainer & Bell	1960
3+	Parthenia In-Violata	Thurston Dart	New York Pub. Lib.	1961

★ The copyist Francis Tregian also made two other collections (Egerton 3665 and Sambrooke MS, N.Y. Public Library), totalling some 2000 compositions.

Code No.	Title	Editor	Publisher	Date
4	The Loyal and National Songs of England	William Kitchiner	Hurst, Robinson & Co.	1823
5	John Bull, Thirty keyboard pieces	Margaret Glyn	Stainer & Bell	1928
6	John Bull, Pieces edited for the Pianoforte	Margaret Glyn	Joseph Williams	1922
7	Twenty-five pieces for keyed instruments from Cosyn's Virginal Book	J. A. Fuller Maitland & W. Barclay Squire	Chester	1923
8	John Bull—Keyboard Music I, *Musica Britannica*, Vol. XIV	John Steele & Francis Cameron	Stainer & Bell	1960
9	John Bull—Keyboard Music II, *Musica Britannica*, Vol. XIX	Thurston Dart	Stainer & Bell	1963
10	My Ladye Nevells Booke (ii) reissued, with a new introduction by Blanche Winogron	Hilda Andrews	J. Curwen & Sons Dover Publications, New York	1926 1969
11	Thomas Tomkins— Keyboard Music *Musica Britannica* Vol. V	Stephen D. Tuttle	Stainer & Bell	1955
12	Orlando Gibbons— Keyboard Music *Musica Britannica* Vol. XX	Gerald Hendrie	Stainer & Bell	1962
13+	Thirty Virginal pieces by various composers	Margaret Glyn	Stainer & Bell	1927
14	Orlando Gibbons— Complete Keyboard works (in 5 volumes)	Margaret Glyn	Stainer & Bell	1925
15	Orlando Gibbons—Ten pieces arranged for the modern organ, from the Virginal Book of Benjamin Cosyn.	J. A. Fuller Maitland	Chester	1925
16	Orlando Gibbons— Edited for the pianoforte	Margaret Glyn	Joseph Williams	1922
17	Thomas Tomkins—nine organ pieces from *Musica Britannica* Vol. V	Stephen D. Tuttle (rev. Thurston Dart)	Stainer & Bell	1955
18	Orlando Gibbons— Eight keyboard pieces (from *Musica Britannica* Vol. XX)	Gerald Hendrie	Stainer & Bell (rev. ed. 1967)	1962
19	Orlando Gibbons— Nine organ pieces (from *Musica Britannica* Vol. XX)	Gerald Hendrie	Stainer & Bell (rev. ed. 1967)	1962
20	Thomas Roseingrave— Ten organ pieces	Peter Williams	Stainer & Bell (rev. ed. 1970)	1961

Code No.	Title	Editor	Publisher	Date
21	Thomas Morley— Keyboard Works (2 vols.)	Thurston Dart	Stainer & Bell (rev. ed. 1964)	1959
22	John Bull—Ten pieces (from *Musica Britannica* Vol. XIV)	John Steele & Francis Cameron	Stainer & Bell	1960
23	William Byrd— Keyboard Music (I) *Musica Britannica* Vol. XXVII	Alan Brown	Stainer & Bell	1969
24+	The Mulliner Book *Musica Britannica* Vol. I	Denis Stevens	Stainer & Bell (2nd ed. 1954, reprinted 1962, 1966)	1951
25+	Early Tudor Organ Music: I Music for the office *Early English Church Music* Vol. 6	John Caldwell	Stainer & Bell	1966
26+	Early Tudor Organ Music: II Music for the Mass *Early English Church Music* Vol. 10	Denis Stevens	Stainer & Bell	1969
27	Thomas Tallis— complete keyboard works	Denis Stevens	Hinrichsen	1953
28	John Redford— Organ Works	Carl Friedrich Pfatteicher	Bärenreiter, Kassel	1934
29+	*Altenglische Orgelmusik* (manualiter)	Denis Stevens	Bärenreiter	1953
30+	Early English Organ Music	Margaret Glyn	Plainsong & Mediaeval Mus. Soc.	1939
31	Thomas Tomkins— Three Voluntaries, *Tallis to Wesley* No. 17	Denis Stevens	Hinrichsen	1959
32+	Two Elizabethan Keyboard duets	Frank Dawes	Schott	1949
33+	Early Keyboard Music (in 5 Vols.)	Frank Dawes	Schott	1951
34	John Lugge—Three Voluntaries for double organ	Susi Jeans & John Steele	Novello	1956
35	Thomas Roseingrave: Compositions for Organ and Harpsichord	Denis Stevens	Penn Music	1964
36	Giles Farnaby: Seventeen pieces transcribed and selected from the *Fitzwilliam Virginal Book*	Thurston Dart	Stainer & Bell	1957
37	William Byrd: Fifteen pieces transcribed and selected from the *Fitzwilliam Virginal Book* and *Parthenia*	Thurston Dart	Stainer & Bell	1956

Code No.	Title	Editor	Publisher	Date
38+	Twenty-four pieces from the *Fitzwilliam Virginal Book*	Thurston Dart	Stainer & Bell	1958
39	Tremain—Six Sonatas or Voluntarys	—	Preston	1810
40	Thomas Tallis—Three organ Hymn Verses and four Antiphons (sel. from ed. 27) *Tallis to Wesley* No. 2	Denis Stevens	Hinrichsen	1953
41	Thomas Tallis: Four pieces (sel. from ed. 27) *Tallis to Wesley* No. 3	Denis Stevens	Hinrichsen	1953
42	William Byrd: Eight Organ pieces, *Tallis to Wesley* No. 8	Philip Ledger	Hinrichsen	1968
43	Orlando Gibbons: Three Organ pieces, *Tallis to Wesley* No. 9	Gordon Phillips	Hinrichsen	1957
44	Thomas Sanders Dupuis: Nine Voluntaries	—	Preston	1800
45+	Stanley, Walond & Boyce: Voluntaries, *Tallis to Wesley* No. 1	Gordon Phillips	Hinrichsen	1956
46	Maurice Greene: Three Voluntaries, *Tallis to Wesley* No. 4	Gordon Phillips	Hinrichsen	1958
47	Maurice Greene: Four Voluntaries, *Tallis to Wesley* No. 15	Francis Routh	Hinrichsen	1960
48+	The Wesleys, *Tallis to Wesley* No. 5	Gordon Phillips	Hinrichsen	1960
49	Matthew Locke: Seven pieces from *Melothesia*, *Tallis to Wesley* No. 6	Gordon Phillips	Hinrichsen	1957
50	Samuel Wesley: Twelve short pieces, *Tallis to Wesley* No. 7	Gordon Phillips	Hinrichsen	1957
51	Henry Purcell: Three Voluntaries, *Tallis to Wesley* No. 10	Gordon Phillips	Hinrichsen	1961
52	Henry Purcell: Organ Works	Hugh McLean	Novello	1957
53	Christopher Gibbons: Keyboard compositions	Clare G. Rayner	American Inst. of Musicology	1967
54	Handel: Six Fugues or Voluntaries, *Tallis to Wesley* No. 12	Gordon Phillips	Hinrichsen	1960
55	Handel: Four Volun-	Francis Routh	Hinrichsen	1961

Code No.	Title	Editor	Publisher	Date
	taries *Tallis to Wesley* No. 19			
56	Samuel Wesley & Dr. Mendelssohn, *Tallis to Wesley* No. 14	Gordon Phillips & Max Hinrichsen	Hinrichsen	1962
57+	John Blow & his pupils *Tallis to Wesley* No. 21	Gordon Phillips	Hinrichsen	1962
58+	Dupuis, Keeble, Travers *Tallis to Wesley* No. 22	Peter Williams	Hinrichsen	1961
59	John Alcock: Four Voluntaries, *Tallis to Wesley* No. 23	Peter Marr	Hinrichsen	1961
60	William Boyce: Four Voluntaries, *Tallis to Wesley* No. 26	Gordon Phillips	Hinrichsen	1966
61	John Stanley: Voluntaries Op. V, VI, VII (New Music Magazine, 51–55)	—	Harrison	1785
62	John Stanley: Voluntaries Op. V, VI, VII	—	Johnson	1748/54
63	John Stanley: Complete Organ Works, *Tallis to Wesley* Nos. 27, 28, 29	Gordon Phillips	Hinrichsen	1967
64	William Walond: Three Cornet Voluntaries, *Tallis to Wesley* No. 20	Gordon Phillips	Hinrichsen	1961
65	William Walond: Three Voluntaries, *Tallis to Wesley* No. 32	Gordon Phillips	Hinrichsen	1962
66	Philip Hart: Fugues for the Organ or Harpsichord	—	Author	1704
67+	Parthenia	E. F. Rimbault	Chappell	1847
68+	Parthenia	Margaret Glyn	Reeves	1927
69+	Parthenia	Kurt Stone	Bronde, New York	1951
70	Harpsichord pieces from Dr John Bull's Flemish Tabulatura	H. F. Redlich	Noetzel, Wilhelmshaven	1958
71	Benjamin Rogers: Voluntary	Susi Jeans	Novello	1962
72	John Robinson: Voluntary in A minor	Susi Jeans	Novello	1966
73+	Geschichte des Orgelspiels und der Orgelkomposition	Gotthold Frotscher	Merseburger, Berlin	1966
74+	Old English Organ Music for manuals (in 6 vols.)	C. H. Trevor	Oxford Univ. Press	1966/71
75+	The first four centuries	John Klein	Associated Mus.	1948

Code No.	Title	Editor	Publisher	Date
	of music for the Organ (in 2 vols)		Pub., New York	
76+	Europäische Orgelmusik des 16.–18. Jahrhunderts	Johannes Piersig	Peters, Leipzig	1958
77+	Alte Orgelmusik aus England und Frankreich	Flor Peeters	Schott, Mainz	1958
78+	Treasury of early organ music	E. Power Biggs	Music Press Inc. New York	1947
79	William Byrd: Keyboard Music (II) *Musica Britannica*, Vol. XXVIII	Alan Brown	Stainer & Bell	1971
80	William Byrd: Dances grave and gay	Margaret Glyn	Winthrop Rogers	1923
81	The Byrd Organ Book	Margaret Glyn	Reeves	1923
82	William Byrd: Fourteen pieces for keyed instruments	J. A. Fuller Maitland & W. Barclay Squire	Stainer & Bell	1923
83	William Byrd: Forty-five pieces for keyboard instruments	Stephen D. Tuttle	L'Oiseau-lyre	1939
84	John Travers: Three Voluntaries	Norman Hennefield	Liturgical Mus. Press, New York	1944
85	Orlando Gibbons: Five selected compositions	Norman Hennefield	Liturgical Mus. Press, New York	1945
86	Anonymous: Voluntary in D minor	Watkins Shaw	Novello	1960
87	John Blow: Two Voluntaries	Hugh McLean	Novello	1971
88	Benjamin Cosyn:★ Three Voluntaries	John Steele	Novello	1959
89	John Bennett: Two Voluntaries	H. Diack Johnstone	Novello	1966
90	John Blow: Complete Organ Works	Watkins Shaw	Schott	1958
91	John Blow: Selected Organ Music	A. Vernon Butcher	Hinrichsen	1956
92	Roseingrave: Six double fugues for the organ or harpsichord	—	Walsh	1750
93	Roseingrave: Voluntarys and Fugues	—	Walsh	1728
94	Matthew Locke: Organ Voluntaries, (Seven voluntaries from *Melothesia* (1673))	Thurston Dart	Stainer & Bell	1957
95	Handel: Twelve Voluntaries and Fugues for the Organ or Harpsichord, with rules for tuning	—	Longman & Broderip	*c.* 1780

★ Doubtful attribution, see p. 66.

Code No.	Title	Editor	Publisher	Date
96	Handel: Six Fugues or Voluntaries for the Organ or Harpsichord (Op. 3)	—	Walsh ii: Harrison	1735 1784
97	Handel: Six Fugues pour le clavecin ou l'orgue, (Op. 3)	—	Unterbreuner Strasse 1152, Vienna	c. 1790
98	Handel: Six Fugues, Op. 3	—	Nägeli, Zurich	c. 1805
99	Handel: Six Fugues, Op. 3	—	Preston	c. 1810
100	Handel: Six Fugues, Op. 3	—	Richault, Paris	c. 1830
101	Handel: Two Voluntaries	Francis Routh	Oxford Univ. Press	1960
102	William Hine: Harmonia Sacra Glocestriensis	A. H. (edited by composer's widow, Alicia Hine)		c. 1731
103	Handel: Two fugues in 'Ten miscellaneous fugues'	J. Diettenhofer	Goulding, Phipps & D'Almaine	1803
104+	Maurice Greene and others: Ten Voluntaries for the Organ or Harpsichord	—	Thompson	1767
105+	Maurice Greene, and others: A collection of Voluntaries for the Organ or Harpsichord	—	Longman, Lukey & Co. ii reissued by Muzio Clementi	c. 1770 c. 1805
106	John Travers: Twelve Voluntaries for the Organ or Harpsichord	—	Thompson	1769
107	Matthew Locke: Melothesia, or certain general rules for playing upon a continued-bass, with a choice collection of Lessons for the Harpsichord and Organ of all sorts (The last seven pieces, pp. 73–84, 'for the organ')	—	Carr	1673
108+	Gibbons and others: Ten selected Voluntaries	—	Longman & Broderip	1780
109+	Handel and others: Ten select Voluntaries	—	Longman & Broderip ii reissued by Muzio Clementi	1780 1805
110	John James: Voluntary in D	Kenneth Simpson	Hinrichsen	1950
111	John Worgan: (Five) Organ Pieces	—	Fentum	c. 1795

Code No.	Title	Editor	Publisher	Date
112	Maurice Greene: Twelve Voluntaries	—	Bland	1779
113+	Maurice Greene, John Stanley and others: for manuals only	Various	Oxford Univ. Press	1960
114+	The Wesleys: *Tallis to Wesley* No. 24	Peter Williams	Hinrichsen	1961
115	Egerton Webbe: Prelude and Fugue in A major, Op. 1	—	J. Alfred Novello	1837
116	John Alcock(jnr.) Eight easy Voluntaries	—	Longman, Lukey & Co.	1775
117	Thomas Adams: 'Quant'è più bella', with variations	—	Clementi & Co.	1812(?)
118	Thomas Adams: Grand Organ Piece	—	Hodsoll	1824
119	Thomas Adams: (four Books of three Voluntaries)	—	Hodsoll	1824
120	Thomas Adams: Six Voluntaries	—	Longman	1820
121	Thomas Adams: Three Organ pieces	—	Novello, Ewer & Co.	1835(?)
122	Thomas Adams: Six Organ pieces	—	J. Alfred Novello	1825
123	Jonathan Battishill: Select pieces for the Organ	John Page	Page, Warwick Square	1805
124	Jonathan Battishill: Two Voluntaries	C. W. Pearce	Hammond	1896
125	Thomas Adams: Six fugues for the Organ or pianoforte	—	Clementi	1820
126	George Guest: Four fugues for the Organ	—	Preston	1815(?)
127	Samuel Webbe(jnr): Three Voluntaries for the Organ or Harpsichord	—	Clementi Banger Collard etc.	1820(?)
128	John Alcock (sen.): Ten Voluntaries for the Organ or Harpsichord	—	C. & S. Thompson	1774
129	John Bennett: Ten Voluntaries for the Organ or Harpsichord	—	Author	1758(?)
130	George Berg: Ten Voluntaries for the Organ or Harpsichord	—	Johnson	1757
131	William Boyce: Six Voluntaries for the Organ	—	Wheatstone	1825

Code No.	Title	Editor	Publisher	Date
	(Nos. 5–10 of Ed. 132 reissued)			
132	William Boyce: Ten Voluntaries for the Organ or Harpsichord	—	Thompson	1785
133	John Stanley: Voluntaries Op. V, VI, VII	—	Button and Whitaker	1809
134	John Stanley: Voluntaries Op. V, VI, VII	—	Thompson	1770
135	Henry Heron: Ten Voluntaries for the Organ or Harpsichord	—	Author	1760
136	John Marsh: An overture and six pieces	—	Preston	1791
137	James Nares: Six fugues with introductory Voluntaries	—	Welcker	1772
138	William Walond: Voluntaries for the Organ or Harpsichord Op. 1	—	Johnson	c. 1760
139	William Walond: Voluntaries for the Organ or Harpsichord Op. 2	—	Johnson	1758
140	John Worgan: Select Organ Pieces (in three Books)	—	Longman & Broderip	1795
141	Thomas Sanders Dupuis: Nine Voluntaries for juvenile Organists	—	Wheatstone	1808
142	James Hook: Ten Voluntaries	—	Whitaker	c. 1815
143	Jonas Blewitt: Twelve Voluntaries (and a treatise on the organ)	—	Longman & Broderip	c. 1795
144	Jonas Blewitt: Ten Voluntaries or Pieces . . . Op. V	—	Culliford, Rolfe & Barrow	1796
145	Jonas Blewitt: Twelve easy and familiar movements, Op. VI	—	Culliford, Rolfe & Barrow	c. 1798
146	Thomas Sanders Dupuis: A second set of pieces . . . for the use of young organists, Op. X	—	J. Dale	1792
147	George Guest: Sixteen pieces or Voluntaries, Op. 3	—	Preston	1808
148	Matthias Hawdon: A choice set of Voluntaries	—	J. Dale	c. 1794
149	Jacob Kirkman: A collection of six Voluntaries	—	Longman & Broderip	c. 1790

Code No.	Title	Editor	Publisher	Date
150	Thomas Sanders Dupuis: — Pieces for the organ or harpsichord . . . for the use of young organists		Preston	1785
151	William Crotch: Twelve — fugues (based on Anglican chants)		R. Mills	1835/7
152	John Marsh: Two fugues —		R. Bremner	1783
153	John Keeble: Select pieces for the organ	—	Author	1777
154	John Keeble: A second set of select pieces	—	Author	1778
155	John Keeble: A third set of select pieces	—	Author	1778
156	John Keeble: the above with a fourth set added	—	Longman & Broderip	1780
157	Charles Burney: Six Cornet Pieces . . .	—	Walsh	1751
158	Benjamin Cooke: Fugues and other pieces for the Organ (2 Books)	—	Birchall	1825
159	Starling Goodwin: Twelve Voluntarys for the Organ or Harpsichord (Book I)	—	Thompson	177?
160	Starling Goodwin: Twelve Voluntarys for the Organ or Harpsichord (Book II)	—	Thompson	1776
161	Starling Goodwin: The complete organist's pocket companion (Psalm-tunes with their interludes. . . .)	—	Thompson	1775
162	Samuel Long: Four Lessons and two Voluntarys for the harpsichord or organ	—	Thompson	c. 1772
163	John Marsh: Eighteen Voluntaries	—	Preston	1791
164	John Marsh: Twenty Voluntaries (second set)	—	Preston	1795
165	George Green: Six Voluntarys for the Organ, pianoforte or Harpsichord	—	Longman, Lukey & Co.	c. 1775
166+	Various Composers: (anon) Six Voluntaries	Edward Kendall	Longman, Lukey & Co.	1775
167	Matthias Hawdon: Six Sonatas Spirituale Op. 4 or Voluntarys, for the	—	Preston	c. 1780

Code No.	Title	Editor	Publisher	Date
	Harpsichord, Organ or Pianoforte			
168	Samuel Wesley: 'Jacky Horner' Rondo	—	Clementi	1810
169	William Russell: Twelve Voluntaries for the Organ or Pianoforte (Book I)	—	Clementi	1804
170	William Russell: Twelve Voluntaries for the Organ or Pianoforte (Book 2)	—	Clementi	1812
171	Samuel Wesley: The Deserters Meditations arranged as a Rondo	—	Chappell	1812
172	Samuel Wesley: Prelude Arietta and Fugue ('Prelude and Fugues . . . No. 1')	—	D'Almaine	c. 1840
173	Charles Wesley: Six Voluntaries	—	Bland and Wellers	1812
174	William Crotch: Fugue on a subject of Muffat	—	Birchall	1806
175	Samuel Wesley: Voluntaries for the Organ, Op. 6	—	Hodsoll	1805
176	Samuel Wesley: Six Organ Voluntaries, Op. 36, for young organists	—	Dean	c. 1830
177	Samuel Wesley: Twelve Voluntaries Op. 6	W. J. Wesbrook	Weekes	1887
178	Samuel Wesley: Voluntary in D	Kenneth Simpson	Hinrichsen	1950
179	Samuel Wesley: No. 1 of Beauties for the Organ	—	Galloway	1820(?)
180	Samuel Wesley: A selection of Pianoforte works	Eliza Wesley	Weekes	1890
181	Samuel Wesley: The Christmas Carol (Rondo)	—	Clementi	1810(?)
182	Samuel Wesley: Moll Pately, a celebrated dance	—	Guichard	1810
183	Samuel Wesley: Variations on a Polish air	—	Birchall	1830(?)
184	Samuel Wesley: Grand duet for the organ	W. Emery	Novello	1964
185	Samuel Wesley: Seventeen movements by Wesley (the Cabinet Organ Books, Vol. 3)	J. Pittman	Boosey	1885
186	Samuel Wesley: Four Sonatas and two Duets for the pianoforte (Op. 5)	—	Lavenu	1800

Code No.	Title	Editor	Publisher	Date
187	Samuel Wesley: An old English melody	A. E. Floyd	Hinrichsen	1955
188	Samuel Wesley: The favourite Air of William Putty arranged as a Rondo	—	Author	1805
189	Samuel Wesley: A sonata for the pianoforte, with a fugue subject by Salomon	—	Birchall	1808
190+	Samuel Wesley, Russell and others: Short melodies for the organ in 6 books	Vincent Novello	J. A. Novello	1848–58
191	Samuel Wesley: Grand Coronation March for the pianoforte or Organ	—	Willis	1830
192	Samuel Wesley: Nine variations on 'The Bay of Biscay' (to Clementi)	—	Monro & May	1825
193	Samuel Wesley: Six introductory movements	—	Clementi, Collard etc.	1815(?)
194	Samuel Wesley: Twelve short pieces with a full Voluntary added	—	Clementi	1815
195	Samuel Wesley: 'Off she goes', arranged as a Rondo	—	Hodsoll	1802
196	Samuel Wesley: Original Hymn Tunes	—	Author	1828
197	Samuel Wesley: The Siege of Badajoz, A characteristic sonata for the pianoforte	—	Preston	1812
198	Samuel Wesley: Three Sonatas, Op. 3	—	Birchall	1789
199	Samuel Wesley: Eight Sonatas for the harpsichord or pianoforte	—	Author	1777
200	Samuel Wesley: Fugue in D for the pianoforte (ii) reissued in Anthologie Classique et Moderne, No. 119	—	Willis	1828
			Augener	1885
201	Samuel Wesley: Rondo on an old English Air 'Kitty alone and I'	—	J. A. Novello	1830
202+	Samuel Wesley & others: A collection of Sacred Music	Joseph Major	Author	1825
203	Samuel Wesley/Handel: —		Author	1826

Code No.	Title	Editor	Publisher	Date
	The Fitzwilliam Music, (three hymns)			
204	Samuel Wesley: Voluntary for the Organ in B flat (to Attwood)	—	Hodsoll	1820
205	Samuel Wesley: A short and familiar Voluntary in A	—	Hodsoll	1820
206	Samuel Wesley: Hornpipe & Variations from an Organ Concerto (Arranged with a new introduction for the pianoforte by the author)	—	Royal Harmonic Institution	1820
207	Samuel Wesley: March for piano duet	—	Hodsoll	1807
208	Samuel Wesley: 'The sky Rocket'	—	Hodsoll	1809
209	Samuel Wesley: 'Scots wha hae wi' Wallace fled'	—	Birchall	1826
210	Samuel Wesley: A favourite Air by Weber (Der Freischütz)	—	Birchall	1826(?)
211	Samuel Wesley: Cobourg Waltz	—	Guichard	1816
212	Samuel Wesley: 'Sweet Enslaver'—Rondo with variations	—	Guichard	1816
213	Various composers: 'The Psalmist' (in four books)	Vincent Novello	Haddon	1835–42

Index